Manet: The Execution of Maximilian

Painting, Politics and Censorship

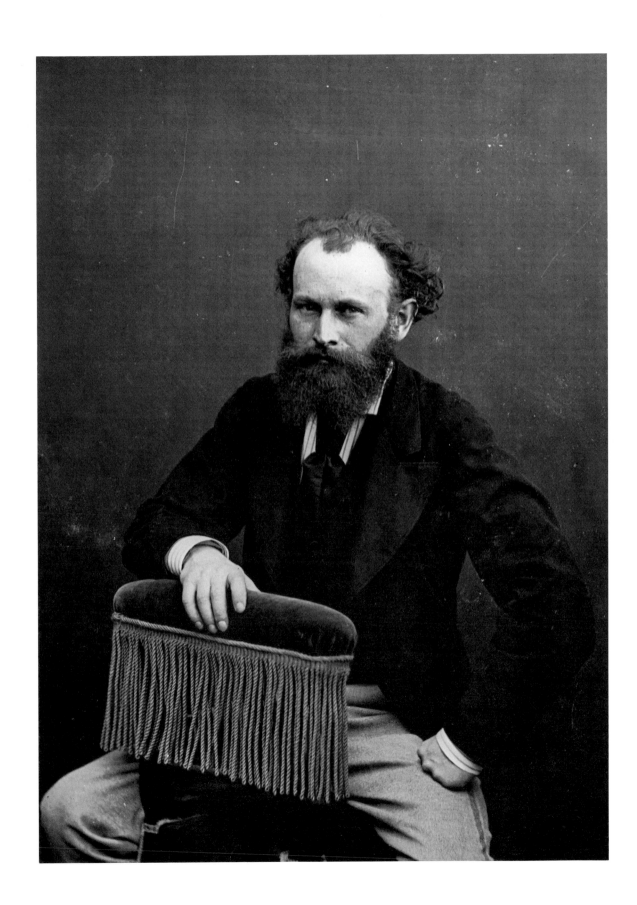

Manet: The Execution of Maximilian

Painting, Politics and Censorship

Juliet Wilson-Bareau

With essays by John House and Douglas Johnson

NATIONAL GALLERY PUBLICATIONS, LONDON

IN ASSOCIATION WITH

PRINCETON UNIVERSITY PRESS

This book was published to accompany an
exhibition at the National Gallery, London,
1 July–27 September 1992

First published in Great Britain in 1992 by
National Gallery Publications Limited
5/6 Pall Mall East, London SW1Y 5BA

Library of Congress Catalog Card Number 92-9919.

ISBN 0-691-03209-2

Clothbound edition distributed in the United States of America
and Canada in 1992 by Princeton University Press

Designed by Peter Guy

Maps by Denys Baker

Printed and bound in Great Britain by
Butler and Tanner Limited,
Frome and London

Fig. 1 Frontispiece: *Edouard Manet*, by Nadar, *c.* 1865.
Paris, Caisse Nationale des Monuments Historiques.

Contents

Preface

The European Arts Festival of 1992 seeks to reveal and reinforce the links that bind this country to our European partners. There can be no more appropriate place to launch the Festival than at the National Gallery, housing as it does some of the greatest manifestations of the genius of European art.

While it is true to say that post-Renaissance European influence in this country came primarily from other quarters, there is no doubt that by the nineteenth century the principal source of inspiration was France. The work of painters from Delacroix to Monet has had a lasting influence on the way we see the world and has given a wide public profound pleasure for over a century.

Among the greatest names of that period is that of Edouard Manet, and it is especially gratifying that the National Gallery has been able to organise an exhibition, not only of impressive scholarship and distinction, but of real historical significance.

I am particularly happy that the funds provided to the European Arts Festival by the Government through the Office of Arts and Libraries, have allowed us to make possible what I am sure will be not only a memorable exhibition, but one that has not occurred before, and is unlikely to be repeated in our time.

John Drummond, CBE
Director European Arts Festival

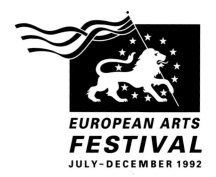

EUROPEAN ARTS
FESTIVAL
JULY–DECEMBER 1992

Foreword

The fragments of Manet's *Execution of Maximilian* are among the most moving and most tantalising pictures in the National Gallery. They are not just parts of a great picture, now damaged; that picture itself was part of a progression which culminated in one of the supreme achievements of nineteenth-century painting.

Napoleon III's attempt to recover the political initiative at home by placing a puppet emperor on the throne of Mexico, squalid fiasco that it was, stirred the conscience of France and of Europe – less, perhaps, for the suffering of the Mexican people, than for the tragic destruction of the young Emperor and his wife. It seemed that for once, as in antique drama, the politics of the 1860s had resolved into the fate of two noble victims, closely related to the rulers of the world: Maximilian, scholarly brother of the Emperor Franz Joseph, abandoned by Napoleon to a Mexican firing squad; Charlotte of Belgium, his wife, first cousin to Queen Victoria, driven insane in her desperate struggle to rally support in Europe for her doomed husband four thousand miles away.

This exhibition brings together for the first time since Manet's lifetime, and for the first time ever in public, the Maximilian paintings from Boston, London and Mannheim – the three stages of Manet's struggle to produce a work of art out of the political shambles of the Mexican debacle.

The succeeding versions suggest that Manet was responding to the ever more precise news bulletins of the execution which slowly filtered through to Europe. More important, they show him transforming contemporary politics into heroic painting, as Géricault had transformed them – after comparable struggle – in his *Raft of the Medusa* forty-five years earlier, and as Picasso was later to do in *Guernica*. Most important of all, they allow us to watch Manet examining more deeply the emotions of the executioners and of the condemned, and indeed of ourselves, the spectators, as we play our part in a drama not just of the 1860s, but of power, reversal and destitution in any age.

The National Gallery could not have put on this exhibition without the unstinting kindness of lenders in many countries, and our gratitude is deep indeed. Sadly, the exhibition will not travel to Boston as originally planned, but we are grateful to Peter Sutton and his colleagues at the Museum of Fine Arts for their generous support. With our partners at the Städtische Kunsthalle, Mannheim, we have enjoyed the happiest co-operation. Among the many museum directors, curators and scholars who have assisted with this project I would like to thank especially David Alston, Henrik Bjerre, Françoise Cachin, Philippe Comte, Douglas Druick, Antony Griffiths, John House, Flemming Johansen, Douglas Johnson, William R. Johnston, Christopher Lloyd, Charles Moffett, Edmund P. Pillsbury, Joseph Rishel, Salvador Rueda Smithers and Edith Varga. His Excellency, the Mexican Ambassador, Bernardo Sepúlveda, and his colleague Raúl Ortiz y Ortiz, offered invaluable advice and kindly assisted with our loan requests from Mexico. Her Majesty's Government has generously contributed to the costs of the exhibition as part of the European Arts Festival, thus enabling us to present the pictures and the new research on them to the British public. That research is the combined achievement of those who have written this catalogue. John Leighton, Curator of Nineteenth-Century Painting at the National Gallery, has carried a heavy administrative burden. But all connected with the exhibition would acknowledge our enormous debt to Juliet Wilson-Bareau, who has shown us all how much may be learnt and what pleasure may be had by looking at Manet again and again.

In London, however, our greatest debt of all is to that earlier British Government, which, in March 1918, in spite of war and financial crisis, nonetheless found the money and the will to buy for the National Gallery the Maximilian fragments from the Degas sale in Paris. Few governments anywhere have shown such faith in the enduring power of art to inspire and to transform. Not the least aim of this exhibition is to vindicate that faith.

Neil MacGregor
Director

Acknowledgements

Manet and the execution of Maximilian in Mexico is a subject that has involved a great many people in a variety of fields. I am indebted to all of them for responding so warmly to different aspects of this project, with general advice or with special expertise in areas such as military weapons and uniforms, the French Foreign Legion or the European and transatlantic cable network.

An essential though all too brief encounter with Mexico was planned with the help of Elizabeth Carmichael, Marcela Ramírez and Mariana Yampolsky, and the generous enthusiasm of Louis Hallard. Salvador Rueda Smithers, Director of the Museo Nacional de Historia now installed in 'Maximilian's palace' at Chapultepec, was immensely helpful and provided stimulating insights into the Mexican point of view, so often ignored in European accounts of Maximilian's death. Thanks to him, it was also possible in a very short time to appreciate the rich holdings of the museum on which the exhibition and its publication have been able to draw. I am also grateful to Raúl Ortiz y Ortiz in London, and am greatly indebted to Brian R. Hamnett, of the University of Essex.

For information and documentation concerning Maximilian, I am very grateful to Rossella Fabiani, curator at the archduke's former home near Trieste, now the Museo Storico del Castello di Miramare. I was particularly fortunate to encounter Ferdinand Anders, an expert on Maximilian, who was a mine of information and a source of images and ideas in Mexico and in Austria. In Vienna, Peter Broucek, Barbara Dossi, Erwin A. Schmidl and Marie Luise Sternath were generous with their assistance, and useful exchanges took place with Konrad Ratz.

Information on military matters and the Foreign Legion were provided by Paul Dubrunfaut in Brussels; Adjudant-chef Glaziou at Aubagne, Commandant Chaduc, Louis Delpérier and Jean-Marcel Humbert in Paris, and Raoul Brunon in Salon-de-Provence; De Witt Bailey and David Penn offered invaluable help in London. John G. Entwhisle of Reuters London office unravelled the mysteries of the transatlantic cable. Photography and the carte de visite, much in evidence here, were studied with the help of Amparo Gómez Tepexicuapan and Olivier Debroise in Mexico; Inge Dupont, Carol Johnson, Lewis Lehr and Patricia Lowinsky in the USA; Michèle Chomette, Gilbert Gimon, Françoise Heilbrun, Bernard Marbot, Catherine Mathon, Commandant Jacques Spitzer and Lieutenant-Colonel Terrasson in France. For assistance with popular prints and the *dépôt légal*, I am very grateful to François Fossier, Jacqueline Lafargue and Frédéric Maguet. Philippe Grand, Claude Jacir, Christian Opriessnig and François Robichon helped to clarify the career of the military painter J. A. Beaucé.

In Brussels, the Royal archives and collections and the Royal Army Museum are essential sources for material relating to Maximilian, Charlotte and the French intervention in Mexico, and I would like to thank Gustav Janssens and Martine Vermeire in the Royal Palace and Richard Boijen and his very helpful staff in the museum, as well as its former print curator Albert Duchesne.

For help of many different kinds, I am indebted to Paul and Marie Van den Abbeel, Jeannine Baticle, Huguette Berès, Henrik Bjerre, François Caradec, Elizabeth Childs, Philippe Comte, Claire Constans, Marlyse Courrech, France Daguet, Eric Darragon, Guy-Patrice Dauberville, France Dijoud, Roland Dorn, Philippe Dupuis, Caroline Durand-Ruel Godfroy, Walter Feilchenfeldt, Anne-Birgitte Fonsmark, Teréz Gerszi, Judit Geskó, Nigel Glendinning, Lennart Gottlieb, Gloria Groom, Anne Hoenigswald, Henry McKenzie Johnston, Alvaro Martínez-Novillo, Michael Pakenham, Theodore Reff, Claudie Ressort, Jane Roos, Anne Roquebert, Eugène Rouir and Barbara Shapiro.

I am particularly grateful to Françoise Cachin, Douglas Druick, Antony Griffiths, Charles Moffett and Joseph Rishel for their enthusiasm and support, and to John House and Douglas Johnson for all their help. Peter Sutton, Robert Boardingham and the conservation team at the Boston Museum of Fine Arts, especially Rona Macbeth and Richard Newman, have done all that was possible to help decipher the first version of the painting, and Manfred Fath and Jochen Kronjäger gave every assistance in investigating the final version in Mannheim.

Finally, this study of Manet's great enterprise has had at its heart the vision and commitment of the staff of the National Gallery in London, where my greatest debt is to Neil MacGregor for his friendship and unfailing support. I would also like to acknowledge the support of Mary Hersov and Michael Wilson, and thank Jo Kent, Sarah Perry and Louise Woodroff for their help. John Leighton and David Bomford have been my principal collaborators and I am grateful for their constant encouragement as much as for their informed and sometimes sceptical questioning. Felicity Luard, Emma Shackleton and Sue Curnow, as well as Denys Baker, Malcolm Greenleaf, and Peter Guy, shared the delights and bore most of the difficulties of producing this publication. It is dedicated to everyone who is interested, as Manet himself put it, in an art 'that has a sense of humanity, a sense of modernity', and can involve us in the issues of our own and other times.

Juliet Wilson-Bareau

Introduction

JOHN LEIGHTON

After Manet's death on 30 April 1883, one of his young friends, Edmond Bazire, prepared a biography that contains a moving account of the artist's deserted studio:

Manet's last studio is on the rue d'Amsterdam . . . a tall, square structure on the far side of a courtyard, away from noise and bustle. . . . It is so arranged that light floods into the space. The furnishings are of the simplest: a curved settee, a divan, some armchairs, a mahogany desk covered in papers and pamphlets, a leather stool, and that is all. Yet this huge hangar appears almost diminutive, its walls almost hidden by canvases of earlier or more recent date. . . . This studio tells the artist's story, the précis of a career devoted to study, shaken by storms. . . . The celebrated *Olympia* hangs in the centre of the largest wall . . . the tremendous *Execution of Maximilian* is suspended over a door . . . these are the works from the earlier period. Then the mood changes; instead of dark backgrounds and violent contrasts there is a move to bright colours and sunshine.

The monumental *Execution of Maximilian* (fig. 76:III), dominating the works of the 1860s in Manet's studio, was the final version of a painting that he tackled in two other canvases (figs. 70:I and 73:II), which were set aside and rolled for storage because they were so large. An oil sketch (fig. 74) and a lithograph (fig. 77) are further evidence of his preoccupation with this theme. None of these works was shown in France during Manet's lifetime and his lithograph was banned by the authorities in 1869.

Manet had chosen to confront one of the most contentious issues of his day – the disastrous end to the French intervention in Mexico. This began in 1862 with Napoleon III's controversial decision to send French troops into Mexico to enforce repayment of debts owed to France by the newly established Republic under the presidency of Benito Juárez. Juárez was forced to leave the capital and in 1864, the Archduke Ferdinand Maximilian, younger brother of Franz Joseph, Emperor of Austria, was installed as Emperor of Mexico by Napoleon III under the protection of an occupying French army. Maximilian's reign as puppet emperor was short lived. When France reneged on a formal treaty and withdrew its troops, Maximilian was soon captured by republican forces loyal to the legitimate government of Benito Juárez. He was executed at Querétaro alongside two of his generals, Mejía and Miramón, on 19 June 1867, the date inscribed on Manet's final canvas.

For the majority of Mexicans, the Maximilian affair was a victory ending a long period of civil war and foreign interference. In France the death of Maximilian was seen as a national humiliation and a shattering blow to the prestige of the French Emperor. Harrowing accounts of the execution and of Maximilian's courage in facing the firing squad only served to enhance the image of an innocent victim betrayed by the ambitious and deceitful policies of Napoleon III.

Manet: The Execution of Maximilian begins with the story of the French intervention in Mexico. Within the scope of this account by Douglas Johnson, the historical events are seen from a largely French perspective, since this was the background to Manet's perception of the Maximilian affair. Manet's response to this episode is examined here by Juliet Wilson-Bareau. An extraordinary variety of prints and photographs of Maximilian circulated in Europe and America in the months after the execution. Even in France, where the imperial censors could suppress unfavourable references to recent events, Manet would eventually have had access to many images as well as to the reports from Mexico that appeared in the press. A notorious critic of 'history painting', he nevertheless set out to fashion an ambitious example of this genre and to bring a sensational contemporary event to the walls of the Paris Salon exhibition.

Manet's republican sympathies are well known, although he left few clues as to how they informed his art. In the 1870s, he painted several works that are obviously influenced by his republican views. These are discussed here, but the Maximilian pictures are also examined in the context of works of the 1860s that may carry a political charge. Manet's innovative approach to history painting is considered in relation to other images of contemporary history presented at the Salon exhibitions in these years.

Ultimately, Manet's endeavour was to end in frustration when his efforts to exhibit his paintings of Maximilian, and to publish his lithograph of the composition, were thwarted by successive French governments, who remained sensitive to the subject long after Maximilian had been laid to rest in the Habsburg crypt in Vienna. The question of political censorship in France is examined in depth by John House who argues that Manet's treatment of his theme was as provocative as his subject.

For a variety of reasons, the story of the life and death of Maximilian has lent itself to partisan or sentimental presentations. We have attempted here to chart the progress and evaluate the significance of Manet's paintings by attending to his own insistence on basing his work on documentary evidence. Precedents for this approach were set by the thesis of Nils Sandblad in 1954 and the remarkable analyses and documentation in the Brown University catalogue of 1981. In the present study, Manet's Maximilian project is viewed not as an isolated outburst of political sentiment but as part of his persistent interest in contemporary history. The artist's direct, personal contacts, close attention to eyewitness accounts and use of 'real' soldiers as models are considered, as are his known feelings about the military and his views on art and politics.

Manet often insisted on the purely artistic nature of his work, yet he was clearly alive to the events that shaped his world. His use of a highly sophisticated though deliberately naïve pictorial language, and his refusal to make his aims explicit, have helped to obscure the fact that he immersed himself in the raw materials of the news reporting of his day. Such materials are gathered here in an attempt to recreate the impact in France of Maximilian's execution at Querétaro, and to see how it was received and understood – or misunderstood – by Manet and his contemporaries.

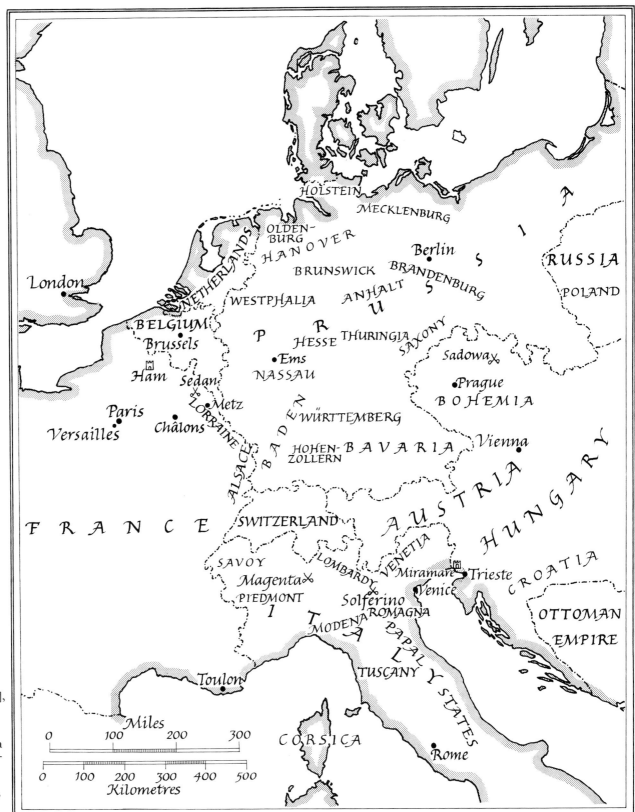

Europe
*c.*1860–70
Based on
Stanford's
*Portable Map
of Europe*,
London [1861],
and showing
France under
the Second
Empire, Prussia
and the Austro-
Hungarian
Empire –
principal states,
cities and
battle sites.

HOLSTEIN

MECKLENBURG

OLDEN–
BURG

HANOVER

Berlin

BRUNSWICK BRANDENBURG

RUSSIA

POLAND

London

NETHERLANDS

WESTPHALIA

ANHALT

S
I
S
U
R
P

BELGIUM

Brussels

HESSE THURINGIA

SAXONY

Sadowa

Ham

Ems

NASSAU

Prague

B O H E M I A

Sedan

Metz

WÜRTTEMBERG

Paris

LORRAINE

Versailles

Châlons

BADEN

HOHEN-
ZOLLERN

B A V A R I A

Vienna

ALSACE

F R A N C E

SWITZERLAND

A U S T R I A

H U N G A R Y

SAVOY

Magenta

VENETIA

LOMBARDY

Miramare

Trieste

C R O A T I A

PIEDMONT

Solferino

Venice

OTTOMAN

MODENA ROMAGNA

PAPAL

EMPIRE

I
T
A
L
Y

TUSCANY

STATES

Toulon

Miles

0   100   200   300

C O R S I C A

0 100 200 300 400 500

Kilometres

Rome

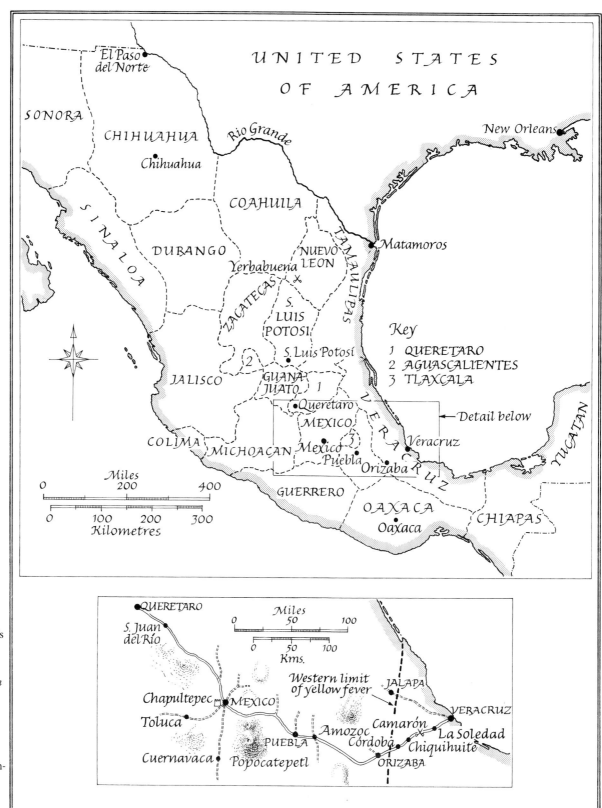

Mexico
*c.*1860–70
Based on A. Vuillemin's
*Nouvelle Carte du
Mexique*, Paris 1862,
and the detail
*Map of the Country from
Vera Cruz to Mexico*
prepared for the
War Office, London
1862. All maps of this
period are unreliable
and reference has
been made to other con-
temporary sources as
well as to modern
maps for both Europe
and Mexico.

UNITED STATES
OF AMERICA

El Paso
del Norte

New Orleans

SONORA

CHIHUAHUA

Rio Grande

Chihuahua

COAHUILA

S I N A L O A

DURANGO

Yerbabuena
×

NUEVO
LEON

Matamoros

TAMAULIPAS

ZACATECAS

S.
LUIS
POTOSI

S. Luis Potosí

Key

1 QUERETARO
2 AGUASCALIENTES
3 TLAXCALA

2

JALISCO

GUANA
JUATO

1

Queretaro

V E R A C R U Z

Detail below

MEXICO

Veracruz

COLIMA

MICHOACAN

Mexico

3

Puebla

Orizaba

YUCATAN

Miles
200   400

GUERRERO

0   100   200   300
Kilometres

OAXACA

Oaxaca

CHIAPAS

QUERETARO

S. Juan
del Río

Miles
50   100

0   50   100
Kms.

Western limit
of yellow fever

JALAPA

Chapultepec

MEXICO

VERACRUZ

Toluca

Camarón
×

La Soledad

Amozoc

Córdoba

Chiquihuite

Cuernavaca

PUEBLA

ORIZABA

Popocatepetl

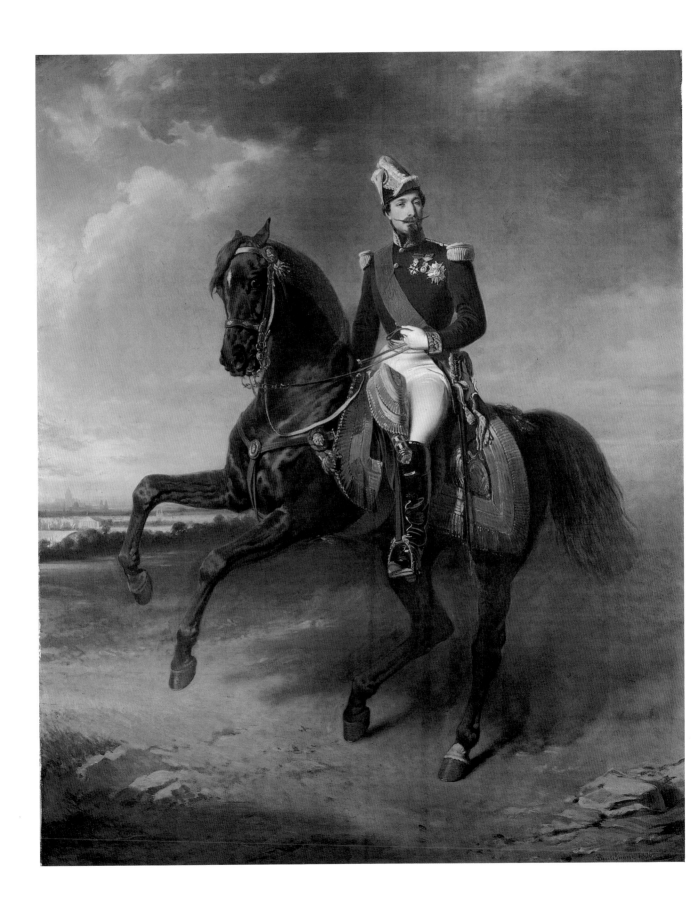

The French Intervention in Mexico
A Historical Background
DOUGLAS JOHNSON

The imperial ambitions of Napoleon III

The story of Maximilian is inextricably entwined with that of Napoleon III, Emperor of the French. But while historians agree on Maximilian's character, as being one where naïvety and pride alternated with courage and a sense of duty, they have always been divided about Napoleon III (fig. 2). For some he was an adventurer, whose only ambition was to manoeuvre himself into a position of power by exploiting the name of Bonaparte. Once he had attained that aim he lacked a firm goal and pursued a number of policies with an inconsistency that both baffled and dismayed observers. The British statesman Lord Palmerston claimed that the Emperor's mind was as full of schemes as a rabbit warren was of holes. But others have seen him differently, as a sophisticated politician, a connoisseur of ideas, a mixture of the enlightened despots of the eighteenth century and the dictators of modern times, someone who was preoccupied with economic progress and welfare.

Any view of Napoleon III has to take account of his early life. Born in 1808, Louis Napoleon was the son of Napoleon I's step-daughter, Hortense de Beauharnais, and his brother Louis Bonaparte, one-time King of Holland – although his paternity was vigorously disputed. However, it was not until the death in 1831 of his elder brother, followed by that in 1832 of Napoleon's only son, the duc de Reichstadt, that the prospect of imperial accession was presented to him.

For many years Louis Napoleon was only a bystander. He lived in exile, the author of occasional pamphlets, the organiser of two hopelessly unsuccessful attempts at *coups d'état*, in 1836 and 1840. The latter resulted in his imprisonment in the fortress of Ham in north-east France until, in 1846, he escaped and fled to England. When, in February 1848, the monarchy of Louis-Philippe was overthrown and the Second Republic established, he was not immediately allowed to return to France. The new Assembly decreed that the President should be elected; in December 1848 Louis Napoleon put his name forward and received an overwhelming majority. But as Prince–President his powers were restricted: he was elected for only four years and was not eligible for re-election. Therefore on 2 December 1851 he arrested many leading politicians, dissolved the Assembly and proclaimed a new constitution that gave him virtually all powers. This constitution was approved by plebiscite, a huge majority again voting in favour. A year after the *coup d'état*, even fewer voters opposed the amendment that gave the President the title of Emperor.

Now that France was once again under imperial rule it was clear that Napoleon III's government was authoritarian, enforced by institutional controls. But he also recognised the importance of public opinion, and the need to please and impress. His latest biographer has subtitled his work 'The Pursuit of Prestige'.[1] This prestige could come from many sources. There was a splendid court, especially after Napoleon III's marriage in 1853 to Eugénie de Montijo, Countess of Teba (fig. 3), the daughter of a Spanish nobleman who had served under Napoleon I. There was the transformation of Paris into an outstandingly beautiful city. There was economic expansion and a programme of public works. There was the association of the Church with the Empire. Prestige could also come by demonstrating the importance of France in the world. Paris became the capital of Europe when the Crimean War – in which France opposed Russia's supposed designs on the Ottoman Empire – was concluded by the Congress held there in 1856. The French army fought in Italy. France made her presence felt in Siam and in what was to become Indo-China, in Syria and in West Africa. Finally there was Mexico, which has been described as the most arresting undertaking of the Second Empire, as Napoleon III's most significant concept, '*la grande pensée de Napoléon III*'.[2]

The French in Mexico during the early nineteenth century

Mexico, independent from Spain after 1821, was a semi-feudal state that by the mid-nineteenth century had a population of some eight million, of which the overwhelming majority was Indian or of mixed race. The country was controlled by the white owners of the large estates, by the army and by the Catholic Church. Mexican history is dominated by the rivalries that existed between these three groups, and which became increasingly complex because of the importance of regionalism in a vast country where communications were exceptionally bad. Military leaders tended to predominate in a series of short-lived regimes, while the United States contributed to the weakness of these administrations both by its official annexations and by the activities of its free-booting agents, such as the raiders known as the Texas Rangers.

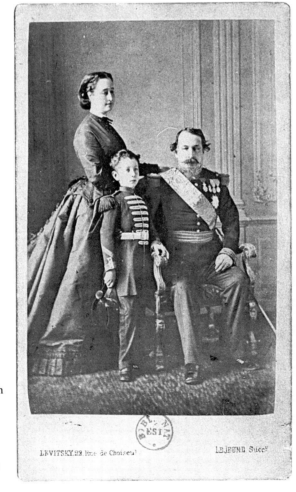

LEVITSKY, 22 Rue de Choiseul   LEJEUNE Succr

Fig. 3
The Imperial Family.
Carte de visite photograph
(enlarged) by Levitsky,
c. 1865.
Paris, Bibliothèque
Nationale.

Napoleon III with the
Empress Eugénie and the
Prince Imperial.

The French community in Mexico, in mid-century, consisted of some 6,000 urban-based traders and craftsmen and was the largest group of foreign, non-Spanish settlers. By 1860 it was no longer expanding, except in the state of Sonora in north-west Mexico, bordering American Arizona, where many French were attracted by hopes of spectacular mineral wealth, especially after the 1848 discovery of gold in California. These expectations were never fulfilled, although they added to the chorus of those who claimed that the prosperity of France would be increased by extending its territories overseas.

Because the French expedition to Mexico and the installation of the Archduke Maximilian of Austria as Emperor (figs. 5 and 6) ended in tragic disaster, this adventure has been seen as an example of Napoleon III's foolishness and untrustworthiness, since he embarked impetuously on an enterprise, only to abandon it when the difficulties that he should have foreseen became overwhelming. The subject has been studied by many historians,[3] and the debate continues, but one aspect of the matter is now established. The Mexican expedition was the culmination of a long-standing reflection, not only on the part of the Emperor as an individual, but also on the part of many Frenchmen who had long thought that France should take an initiative in Central or South America.[4]

It was as early as 1817 that the French Prime Minister under Louis XVIII, the duc de Richelieu, began to entertain the possibility of Bourbon princes playing a role in South America. Although there were no French Bourbons available, he considered that the position of the newly restored monarchy in France would be strengthened if the Bourbon family extended its power.[5] In the 1820s several European governments believed that the Spanish colonies in America could be recovered, with the use of relatively small forces, but it seemed, at least to the alert British statesmen Castlereagh and Canning, that it was the French who were the most likely to take action, whether by intrigue or by positive plans for intervention. There is no evidence of any ambition to make Mexico a French colony, but it was widely believed that Mexico, since Agustín de Iturbide had proclaimed independence from Spain in 1821, preferred to be governed by a monarchy, and that a monarchical government established there with French support would further French economic interests.

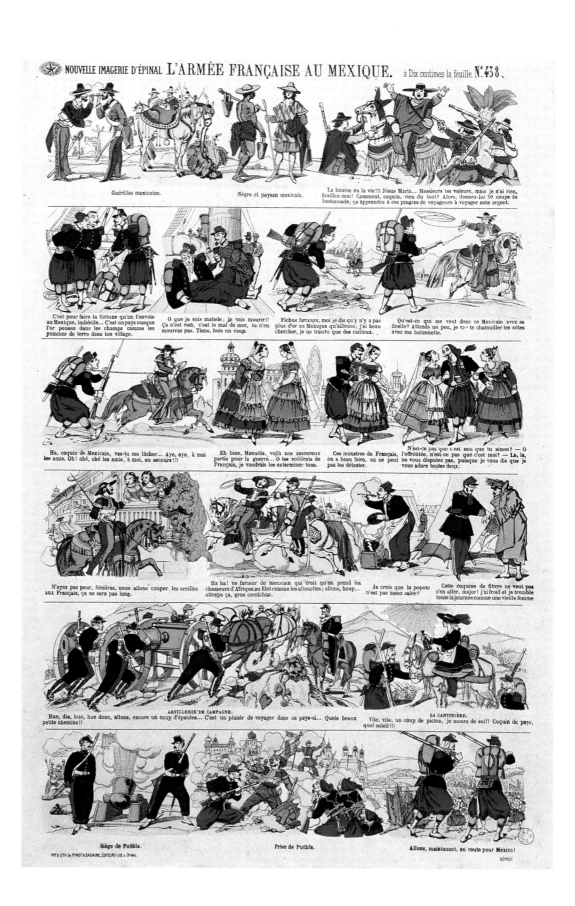

Fig. 4 (cat. 8)
The French Army in Mexico.
Coloured and gilded lithograph, 40.5 x 27.9 cm, by Pinot & Sagaire, Epinal and Paris, June 1863. Paris, Musée National des Arts et Traditions Populaires.

The print sets the scene for the French intervention in Mexico, with guerrilla fighters, a poor Indian and peasant, and a traveller surprised by brigands. The French forces, hoping to find gold, deal with Mexican guerrillas and their *señoritas*, suffer from yellow fever at Veracruz, and force a way over difficult terrain to Puebla, where they take the town and then head for Mexico City.

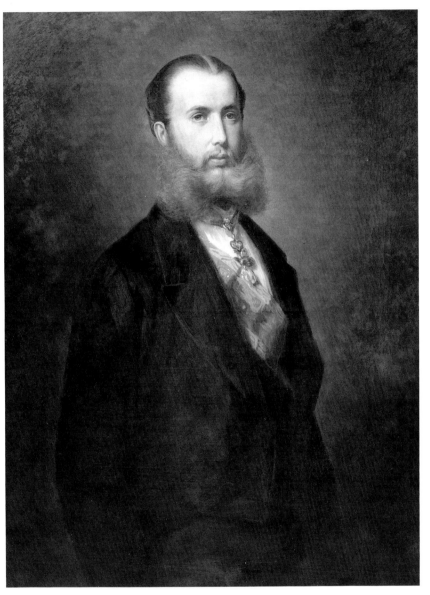

Fig. 5 (cat. 11)
Alfred Graefle
(after Winterhalter),
*Maximilian, Emperor of
Mexico*, 1867–8. Oil on
canvas, 100 x 76.2 cm.
The Royal Collection.

Winterhalter painted
portraits of Maximilian and
Charlotte in Paris in 1864
(now in Hearst Castle,
California). They were
both copied by Graefle in
about 1867–8 for Queen
Victoria.

compensation was supposedly a pastry cook). This action, however, failed to establish a predominant position for the French in Mexico.[7]

French opinion was divided as to what attitude France should adopt with regard to the expansion of the United States, as it began over a period of years to absorb the Spanish Floridas, the Mexican domain of Texas, New Mexico and California. The political philosopher Alexis de Tocqueville prophesied that the Americans and the Russians were marked out by the will of Heaven to sway the future of half the globe. Guizot, who dominated French policy in the 1840s, accepted that while the United States, Russia and Great Britain continued to expand in their different ways, France had no need to imitate them. Although he was critical of the American Monroe Doctrine of 1823, which warned European powers against intervention in the New World, he did not want to join Great Britain in opposing American action in Texas, and it seems that he did not consider American expansion as necessarily hostile to France.[8]

Napoleon III's Grand Design

Louis Napoleon had a greater knowledge of, and greater interest in, the New World than any of his predecessors in French government. He had himself stayed briefly in America, and had family contacts there through his uncle Jérôme Bonaparte's first wife, Elizabeth Patterson of Baltimore, and through his cousin Achille Murat, who had emigrated to Florida in 1823 and who wrote several books about life on the frontier. An important source of Louis Napoleon's interest in Latin America was his early participation in a project to build a canal across Nicaragua that would join the Atlantic and the Pacific Oceans and he published a pamphlet on the subject in 1846 that stressed the commercial advantages of such a construction.[9] But the canal was in fact only part of a greater political scheme for a united Central American state under British protection, with Louis Napoleon at its head (he seems to have envisaged Nicaragua, Honduras, Guatemala, Costa Rica and San Salvador as being included). He was apparently approached by 'several influential men' from Central America as early as 1842, while he was imprisoned at Ham, by the Nicaraguan envoy in 1844, and by his friend Lord Malmesbury, on behalf of the British government who were to intercede with the French King

It is significant that it always seems to have been a small number of important individuals who pressed for these ideas to be put into practice – such as Chateaubriand, who was for a time Foreign Minister – yet they found it difficult to understand the political upheavals to which Mexico was subject or to persuade successive French governments that they should take positive action to ensure favoured treatment for French subjects resident in or trading with Mexico.[6]

But in 1837 the French government did take action and in an effort to recover unpaid debts started an inconclusive war against Mexico, known as 'the Pastry War' (because one of the claimants for

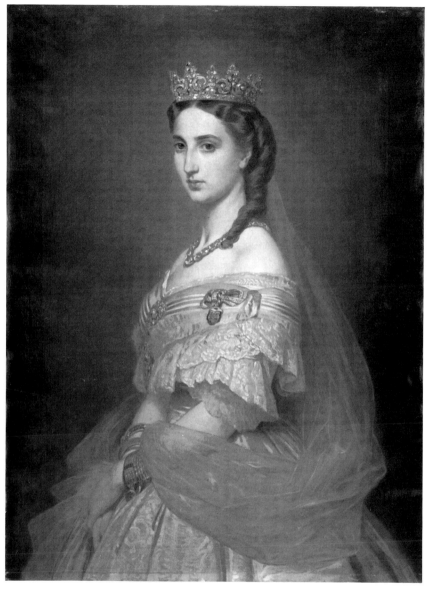

Fig. 6 (cat. 12)
Alfred Graefle
(after Winterhalter),
Charlotte, Empress of Mexico,
1867–8. Oil on canvas,
99.4 x 74.3 cm.
The Royal Collection.

Charlotte, the daughter of
Leopold I, King of the
Belgians, married Max-
imilian, Archduke of
Austria, in Brussels on
27 July 1857.

ruler and supported by European power and capital, could transform Latin America into an area that would have the prosperity and the strength to resist the encroachments of the United States.

When Louis Napoleon was elected President in 1848, he assured the Mexican chargé d'affaires that he would always do everything in his power to maintain peace and closer ties with Mexico.[11] In 1853 General Antonio López de Santa Anna, 'the Bonaparte of the West', made himself dictator in Mexico and, with his collaborators, asked Napoleon III for French protection (he also appealed to the British government), saying that he would step down in favour of a European ruler. He ordered a former Mexican Conservative minister, José María Gutiérrez de Estrada (see fig. 13), a fervent monarchist, exiled since 1840, to search for a likely prince. In 1856, after a Liberal victory had again driven Santa Anna from Mexico, and subsequently, a French diplomat, the marquis de Radepont, acting with the collaboration of the French Minister in Mexico, the vicomte de Gabriac, endeavoured unsuccessfully to persuade the French government that the fourth son of the deposed Louis-Philippe, the duc d'Aumale, should be given the throne of Mexico.

The Crimean War, which lessened the likelihood of Britain and France taking any resolute action in South America, nevertheless provided an interesting analogy. If these European powers were prepared to go to war in order to prevent Russia from absorbing Turkey, why should they not protect Mexico from the United States? The question appeared all the more pressing since a plan existed (in which Napoleon III was very interested), for the canal linking the Atlantic and the Pacific to pass through the Mexican Isthmus of Tehuantepec, and it was thought essential that the United States should not control such an important channel of communication.[12]

There were other considerations. Many contemporary politicians urged the cause of European, particularly French, intervention in Mexico, and stressed the possibilities of Mexican development, because of its favourable geographical situation, if only it could escape the threat of American expansion.[13] There were refugees from Mexico, some of whom had access to the French court and could influence official opinions. There was also the Empress. She was Spanish and regretted the loss of the Spanish Empire. As a devout Catholic she

Louis-Philippe to obtain his release from Ham on condition that he would never again return to Europe.[10]

These negotiations, although unsuccessful, are important because they show how Latin American states were reportedly turning to Europe, not only for diplomatic and economic assistance, but also for their rulers. This is in line with the ideas of the French ministers plenipotentiary in Mexico who in 1844 and 1856 made detailed proposals for the introduction of a European prince into Mexico. The Nicaraguan discussions are also significant because they indicate Louis Napoleon's belief that a strong and active government, led by a European

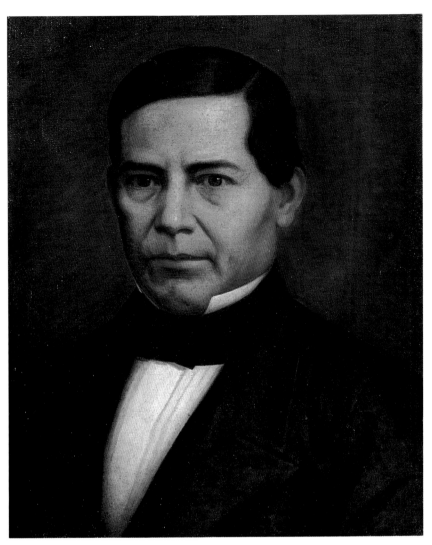

Fig. 7 (cat. 5)
Artist unknown,
Benito Juárez, c. 1868. Oil
on canvas, 50.5 x 41.5 cm.
Mexico City, INAH,
Castillo de Chapultepec.

This anonymous portrait
was probably based on a
photograph of Juárez, the
republican President of
Mexico, who defended his
country against the French
intervention, and approved
the execution of Max-
imilian in June 1867 (see
cat. 22).

Emperor acted under pressure from his wife and
from a few exiles who were ignorant of the real
situation in Mexico can be taken seriously. Eugénie
played an undeniable role in promoting the expedition, but it was far from being as vital as some
(including herself) have imagined.[14]

The diplomatic representatives of France in Mexico tended to be forceful characters, spurred on
sometimes by their memories of the Napoleonic
wars and invariably by their contempt for Mexicans
and for Mexican institutions. But in such a divided
society there were bound to be disputes as foreign
companies fought for concessions and, in an atmo-
sphere of confusion and corruption, alleged that
promises had not been kept and that legal obliga-
tions had been broken. The greatest faults of successive Mexican governments were overspending
and their consequent recourse to borrowing money
and raising loans from foreign banks. They were
therefore constantly in debt and had the greatest
difficulty in paying the often exorbitant interest
rates that they had incurred.

A particularly severe crisis developed with the
revolution of 1855, when Santa Anna was ousted
from power by Colonel Ignacio Comonfort. The
government that replaced him included the man
who was to personify Mexican aspirations for many
years, Benito Juárez, an Indian, born in 1806 (fig.
7). Juárez, who as a poor orphan boy walked bare-
foot the forty miles from the village of San Pablo
Guelatao, where he was born, to Oaxaca, who was
educated there at the Holy Cross Seminary, and
who became a lawyer and a member of the state
legislature, is the embodiment of progress. As
Minister of Justice, he and his associates were
responsible for the liberal Constitution of 1857,
which made Mexico a constitutional republic and
abolished slavery. But it was the measures limiting
the powers of the Church and abolishing many of
its privileges that led most directly to an unpre-
cedentedly vicious civil war. Comonfort, elected
President in 1857, was soon overthrown by the
Conservative General Zuloaga and went into exile
in 1858. Juárez, who became acting President,
withdrew his ministers from Mexico City, while a
rival government was set up there under the
presidency of Miguel Miramón (fig. 8). By the end
of 1860 the Conservative and clerical parties had
been defeated and in June 1861 Juárez became
President of the Mexican Republic. He had to face
many problems and his position was far from

responded readily to suggestions that a French
expedition would save the Catholic Church in Mexico, which was threatened by the Liberal and anti-
clerical regime and by American Protestantism. She
was in touch with Mexican expatriates, in particular
with José Hidalgo (see fig. 13), and may have
played an important part in persuading the
Emperor to undertake the Mexican expedition. It
has been suggested that her influence was all the
greater because by the late 1850s she was particularly distressed by her husband's affairs with various
women, and at times threatened to go and live with
her son in Rome. The Emperor, it was said, would
set all Europe afire in order to escape a domestic
quarrel and if his wife wanted a new crusade then
he would give her one.

It is doubtful that the allegations that the

secure, but it was Mexico's economic difficulties that precipitated the next war. The treasury was in deficit and there was scarcely any currency circulating in the country. Therefore when Mexico's European creditors demanded repayment Juárez felt that he had no option but to declare a two-year moratorium on the foreign debt.[15]

The European punitive expedition

The European response was the Tripartite Convention of London, of 31 October 1861, by which Britain, France and Spain agreed to coerce Mexico into paying its debts by occupying its coasts. The result of this treaty was the arrival at Veracruz of some 6,000 Spaniards, followed by a small British force and some 2,000 French troops. But the aims of the three powers were very different. The Spanish force was led by General Juan Prim (fig. 113), the Catalan hero of his country's war in Morocco, who saw himself as the natural leader of the expedition. He believed that it was possible to come to an agreement with Juárez. He saw no possibility of occupying Mexico, and he did not believe that the Mexicans were monarchists. The

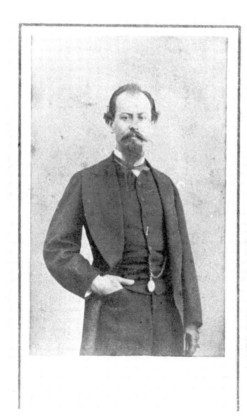

Fig. 8
General Miguel Miramón.
Carte de visite photograph by Aubert, *c.* 1865–7. Commandant Spitzer Collection.

Miramón was acting President of Mexico 1859–60, in opposition to the Liberal government of Benito Juárez. He later fought for Maximilian against Juárez and died with the Emperor at Querétaro in 1867.

British were timid. The British Foreign Secretary, Earl Russell, had made it clear from the outset that 'without at all yielding to the extravagant pretentions implied by what is called the Monroe Doctrine', he did not wish to arouse the ill feelings of the United States 'unless some paramount object were in prospect and tolerably easy of attainment'.[16] But the French were more ambitious and it was this that led to the break-up of the Tripartite Convention and to France acting alone.

Napoleon III was influenced by many considerations. He was convinced that the American Civil War, which began in April 1861, was going to be a long-drawn-out affair, and that the Americans would not be in a position to help Juárez (they had recognised his Liberal government in 1859). He had received many assurances that the conquest of Mexico would be easy. A further excuse was provided by the affair of the Jecker bonds, when a Swiss banker claiming French nationality, who had loaned Miramón's government three million francs in return for treasury bonds, sought aid from Napoleon III's half-brother, the duc de Morny, in pressing his colossal claim against Mexico.[17] There was also the possibility of particular economic advantage coming to France with the formation of a French-sponsored railway company in Mexico associated with a United States senator (and later Confederate leader), Judah P. Benjamin.[18]

But although these considerations were important (and French insistence on getting satisfaction over the Jecker bonds was one of the reasons for the break-up of the Tripartite Convention), Napoleon III was pursuing two major aims. The first was to prevent the United States from becoming the sole power in America and the sole dispenser of the products of the New World.[19] The other was to propose that, with French support, the Archduke Maximilian, younger brother of the Emperor of Austria, and former Governor of Lombardy, which until recently had been under Austrian rule, should be the Emperor of Mexico. Thereby Napoleon would achieve his primary diplomatic aim in Europe: that of creating a Franco–Austrian alliance. Such an alliance would enable France to dominate European diplomacy and to settle outstanding questions (particularly that of completing Italian independence by freeing Venetia from Austrian rule). By the autumn of 1861 Napoleon III was giving direct encouragement to Maximilian's candidature.[20]

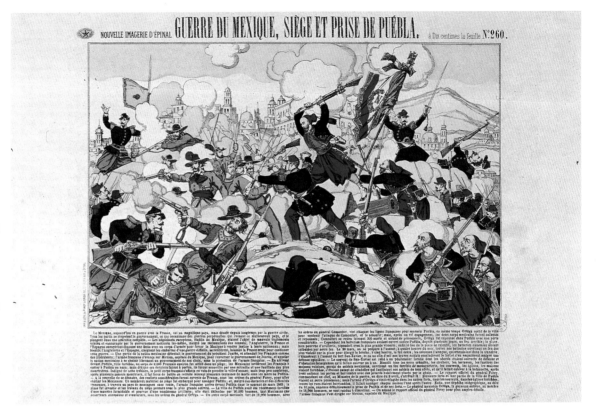

Fig. 9 (cat. 9)
War in Mexico, Siege and Capture of Puebla.
Coloured and gilded lithograph, 27.6 x 41 cm, by Pinot & Sagaire, Epinal and Paris, June 1863.
Paris, Musée National des Arts et Traditions Populaires.

The lengthy text justifies the French intervention on behalf of 'a part of the Mexican nation that hated President Juárez's government and looked on the French as liberators', and gives a detailed account of the long and difficult engagement at Puebla.

Fig. 10
Marshal Bazaine and his Staff, photograph by François Aubert, 1866.
Albumen print, 11.5 x 18 cm.
Brussels, Musée Royal de l'Armée.

Aubert's photograph of Bazaine in Mexico, originally printed in reverse, is inverted here, showing military decorations correctly worn over the left breast.

Fig. 11
Jean-Adolphe Beaucé, *Combat at Camarón (Mexico), 30 April 1863*, Salon of 1869. Oil on canvas, 150 x 235 cm.
Aubagne, Musée de la Légion Etrangère.

The scene shows a handful of Legionnaires making their last stand against overwhelming Juarist forces in a ruined *hacienda*.

The French campaign in Mexico

But the French expeditionary force in Mexico was not immediately successful. The first priority was to advance on Mexico City from the port of Veracruz, keeping the supply lines open. This meant securing the cities of Orizaba and Puebla (see map page 13). After the departure of the Spanish and the British, advancing French troops were defeated at Puebla in May 1862, at the hands of Generals Ignacio Zaragoza and Porfirio Díaz (later to become President of Mexico). Reinforcements were sent and the French took their revenge at Puebla the following year, after a difficult siege (fig. 9).

It was in order to protect supplies to the French forces besieging Puebla that the Foreign Legion engaged in one of its most celebrated exploits, that at Camarón (fig. 11). There, in April 1863, some sixty-five soldiers who had been in Mexico for less than a month, held out in an abandoned hacienda for ten hours against a force of 2,000 Mexicans, losing fifty-two men but dissuading the enemy from making further attacks on French convoys.

Juárez then evacuated Mexico City, and General

Bazaine entered the capital, followed on 10 June 1863 by the French commander, General Forey (fig. 12). A week later Forey announced the formation of a provisional government that was essentially Conservative and clerical, and shortly afterwards a hastily convened assembly of notables voted that they would offer the imperial crown of Mexico to Maximilian. The offer was delivered to Maximilian by an official delegation in October led by Gutiérrez de Estrada (fig. 13).

This was what Napoleon III had wanted. None the less, he was very alarmed. He had given instructions that General Forey should not appear to be in power, and that it was the Mexicans who should seem to be choosing Maximilian. He was also disappointed that although some 38,000 French troops had been sent to Mexico since 1861 there was no sign of any general monarchist rising. Even more perturbing to Napoleon was the condemnation by the opposition at home of this French commitment in a distant country, a commitment that was absorbing a great deal of money and costing thousands of lives.[21]

He therefore requested the replacement of Forey

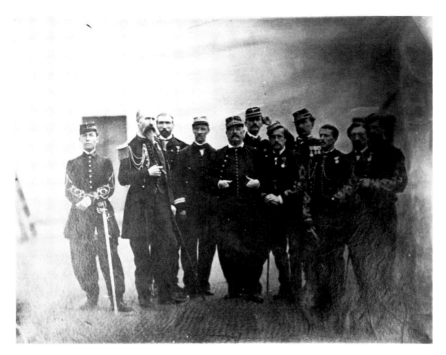

by Bazaine (fig. 10), who had orders to pacify the country rather than conquer it, and to organise a Mexican force that would allow French troops to return home and thereby reduce French expenditure.[22] Bazaine showed great qualities. He got rid of the reactionary groups that Forey had installed. He was generous to his opponents, and as a fluent Spanish speaker he made many allies. Initially he had considerable military success, and was able to popularise the idea of the Empire, particularly among the Indian population.

Meanwhile Maximilian was agonising over whether he would or would not accept the throne. Now that Lombardy was no longer ruled by Austria he had no official position, and lived retired at his castle of Miramare near Trieste. He consulted many people and posed a great many conditions, most of which he eventually abandoned. But the essential meeting between Maximilian and Napoleon III took place in Paris in March 1864. To reassure Maximilian, Napoleon promised to

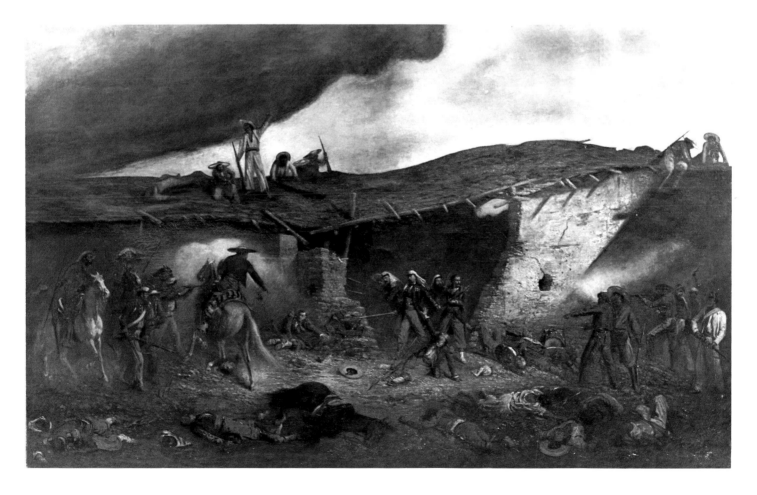

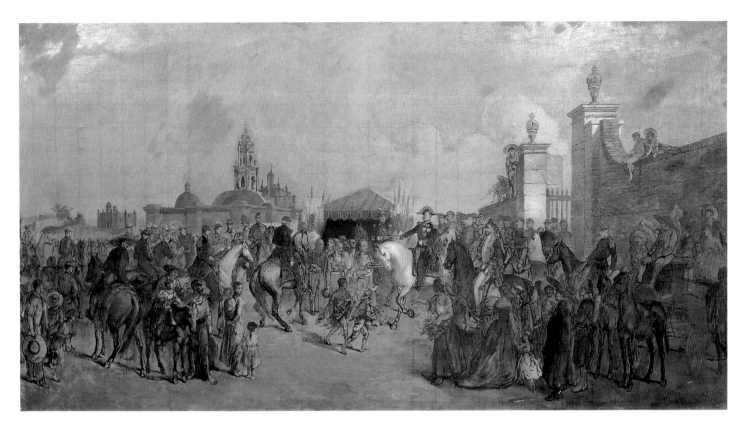

Fig. 12 (cat. 10)
Jean-Adolphe Beaucé,
*General Forey leading the
French Expeditionary Force
into Mexico City*, 1867–8.
Oil on canvas,
79 x 148 cm.
Aubagne, Musée de la
Légion Etrangère.

This preparatory sketch has
been squared-up to transfer
Beaucé's composition to
the very large canvas
(Château de Versailles),
exhibited in the Salon of
1868.

Fig. 13 (cat. 13)
Cesare dell'Acqua,
*The Mexican Delegation at
Miramare*, photograph by
Ghémar Frères, Brussels,
*c.*1865. Mounted albumen
print, 34 x 50 cm (with
letters, 43.6 x 58 cm).
Brussels, Musée Royal de
l'Armée.

Ghémar's photograph of
dell'Acqua's painting identifies the members of the
delegation, including
J. M. Gutiérrez de Estrada
and J. M. Hidalgo.

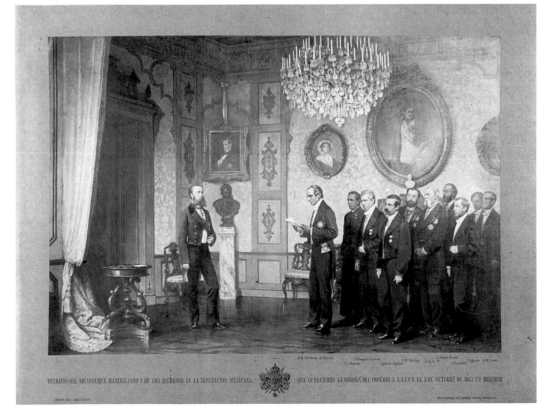

keep 25,000 French soldiers in Mexico until they were replaced by native forces, and that the Foreign Legion would maintain a force there of some 8,000 troops for at least six years. But the French were exacting when it came to demanding that Maximilian should reimburse them for the expenses they had incurred, as well as repay Mexico's outstanding debts, including the Jecker bonds. The agreement was ceremoniously ratified at Maximilian's Adriatic home.

So it was that the thirty-two-year-old Maximilian and his twenty-four-year-old wife Charlotte, daughter of Leopold I, King of the Belgians, set off on the long journey from Trieste to Veracruz (fig. 14). On 28 May 1864 they reached that fever-stricken city and were told by an irritable French rear-admiral that they had arrived too early. It was not an auspicious beginning for the young Emperor and his consort.

The arrival of the Emperor Maximilian

Maximilian and Charlotte made a royal entry into Mexico City on 12 June. At first there was success. Maximilian liked the country. He established a good working relationship with Bazaine. It was thought that more than two-thirds of the population supported him. Some 6,000 Austrian and more than 2,000 Belgian troops came to join his forces. He began the reconstruction of Chapultepec Castle (fig. 16), which was to be his official residence, and he saw himself strolling in the gardens where the Aztec emperor Montezuma II had walked as he wondered how to repulse the advancing Spanish conquistadors of Hernán Cortés. Maximilian had plans for improving the lot of the ordinary people, yet at the same time he wished to import 2,000 birds from Europe to inhabit the woods around Chapultepec and he drew up a

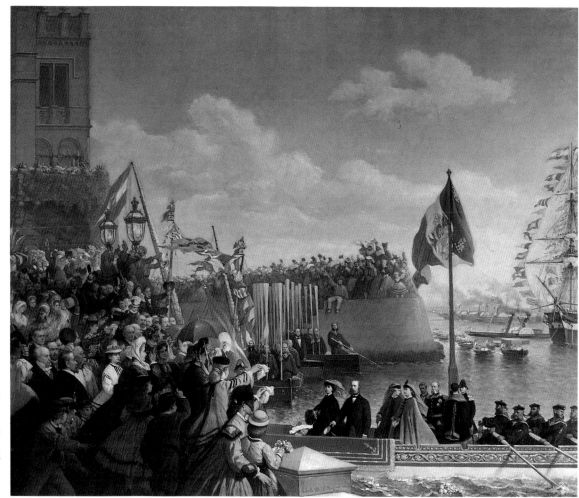

Fig. 14
Cesare dell'Acqua,
The Departure of Maximilian and Charlotte from Miramare for Mexico,
1866. Oil on canvas,
129 x 182 cm.
Trieste, Castello di Miramare.

The imperial couple sailed from Miramare on 14 April 1864 in the *Novara*, the ship that was to bring Maximilian's corpse back to Trieste less than four years later. Dell'Acqua's historical scenes, painted in Brussels, were commissioned for the castle at Miramare.

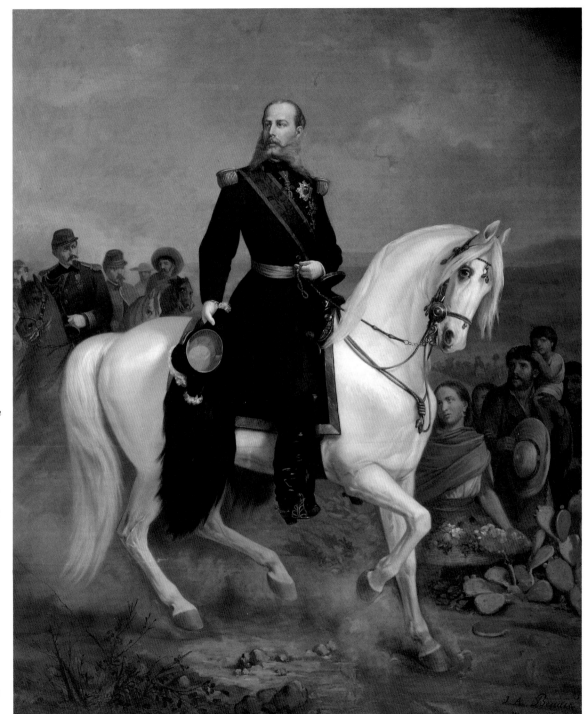

Fig. 15
Jean-Adolphe Beaucé,
*The Emperor Maximilian on
Horseback*, 1865. Oil on
canvas, 255 x 168 cm.
Mexico City, INAH,
Castillo de Chapultepec.

Beaucé's huge equestrian
portrait of Maximilian still
hangs in the palace at
Chapultepec. The painting
was photographed by
Aubert (cat. 14) and also
distributed as a carte de
visite photograph.

Fig. 16 (cat. 15)
The Castle at Chapultepec,
photograph by François
Aubert, *c.* 1864. Albumen
print, 26.2 x 36.8 cm.
Brussels, Musée Royal de
l'Armée.

Maximilian and Charlotte
chose to live in this castle
on the outskirts of Mexico
City in preference to the
palace near the cathedral.

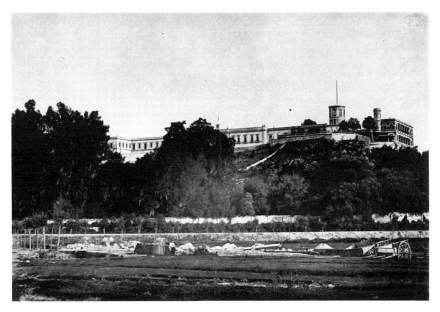

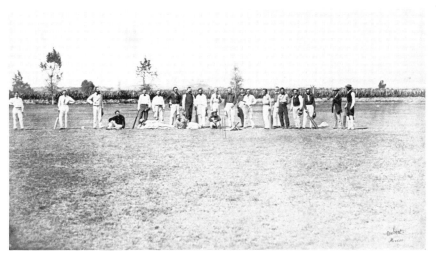

Fig. 17 (cat. 16)
Maximilian and his Court playing Cricket (detail), photograph by François Aubert, *c.* 1865. Albumen print, 28.2 x 37.3 cm. Brussels, Musée Royal de l'Armée.

Maximilian, in a dark shirt and white trousers, stands behind the cricket stumps. On his right is the English Ambassador, Sir Charles Wyke.

detailed etiquette for his court.

Juárez and the ministers of his Republican government were driven further north, eventually to a town on the United States border, and Maximilian seemed triumphant. Aided by moderate advisers, he had drafted a constitution that established equality before the law and, most important, freedom of labour, so that a labourer could leave his employment at will. Child labour was to be controlled, the corporal punishment of labourers was forbidden and Indian villages were given the right to own communal property. As Juárez's mandate as elected President was due to expire on 1 December 1865, his position was obviously weakening.

But difficulties were never absent. Within the court of the Mexican Emperor there were innumerable intrigues and confusions that increased as time went by. There was the Catholic party, supported by the Papacy, which demanded that the lands and the rights of the Church should be restored. There were those who were hostile to the French. Moderate Liberals were thought to support Maximilian, but since they were not convinced that he would remain they added their weight to those who jostled for power and influence in an imported court supported by a foreign army.

The military situation began to deteriorate. When Maximilian arrived a token French force was sent back to France, ostensibly to demonstrate that Mexico was independent, although many units of the French army wanted to return home. It had always been difficult for them to work with the Mexican forces in the Imperial army, and they had found the conduct of guerrilla war complicated. The French hired bandits, such as the self-styled general and bandit chief Ignacio Butrón, to attack the enemy, but such were the bandits' continued depredations and assassinations that they then felt obliged to arrest them. Butrón and others were court-martialled and shot, thus creating enormous controversy and bitterness. Juarista activity increased in the northern provinces, although a rumour came in September 1865 that Juárez had fled from Mexican soil. The result was Maximilian's fierce decree of 3 October that set up a system of instant courts martial with power to execute immediately any members of unauthorised armed bands. Although it appears that Bazaine approved this decree, its extremism suggested a return to old Mexican authoritarianism, and as such was inherently anti-French.[23]

The French withdraw from Mexico

From then on there was a steady decline in the affairs of the Empire. Maximilian ceased to trust Bazaine; Bazaine complained that he was not getting co-operation from Mexican officials; French officers believed that Paris was not being properly informed about the state of affairs in Mexico. At what point Napoleon III began to realise that the Grand Design had been a failure is not clear. As early as August 1865 in conversation with the American Ambassador to Brazil, then in Paris, he stated that he had gone into the Mexican affair

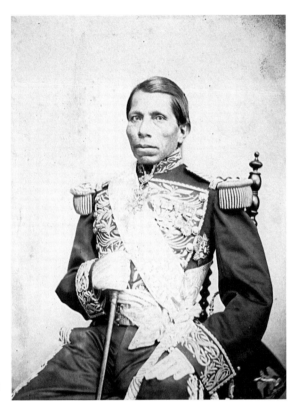

Fig. 18 (cat. 17)
General Tomás Mejía,
photograph by François
Aubert, *c.* 1864. Albumen
print, 17.3 x 13 cm.
Brussels, Musée Royal de
l'Armée.

Mejía, of pure Indian
blood like Benito Juárez,
was Maximilian's most
loyal general and was
executed with the Emperor
in 1867.

'very unintentionally',[24] and by January 1866 he was telling Bazaine that he should withdraw French troops within a year or eighteen months. From then onward French forces worked with the idea of evacuation in mind.

Undoubtedly Napoleon was apprehensive of a military collapse and the loss of his army. But this belief in the possibility of failure was sharpened by fears of American action. As the Civil War drew to its close it became clear that American supplies to the Juaristas had become considerable and there were many reports and rumours of direct intervention across the frontier.[25] The American Secretary of State, William H. Seward, insisted that the French should speed up their withdrawal and told his ambassador to ask repeatedly whether this was being done. He also refused to admit to the possibility of the Mexican Empire surviving and officially received Doña Margarita, the wife of Juárez, in Washington.[26]

The total defeat of Austria by Prussia at Sadowa in July 1866 underlined the ineffectiveness of French diplomacy and the extent of Prussia's military power under Bismarck. It also reduced the value of the Franco–Austrian alliance, which had been one of the main reasons for supporting the Austrian candidate in Mexico. Napoleon was harassed by the opposition at home, who were able to point out that the weakness of France in Europe was being increased by the Mexican venture, which was in every way '*une expédition ruineuse*'. Indeed as the European balance of power became more unfavourable towards France, the prospect of important units of the French army remaining in Mexico became positively dangerous.

Two dramatic incidents did not improve the situation. One was Charlotte's return to Europe to seek aid for Maximilian, and her violent interviews with Napoleon and Eugénie, which precipitated her mental breakdown. The other was the special mission of General François de Castelnau to Mexico, in order to persuade Maximilian to abdicate. The mission ended in controversy, with Castelnau maintaining that Bazaine was trying to persuade Maximilian not to abdicate, because of the influence of his Mexican wife, Josefa de la Peña, whom he had married in 1865. This allegation was never satisfactorily proved.[27]

But Maximilian decided not to abdicate, and at times talked wildly of how his Indian general Tomás Mejía (fig. 18) would continue the war with him. Bazaine arranged with the Juaristas that the evacuation of the French troops would not be hampered by them, and ordered his army to withdraw in an orderly manner. On 3 February 1867 he issued a proclamation to the Mexican people announcing that the French troops were leaving Mexico City. By 13 March the last of the French troops had sailed from Veracruz leaving some 7,000 dead behind them. None of the diplomatic or economic advantages that had been envisaged by the French government had been achieved. While it is impossible to say which considerations influenced Napoleon most, it is certain that he was never indifferent to public opinion at home and that this opinion was concerned with four factors: the financial costs of the expedition, the loss of French lives, fear of war with the United States and apprehension about the growing power of Prussia.

Maximilian's defeat and execution

Profiting from the withdrawal of the French, Juárez was able to move south, Porfirio Díaz recaptured Oaxaca, and although Maximilian's audacious General Miramón made a lightning raid on Zacatecas in central Mexico and nearly took Juárez

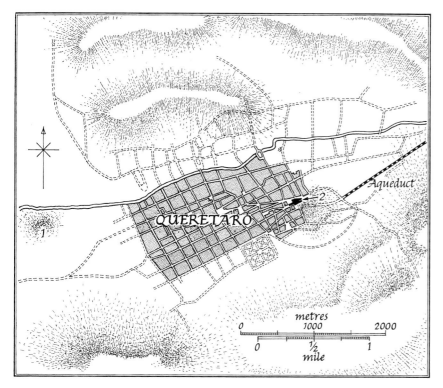

prisoner, only Mexico City, Veracruz and a number of scattered areas remained under imperial control. It was to one of these, Querétaro (figs. 19 and 20), 125 miles north of the capital that Maximilian took his 9,000 troops in order to make a last stand (although he attempted negotiation with both Juárez and Díaz). This town was inhabited by Indians who were devoted to General Mejía and who gave Maximilian a great welcome. But it lay between two ridges of desert mountains and soon these heights were occupied by between 20,000 and 30,000 Republican troops. The whole town was surrounded and the siege began. Maximilian's attempts to bring reinforcements from Mexico City failed, and it seemed that he could only be saved by a break-out. But the Imperial forces were betrayed by Colonel Miguel López, an officer trusted by the Emperor (who was godfather to one of his children). The Republicans entered Querétaro and on 15 May 1867 Maximilian and his entourage surrendered.

It was immediately announced that Maximilian, and his two generals, Miramón and Mejía, must

Fig. 19
Plan of Querétaro
(based on the plan in Prince Salm-Salm's memoirs of 1868).

To the west, outside the town, is the Cerro de las Campanas (1), the hill where Maximilian surrendered to General Escobedo and was later executed; at the opposite end of the town is the Convent of La Cruz (2), which was the Emperor's headquarters during the siege.

Fig. 20 (cat. 18)
Exterior View of the Convent of La Cruz, photograph by François Aubert, June 1867. Albumen print, 16.5 x 22.8 cm. Brussels, Musée Royal de l'Armée.

The Liberal troops broke in through the convent's boundary wall. This view, showing broken cacti in the foreground and what appears to be an execution taking place in the distance, was also circulated as a carte de visite photograph.

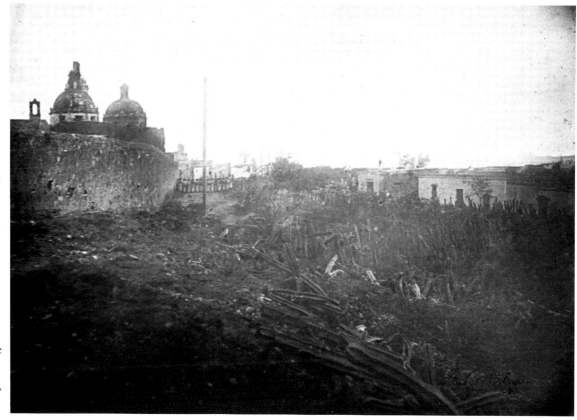

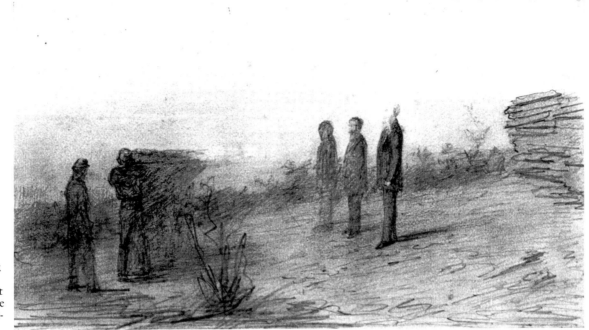

Fig. 21
François Aubert,
*The Execution of Max-
imilian, Miramón and
Mejía*, 19 June 1867.
Graphite, 15 x 26.8 cm.
Brussels, Musée Royal de
l'Armée.

An inscription on the back
of the sheet, possibly by
Aubert's son, indicates that
the sketch was made by the
photographer. It was probably done after the event.

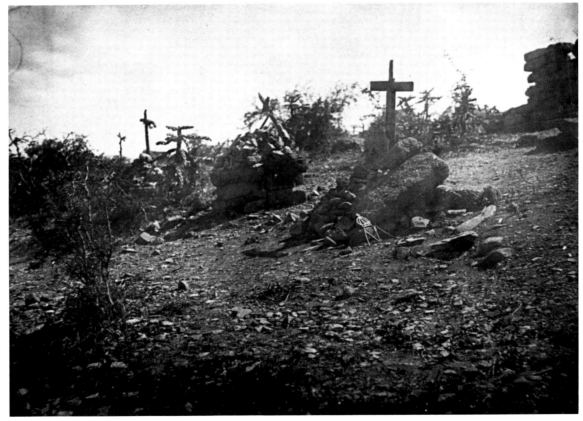

Fig. 22 (cat. 19)
*The Three Crosses on the
Cerro de las Campanas*,
photograph by François
Aubert, June 1867. Albu-
men print, 16 x 22.4 cm.
Brussels, Musée Royal de
l'Armée.

The photograph shows the
places where the three victims stood at their execution. Maximilian's position
in the foreground is
marked with a metal crown
and the letter M.

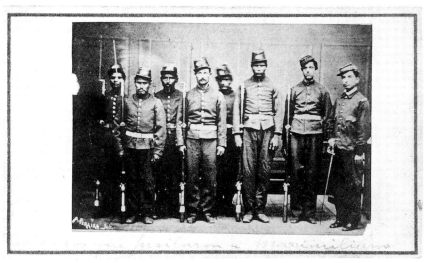

Fig. 23
The Execution Squad standing to Attention. Carte de visite photograph (slightly enlarged) by Agustín Peraire (after Aubert), 1867.
Mexico City, INAH, Castillo de Chapultepec.

This rare photograph (originally taken by Aubert), is normally seen in a widely circulated version in which the setting is painted out (fig. 51).

stand trial before a military tribunal and that they could be executed according to the law that had been promulgated by Juárez in April 1862, pronouncing death to those who aided foreign intervention. When the court-martial officers indeed voted unanimously for the death sentence, Juárez supported their decision in spite of a host of cables that crossed the Atlantic from many diverse personages, such as Garibaldi and Victor Hugo, and from those who pointed out that Maximilian was the brother of the Emperor of Austria, the brother-in-law of the King of the Belgians, and a relative through marriage of Queen Victoria. Attempts were made to arrange an escape through bribery, but they came to nothing.

It was on 19 June 1867 that the executions took place, on the Cerro de las Campanas (Hill of Bells), which overlooked the city. There is no one authoritative account (see pages 48–50), but the three men were evidently executed together, wearing civilian clothes – Maximilian was dressed in black. He stood on the right (fig. 21), insisting that General Miramón, who was a brave soldier, should have the place of honour, in the middle. His last words expressed the hope that his blood would bring an end to the misfortunes of Mexico.

Maximilian was respected for his courage and for the classical nobility of his death. According to his aide, he seems to have likened his betrayal and sacrifice to those of Jesus Christ.[28] More critical assessments emphasise his misfortunes. The Liberals to whom he appealed would not give him their full military support, so that he was obliged to turn to the Conservatives who distrusted his poli-

cies. As he explained many times, he did not understand the policies of Napoleon III, whose troops would capture a stronghold, only to withdraw almost immediately afterwards. He can be criticised for his failure to grasp reality, but perhaps this was because he could not grasp the full nature of his betrayal and abandonment.

If Maximilian is a martyr, Juárez is a national hero. He has the reputation of having remained scrupulously honest as he rose to be Governor of Oaxaca and President of Mexico. He personified the struggle against the French and the fight for Mexican nationalism. His presence, and that of his followers, demonstrated that it was a miscalculation to assume that Mexico was a *tabula rasa*, a malleable society that could be adapted to the requirements of European economics and the formalities of European courts. Many Mexicans have seen his decision to execute Maximilian as a prudent measure, since it prevented further European interventions in their country. After the execution, Juárez re-entered his capital and was re-elected President. He was elected President again in 1871, and died in office in July 1872. The simple clothes that he wore, and the plain black coaches that he used, are preserved in Chapultepec Castle. His memory is perpetuated in the popular slogan, 'Benito Juárez is Mexico, Mexico is Benito Juárez.'[29]

The news of Maximilian's execution reached Paris ten days after the event. Napoleon had been celebrating the Exposition Universelle of 1867 in the presence of visiting emperors and kings, and a multitude of royal personages, and the news was confirmed by the absence from the prize-giving ceremony of Charlotte's brother the Count of Flanders, and by the abrupt departure from it of the Austrian Ambassador, Prince Metternich. The Emperor Franz Joseph cancelled the visit that he was to have made to Paris. In August 1867 Napoleon and Eugénie travelled to Austria to offer their sympathy to Franz Joseph and the Empress Elisabeth. Maximilian's mother, the Archduchess Sophia, refused to be present at the meeting.

Three years later it was General Prim who, as one of the leaders of a revolution in Spain, arranged for Leopold of Hohenzollern to take the Spanish throne, vacated by Queen Isabella. The French opposed this candidacy and out of the diplomatic imbroglio that followed came the Franco–Prussian War and the overthrow of the French Empire. Prim was assassinated in Madrid, Napoleon died in exile in England, and his son was killed fighting with the British against the Zulus in South Africa. Bazaine was disgraced in the Franco–Prussian War and died in exile in Spain. An almost blind Eugénie lived on until 1920; the mad Charlotte until 1927, dying at the age of eighty-seven. The embalmed body of Maximilian was committed to a tomb in the Habsburg crypt beneath the Augustiner Church in Vienna.

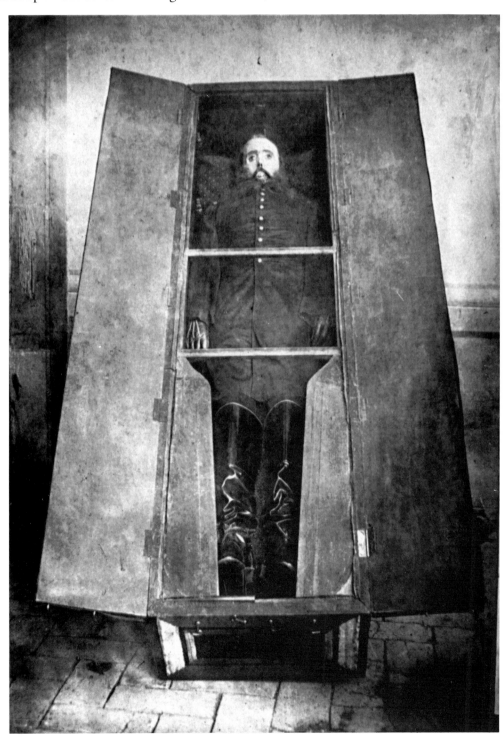

Fig. 24 (cat. 21)
The Corpse of Maximilian in his Coffin, photograph by François Aubert, June 1867. Albumen print, 22.3 x 16.5 cm. Brussels, Musée Royal de l'Armée.

Maximilian's embalmed corpse was given dark-coloured glass eyes, dressed in the clothes he habitually wore (see fig. 52), and laid in a glass-covered coffin; the compartments on either side, near the feet, held his vital organs. All these memorial images (figs. 22–4) were issued as carte de visite photographs (see cat. 22).

Notes

I would like to thank Dr Christopher Abel of University College, London, for the valuable help that he gave me in preparing this article.

1. H. W. C. Smith, *Napoleon III: the Pursuit of Prestige*, London 1991.
2. A. Guérard, *Napoleon III*, Cambridge 1943. C. Schefer, *La Grande pensée de Napoléon III: les origines de l'expédition du Mexique*, Paris 1939.
3. The historiography of the Maximilian affair has been studied in Quirarte 1970. Since the publication of this work, citing nearly three hundred books, many more have appeared.
4. Many of these questions were discussed in Barker 1979, and in N. N. Barker, 'Monarchy in Mexico: Harebrained Scheme or Well-Considered Prospect?', *Journal of Modern History*, 48, 1976, pp. 51–68. Professor Barker writes with great authority and I am much indebted to her publications, and to the advice she gave me when we met at the University of Texas in Austin.
5. I am grateful to Dr Philip Mansel for the information concerning the duc de Richelieu.
6. H. W. V. Temperley, 'French Designs on Spanish America in 1820–1825', *English Historical Review*, 40, 1928, pp. 34–53. W. S. Robertson, *France and Latin-American Independence*, Baltimore 1939.
7. Barker 1979, pp. 57 ff. W. S. Robertson, 'French Intervention in Mexico in 1838', *Hispanic American Historical Review*, 24, 1944, pp. 222–52. J. F. Cady, *Foreign Intervention in the Rio de la Plata, 1838–1858*, Philadelphia 1929.
8. D. Johnson, *Guizot: Aspects of French History 1787–1874*, London and Toronto 1963, pp. 263 ff.
9. L. N. B. (Louis-Napoléon Bonaparte), *Canal of Nicaragua, or, a project to connect the Atlantic and Pacific Oceans by means of a canal*, London 1846.
10. Three documents in the papers of Sir Robert Peel in the British Library illustrate this episode. They are reproduced and commented upon in E. W. Richards, 'Louis Napoleon and Central America', *Journal of Modern History*, 34, 1962, pp. 175–84.
11. The Mexican chargé d'affaires Mangino reported this conversation on 29 January 1849, quoted in Barker 1976 (cited in note 4), p. 58.
12. These activities and considerations are described in Barker 1979, and in Hanna and Hanna 1971.
13. Among the most notable of the publications was M. de Fossey, *Le Mexique*, Paris 1857.
14. The legend of the influence of the Empress and of certain expatriates was put forward in the authoritative work by Corti 1928, and has been embellished by many other biographers. See G. Smith, *Maximilian and Carlota: The Habsburg Tragedy in Mexico*, London 1974. N. N. Barker, *Distaff Diplomacy: The Empress Eugénie and the Foreign Policy of the Second Empire*, Austin 1967, presented a very scholarly appraisal of the question, although in subsequent publications she has modified her view of the Empress's importance.
15. See M. C. Meyer and W. L. Sherman, *The Course of Mexican History*, New York 1979. L. B. Simpson, *Many Mexicos*, Berkeley 1952. Roeder 1947.
16. Quoted in W. S. Robertson, 'The Tripartite Treaty of London', *Hispanic American Historical Review*, 20, 1940, pp. 172–3.
17. N. N. Barker, 'The Duke of Morny and the Affair of the Jecker Bonds', *French Historical Studies*, 6, 1970, pp. 551–61.
18. The suggestion is tactfully put forward in Barker 1979, pp. 162–3, that the French Minister stood to gain financially from this venture, which never materialised.
19. Napoleon III to General Forey, 3 July 1862, as quoted in Hanna and Hanna 1971, pp. 77–81.
20. Napoleon III to Flahaut (French Ambassador in London), 9 October 1861, quoted in C. H. Bock, *Prelude to Tragedy: the Negotiations and Breakdown of the Tripartite Convention of London, October 31, 1861*, Phildalphia 1966, pp. 495–7. N. N. Barker, 'France, Austria and the Mexican Venture, 1861–1864', *French Historical Studies*, 3, 1963, pp. 224–45.
21. L. M. Case, *French Opinion on the United States and Mexico 1860–1867. Extracts from the Reports of the Procureurs Généraux*, New York 1936 (reprinted 1969).
22. P. Gaulot, *L'Expédition du Mexique 1861–1867*, Paris 1906 edition, vol. 1, pp. 18 ff.
23. See the discussion in J. A. Dabbs, *The French Army in Mexico 1861–1867*, The Hague 1963, pp. 146–7.
24. Hanna and Hanna 1971, p. 272.
25. L. Gordon, 'Lincoln and Juárez: A Brief Reassessment of Their Relationship', *Hispanic American Historical Review*, 46, 1968, p. 77, suggests that the accounts of Lincoln's support for Juárez are open to question. R. R. Miller, 'Matías Romero: Mexican Minister to the United States during that Juárez-Maximilian Era', *Hispanic American Historical Review*, 45, 1965, pp. 228–45, describes how hundreds of thousands of guns and millions of rounds of ammunition were sent to the Juaristas.
26. Hanna and Hanna 1971, pp. 270 ff.
27. Dabbs 1963 (cited in note 23), pp. 190–202.
28. Prince Salm-Salm, quoted in Providence 1981, p. 97.
29. Bazant 1988, pp. 423–70; J. Haslip, *The Crown of Mexico*, New York 1971; I. E. Cadenhead Jr, *Benito Juárez*, New York 1973; F. C. Turner, *The dynamic of Mexican Nationalism*, Chapel Hill 1968; R. N. Sinkin, *The Mexican Reform 1855–1876. A Study in Liberal Nation-Building*, Austin 1979.

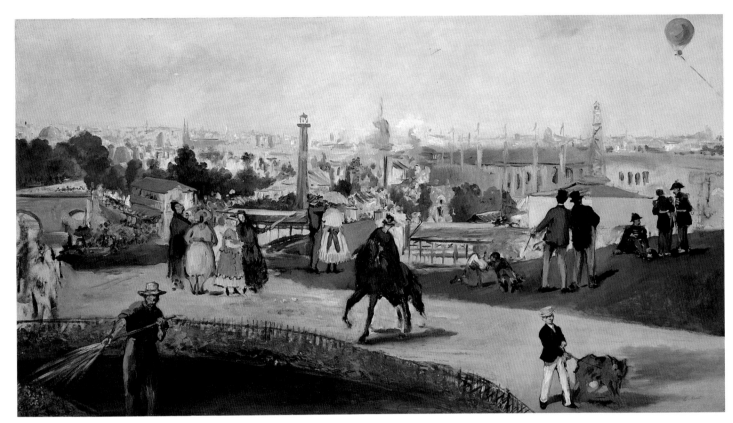

Fig. 25
Edouard Manet,
*View of the Exposition
Universelle of 1867*. Oil on
canvas, 108 x 196.5 cm.
Oslo, National Gallery.

Manet's panoramic view
embraces the Pont de
l'Alma on the left and the
Pont d'Iéna leading into
the Exposition grounds,
with the twin spires of Ste
Clotilde and the dome of
the Invalides in the
distance.

Manet and The Execution of Maximilian

JULIET WILSON-BAREAU

The Exposition Universelle of 1867

In January 1867, the Emperor of Mexico was agonising over whether or not he should abdicate the throne and return to Europe – 'Does he *want* to leave and *can't*? or *can* he leave and *won't*?', asked a baffled Belgian paper, while *Le Charivari* complained that the January fogs were as thick in Mexico as in Paris.[1] For Manet, the year began with a warm and welcome ray of light. On 1 January Emile Zola (fig. 106) published a resounding defence of his art,[2] and Manet responded by thanking the critic and announcing a major project. An Exposition Universelle, or World Fair, was to be held in Paris that year, but Manet told Zola that he had decided to mount an independent one-man exhibition, rather than submit his pictures to the mercies of the official jury.[3]

The fashion for international exhibitions had been established with the Great Exhibition at the Crystal Palace in London in 1851, followed by the Paris Exposition Universelle of 1855. To another London exhibition in 1862, France responded with the Exposition Universelle of 1867. Napoleon III's active promotion of the Exposition, magnificently installed beside the Seine, and his lavish entertainment of foreign heads of state (see fig. 27), were intended to place Paris and the French business community at the centre of world affairs. What no one could have foreseen was that Paris would serve that summer as a stage on which the Mexican drama would be brought into embarrassingly sharp focus.

The authorities responsible for the art exhibitions at the Exposition and the Salon that year (see page 87) were determined to keep them under firm control. For the Exposition, artists were invited to send a list of proposed works, but if not accepted on this basis, they were obliged to submit the works to a jury. Manet found himself in this position, after the stormy response to *Le Déjeuner sur l'Herbe* and *Olympia* (Paris, Musée d'Orsay) in

1863 and 1865, followed by the rejection of both his pictures for the Salon of 1866, *The Tragic Actor* (Washington, DC, National Gallery of Art) and *The Fifer* (fig. 82). On that occasion, Zola had come to Manet's defence in a series of articles[4] in which he attacked the jury system and supported the development of a new, realistic and individual form of art. Referring to *Le Déjeuner sur l'Herbe* as a 'masterpiece' and praising '*The Fifer*, the canvas rejected this year', he had criticised the Salon administration and ridiculed the kind of sentimental, anecdotal art enjoyed by the vast majority of the Salon's hundreds of thousands of visitors.

The expanded and more forceful version of Zola's text on Manet, which appeared on New Year's Day 1867, must have strengthened the artist's determination to hold a major one-man exhibition alongside the official Exposition Universelle. He also counted on the support of his family and in particular on financial help from his widowed mother, a strong-minded woman who attempted to exert some control over her son's finances and even over his way of life. By the end of 1866 she had expressed her view that it was high time to call a halt on a 'ruinous downhill path'.[5] She nevertheless lent Manet further substantial sums between January and December 1867, including 6,000 francs for his exhibition pavilion. By the end of that year, Manet's exhibition had ended without any tangible success, and he was already committed to turning the execution of Maximilian into a major history painting. In January, however, all this was unforeseen.

The Exposition Universelle, a symbol of universal harmony and progress, was installed on the Champ de Mars – the 'Field of the god of War' – in front of the French military academy. The nations of Europe were just then displaying anything but peaceful behaviour, while across the seas French troops, with Austrian and Belgian volunteers, had been fighting on Maximilian's behalf in Mexico. Caricaturists were quick to point up the irony of

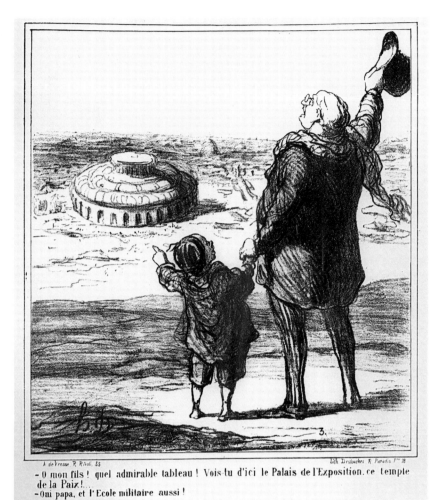

- O mon fils ! quel admirable tableau ! Vois-tu d'ici le Palais de l'Exposition. ce temple de la Paix!...
- Oui papa, et l'Ecole militaire aussi !

Fig. 26
Honoré Daumier,
'Well, my boy! What a splendid sight! Look how well we can see the Palace of the Exposition, that great Temple of Peace, from here!' – 'Yes, Papa, and the Military Academy as well!'.
Lithograph in *Le Charivari*, 16 January 1867.

the situation. On 5 January 1867, Daumier's *Project for a Statue of Peace for the Exposition Universelle* showed 'France' carving cannon balls at the base of a great gun, and 'Peace' with a sword and musket with fixed bayonet. He followed this with a cartoon showing M. Prudhomme, the archetypal bourgeois, hailing the Exposition building as a 'Temple of Peace', while his small son points out the Ecole Militaire nearby (fig. 26).[6]

In spite of criticism from many quarters, the Exposition was of course presented officially in celebratory fashion. Inaugurated by the Emperor on 1 April (fig. 28), it remained open until the end of October, and was visited by the Tsar of Russia and the Ottoman Sultan (see fig. 27). Many views of the exhibition buildings were published, seen from the vantage point of the Trocadéro, the sloping ground on which M. Prudhomme stands with his son and which was laid out for the occasion as a

public park. Manet, too, depicted the Exposition from this viewpoint (fig. 25), the short shadows suggesting a midsummer day in June. Groups of visitors are seen looking out over the exhibition grounds or towards the giant balloon, and the 'slice of life' view includes a Chinaman and a rotund Turk, some of the exotic peoples brought to Paris by the Exposition, as well as three soldiers of the Imperial Guard, and Suzanne Manet's young son Léon walking the family dog.[7]

News of the execution of Maximilian reaches Europe

On 1 July, the day of the prize-giving ceremony for the Exposition (fig. 28), Napoleon III received official news from Vienna of the execution of Maximilian in Mexico. At the ceremony held in the presence of the Sultan of the Ottoman Empire, the Viceroy of Egypt and a host of European princes, Rossini's grandiose *Hymn to the Emperor* was accompanied by the booming of cannon and ringing of bells, and the French Emperor made a speech – in suitably 'imperial style' as one report put it – on the beneficent effects of the Exposition Universelle and its demonstration of France's pacific and progressive role in world affairs.[8] He made no reference to the disaster that had just occurred, although speculative reports of Maximilian's death had already appeared in the press, and the Count of Flanders, Maximilian's brother-in-law, was conspicuous by his absence from the ceremony.

News of the execution, sent throughout Europe by telegraph, was 'scooped' by the foreign press and the first announcement appeared in the liberal *L'Indépendance belge*, distributed in Paris on the afternoon of 1 July. A terse bulletin, dated from Vienna, Sunday 30 June, stated that: 'It appears from official despatches from the Austrian Minister in Washington and from the commander of the Austrian steamship *Elisabeth*, stationed at Veracruz, that the Emperor Maximilian was executed on 19 June.' In the same edition, another bulletin from Paris, dated 1 July, announced that news of the execution was regarded there as untrue. In fact, the publication of the news caused the French authorities considerable embarrassment. Although the announcement was carried in the English press on 1 and 2 July, it did not reach the columns of *Le Figaro* or the 'official' *Mémorial diplomatique* in

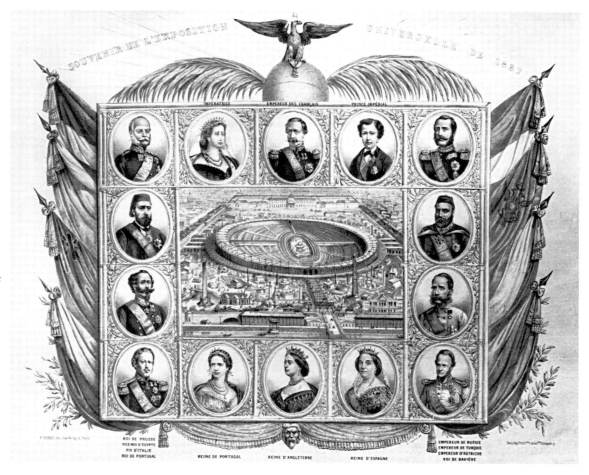

Fig. 27
Souvenir of the Exposition Universelle of 1867. Lithograph, 28.7 x 40.4 cm, by C. Legrand and Herbet Editeur, 1867. Paris, Musée Carnavalet.

Portraits of royalty surrounding a view of the Exposition buildings, include the French Emperor, Empress and Prince Imperial (above), the King of Prussia and the 'Emperors' of Russia, Turkey and Austria (to the sides), and the Queens of Portugal, Great Britain and Spain (below).

Fig. 28
Solemn Distribution of Prizes . . . on 1 July 1867 in the Palais de l'Industrie from *Souvenirs of the Exposition Universelle of 1867*. Wood engraving reprinted from *L'Illustration*, 1867. Paris, Musée Carnavalet.

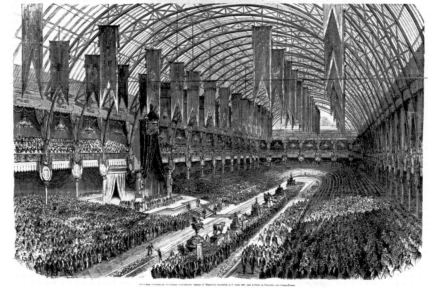

Paris until 3 July, while *Le Moniteur universel, Journal officiel de l'Empire Français*, delayed reporting the news until 5 July, by which time official confirmation of the execution had been received in Vienna. It was not until 6 July, after this formal announcement, that *Le Mémorial diplomatique* appeared with a black border on its front page.[9] The press reflected every shade of political opinion, the official French organs responding with alarm and indignation to any suggestion of blame attaching to France, her government or the Emperor himself.

If written comment was relatively free, the same was not true of visual imagery, where censorship remained very vigilant. Not a single reference to Maximilian's execution appeared in the daily caricatures by Daumier and his colleagues in *Le Charivari*, although its journalists' analyses of the events in Mexico and the French government's response were sharp and critical. Portraits of Maximilian and the generals who died with him were acceptable (figs. 30, 56 and 57), and one or two popular prints of the execution were sooner or later allowed past the censors (figs. 47 and 48), but photographs of the execution squad and the Emperor's clothes were banned (figs. 51, 53 and 54). Manet himself, whose republican opinions were no secret, was to feel the force of this censorship since it prevented the exhibition of the painting inspired by the tragedy and the publication of his lithograph.

The background to Manet's project

Following the announcement of the execution, Manet began to sketch out a composition on this theme on a large canvas. Between July 1867 and early 1869, he painted three very large pictures (figs. 70:I, 73:II and 76:III), showing Maximilian and his fellow victims, Generals Tomás Mejía and Miguel Miramón, facing a firing squad commanded by an officer, with a soldier standing by to deliver the *coup de grâce*. The figures are two-thirds or almost life-size and the subject was conceived as a major history painting, on a scale appropriate to the Paris Salon.

The existence of the three large canvases and Manet's unsuccessful fight to get his lithograph published (fig. 77) are evidence of the impact the event had on him, and it certainly provided the only kind of theme – contemporary and political – that could have inspired him to create a 'history painting'. This was still considered the highest category in the Salon (see page 87), but Manet consistently expressed his contempt for it and the way in which it was practised by his contemporaries. He used the term *peintre d'histoire* as the worst of insults.[10] However, Manet was certainly not indifferent to history in terms of contemporary, real-life drama. Three years earlier, in the summer of 1864, he had painted a sensational incident connected with the American Civil War, when a Confederate gunboat that had been sheltering in the harbour at Cherbourg was sunk off the French coast by a Union corvette (see page 76). Manet's painting of *The Battle of the Kearsarge and the Alabama* (fig. 90) had been displayed shortly after the event took place, in the window of a Paris art dealer.[11]

In 1867 the context was much more complex. The Mexican affair was of concern to liberals and conservatives alike. It involved crucial debates about constitutional government and domestic and foreign policy, and remained a burning issue in France for many months. The execution itself was greeted with universal horror and condemnation, and Manet's immediate response may have been to consider adding a rapidly brushed canvas to his exhibition pavilion, sited just across the river from the Exposition Universelle.[12] His exhibition was not due to close until October and the addition of a large canvas on such a topical and dramatic subject would certainly have appealed to him as a way of drawing the attention of a wider public.

Manet would have had to act quickly in order to show such a picture. However, details of the event could not be expected for some time. Mexico was a vast country, its communications disrupted by war, and despatches travelling overland and by sea to Europe took at least a month to arrive. The first successful Atlantic cable had been laid only the previous year and used by Maximilian to send greetings from Mexico on 15 August 1866 for the French Emperor's official birthday.[13] Use of the cable was restricted to telegrams and coded diplomatic messages, and in the early weeks after the news of Maximilian's death newspaper reports were confused and contradictory. The first authentic eyewitness account did not appear until 22 July, followed by further accounts up to 10 October. Photographs also began to reach Paris in August. But if Manet had to wait for details of the execution itself, there were immediate sources of information of a more general nature to which he could turn, in particular the artists and officers recently returned from Mexico when the French forces were withdrawn.

A French artist returns from Mexico

In the Salon that year was an enormous painting celebrating the French victory at Puebla in 1863 (see fig. 29), as well as a portrait of Marshal Bazaine as commander-in-chief of the Mexican campaign (Musée National du Château de Versailles). These two commissioned works were painted by Jean-Adolphe Beaucé, an artist who specialised in military subjects. He had accompanied the French troops on their campaigns in Algeria, the Crimea and Syria, and his vast *Battle of Solferino* (fig. 100) was included in the Exposition Universelle that year. Following the victory at Puebla in May 1863 (see page 22), Beaucé applied for an official mission and sailed for Mexico in June, remaining there until

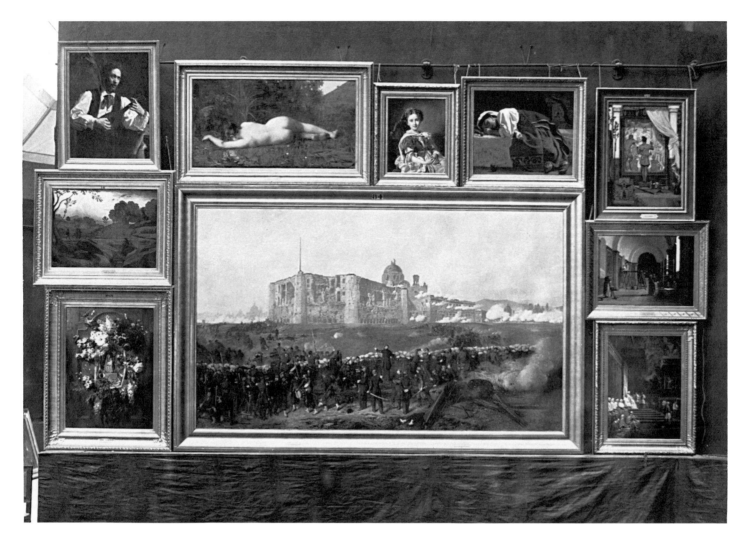

Fig. 29
Jean-Adolphe Beaucé's
Capture of the Fort of San Xavier, near Puebla, 29 March 1863, and other works in the Salon of 1867. Albumen print in Charles Michelez's album, 1867.
Paris, École des Beaux-Arts.

Beaucé's very large picture for the museum at Versailles was photographed, together with other works commissioned or acquired by the state, for the annual album published by Michelez.

late 1865.[14] He sent small pictures to the Salon from Mexico,[15] but the huge commissioned painting at the Salon of 1867 was a careful reconstruction of the event, painted after his return to Paris. In the same Salon, a Mexican battle scene by Alphonse de Neuville was probably based on the type of sketches and descriptions sent back by many serving officers, such as the prolific Lieutenant Jules Brunet.[16]

Around late August or early September, Beaucé was featured in the *Album autographique* (fig. 30), which was published weekly during the period of the Salon.[17] Although his paintings hung in the Exposition as well as the Salon that year, he was a relatively minor figure, and the front-page feature, with its emphasis on his activities in Mexico and reproductions of a portrait of Maximilian and a detachment of Juárez's guerrillas, was probably

intended more as a discreet homage to the dead Emperor than as a reflection of Beaucé's artistic importance. He is interesting in the context of Manet's *Execution of Maximilian* both as the practitioner of an approved style of military painting, and for his first-hand experience of Mexico, where he stayed for more than two years and painted several works for the imperial court, including a large equestrian portrait of Maximilian (fig. 15).[18] After Beaucé's death in 1875, Manet was asked to contribute to a benefit auction for the artist's widow and daughter, and it is quite possible that the two artists knew each other personally.[19]

If Manet visited Beaucé's studio in 1867, he would have found him engaged on a further state commission showing the French expeditionary force entering Mexico City. Painted from a large, squared-up oil sketch (fig. 12), this huge pendant

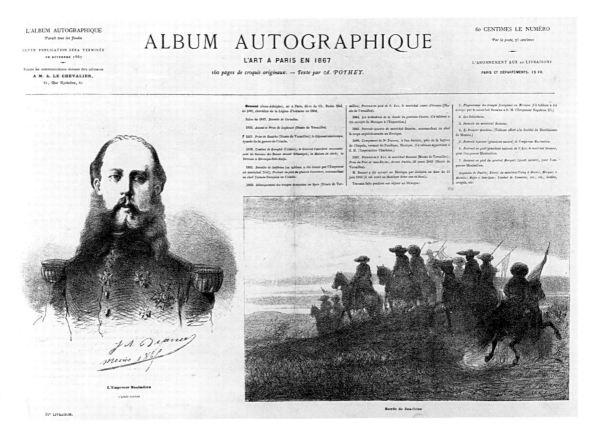

Fig. 30
Front page of the *Album autographique. L'Art à Paris en 1867*, August–September 1867, with reproductions of Jean-Adolphe Beaucé's portrait of Maximilian, dated 1865, and a sketch of a *Band of Juaristas*.

to the taking of the fortress at Puebla was shown at the Salon of 1868, together with a smaller battle scene (fig. 109). In 1867 Beaucé may also have been planning, if he was not actually painting, two works shown at the Salon of 1869, which included the final, dramatic moment in the *Combat at Camarón* (fig. 11), the supreme symbol of the courage and devotion to duty of the French Foreign Legion.[20] Beaucé is known to have worked from photographs taken by François Aubert and Auguste Mérille in Mexico,[21] and he probably brought back to France a variety of photographic studies as well as his own sketches.

There is no record in the Manet archives of the people to whom he turned or the materials he used to construct his paintings – no newspaper cuttings or illustrations, no photographs, notes or rough sketches.[22] Although a historical or military subject might seem to be outside his province, Manet was in fact well-equipped to deal with such matters since he had close connections with the military. His uncle, Colonel Edmond Fournier, who had encouraged his early interest in art, had a son, born

in the same year as Manet, who was killed in action during the capture of the Malakoff Tower at Sebastopol in 1855 (see fig. 99).[23] Thomas Couture, in whose studio Manet spent many years, was involved with military themes, and Auguste Raffet, whose fame derived mainly from his lithographs of army life, was an early supporter of Manet.[24] Most importantly, through the Manet family's friendship with Commandant Hippolyte Lejosne, he could have had access to military information as well as models – the boy musician who posed for *The Fifer* (fig. 82) in 1865–6, and the soldiers who were to play the role of executioners in the second and final versions of *The Execution of Maximilian*.[25]

Before any detailed descriptions or photographs relating to the execution reached France, Manet could already have learnt much about Mexico from informal, personal contacts, and from the news reports and pictures that had been available throughout the years of the French intervention. But the art of the past and his own earlier works provided equally important sources and influences for his composition.

Sources and analogies

Events in France and the repercussions of Napoleon III's ambitions in relation to the rest of the world were certainly of concern to Manet as an intelligent, politically conscious citizen. However, his interest in the themes of modern life in Paris, as an artist *flâneur*, has distracted attention from the possibility of political issues in his work. While his early republican sympathies and antipathy to Napoleon III have been noted, there has been no consistent attempt to relate his work to the wider political scene. A subject such as *The Battle of the Kearsarge and the Alabama* (fig. 90) has always been seen more in terms of a sensational incident of interest to the Parisian public than as evidence of Manet's personal concern with the issues involved.

It was not until a decade ago that one of Manet's earliest and most famous prints, his 1862 lithograph known as *The Balloon* (fig. 93), was recognised as a veiled but specific political allegory.[26] It shows a crowd gathered on the Esplanade des Invalides to celebrate the Emperor's official 15 August birthday with the launching of a balloon, a potent symbol of progress (see fig. 25). But the balloon masks the dome of the Invalides, where Napoleon I lies enshrined, and the image has now been revealed as a statement about the ironic contrasts of civil festivities and military parades, of talk of martial strength and peace, of the ostensibly care-free crowd of citizens and the central, foreground figure of the cripple. If the Hôtel des Invalides is the symbol of Napoleonic fervour, it is also the home of the nation's wounded soldiers, and while France might celebrate her Emperor's aspirations in the summer of 1862, her citizens were simultaneously mourning the losses caused by his Mexican intervention.

In May that year, the French expeditionary force had suffered a devastating and humiliating defeat when it tried to take the town of Puebla on the route to Mexico City (see page 22). Although the disaster was whitewashed and news heavily censored, *L'Indépendance belge* between 15 and 17 June gave its usual clear analysis of the conflicting accounts in French and British newspapers, while all the papers gave graphic, often verbatim eyewitness reports from soldiers of the difficulties facing the expeditionary force in Mexico, and the 'enormous losses' suffered during the attack on Puebla. Napoleon III immediately ordered over 20,000 troops to embark for Veracruz. Seen in this context, the presence of a sailor and a 'Spanish'-looking waterseller in the apparently festive crowd in Manet's lithograph suggests the possibility that he may also have had events like these in mind.

The French forces took their revenge at Puebla a year later (figs. 9 and 29), and 'the sound of cannonfire at the Invalides told the Parisians that the French army had finally entered the Mexican Saragossa' – an allusion to the two sieges of that city during Napoleon I's invasion of Spain.[27]

In the winter and spring of 1863–4, Manet completed two paintings for the Salon, *The Dead Christ and the Angels* (New York, Metropolitan Museum of Art) and *Incident in a Bullfight*. He subsequently cut up the bullfight canvas, reworking two fragments, one of which was catalogued as *The Dead Man* in his 1867 exhibition (fig. 31).[28] The original Salon painting, which attracted very adverse criticism, showed a bullfighter lying in the foreground, with a bull charging across the ring behind him, and several *toreros* in the background. The composition was caricatured in the press (fig. 34) and is revealed in X-rays of the two fragments (fig. 32),[29] which also show a mounted picador and other *toreros* in place of the bull at an earlier stage of the composition.

The perceptive critic Théophile Thoré, alias William Bürger, believed he had identified the direct source of Manet's foreground figure in a painting then considered an authentic masterpiece by Velázquez, the *Dead Soldier* (fig. 33), in the Pourtalès collection in Paris. Although Baudelaire denied this, it is quite possible that Manet saw at least a photograph of the 'Velázquez' when he was working on his *Bullfight*, and the picture itself before he cut out and repainted the figure of the dead toreador.[30]

Manet made such extensive alterations to his picture, both in its original form and in the repainting of the fragments, that its precise design will probably remain unclear. But for all its awkwardness – and criticism was directed particularly at the unsatisfactory perspective effect – the original *Incident in a Bullfight* was a powerful image of considerable size. The sense of heroism and violence in this strange composition, apparent even in the X-ray and caricature, suggests something more significant than its immediate subject, or more specific than a generalised allegory of death and fatality implicit in the bullfight theme.[31] In his review

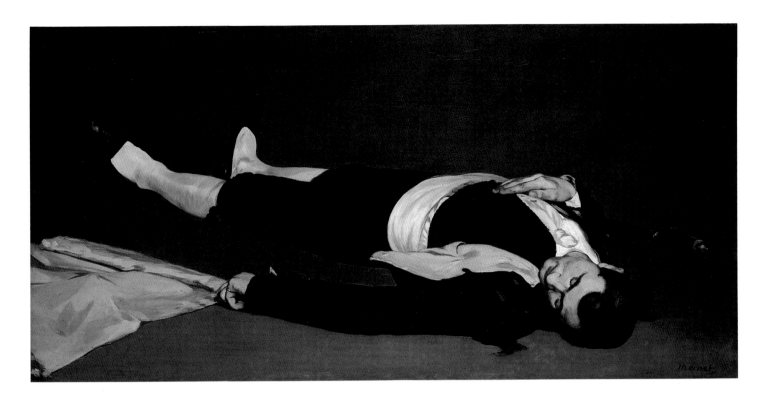

Fig. 31 (cat. 26)
Edouard Manet,
*The Dead Man (The Dead
Toreador)*, 1864–5. Oil on
canvas, 76 x 153.3 cm.
Washington DC, National
Gallery of Art.

The picture was extensively
repainted by Manet after
being cut from his *Incident
in a Bullfight* (see fig. 32).

Fig. 32
Composite X-ray of the
two fragments of Manet's
Incident in a Bullfight,
exhibited at the Salon
of 1864.
New York, Frick Collec-
tion, and Washington DC,
National Gallery of Art.

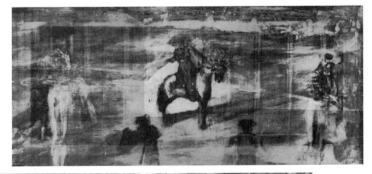

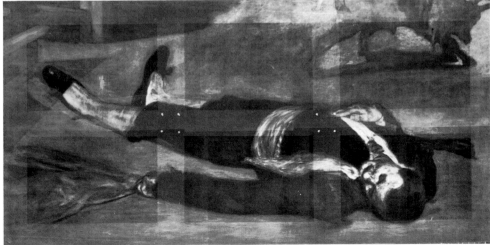

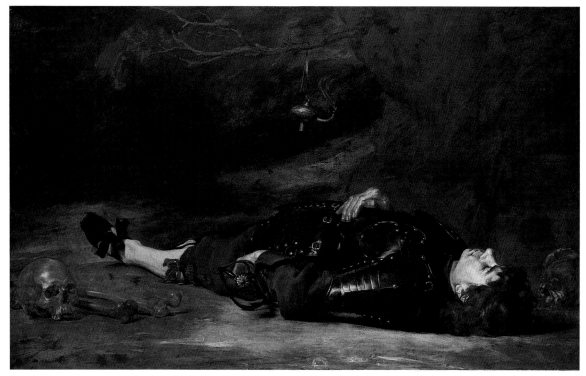

Fig. 33 (cat. 25)
Artist unknown (Italian
School, seventeenth
century),
A Dead Soldier, also known
as *Roland mort*. Oil on can-
vas, 104.8 x 167 cm.
London, National Gallery.

Formerly in the Pourtalès
Collection, Paris; a photograph of the picture was
published by Goupil in
1863 and the work itself
was exhibited in Paris early
in 1865.

Fig. 34
Cham, caricature of
Edouard Manet's
Incident in a Bullfight
(exhibited in the Salon of
1864). From 'Une promen-
ade au Salon. Croquis par
Cham', in *Le Charivari*,
22 May 1864.

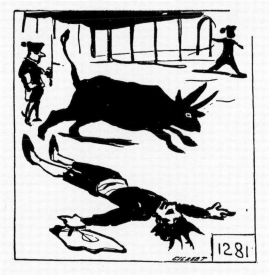

MANET.

Ayant eu à se plaindre de son marchand de couleurs,
M. Manet prend le parti de ne plus se servir que de son
encrier.

Thoré-Bürger wrote of its evidence of 'the ferocity
of human nature', but his discussion of the picture
immediately follows a powerful evocation of Désiré
Laugée's *Incident in the Polish Wars in 1863*, judged
a 'terrible argument against the violent repression'
of the people of Poland.

When a group of Manet's paintings was shown,
early in 1863, at Martinet's fashionable galleries on
the boulevard des Italiens, a critic likened the artist
to 'Goya in Mexico, gone native in the heart of the
pampas and smearing his canvases with crushed
cochineal'.[32] In the *Incident in a Bullfight* of 1864,
Thoré-Bürger spotted an allusion to a classic war-
rior figure by a great master of the past (fig. 33),
but also noted that the 'bourgeois' public was
infuriated by what he described as Manet's 'bizarre
and splendid colouring'. To the average bourgeois
visitor, Manet's Salon picture probably appeared to
have more in common with the crude colouring
and naïve composition of a vulgar Epinal print (see
fig. 9) than with the traditions of 'high art' to
which it appeared to aspire through its scale. The
comparison between Manet's *Incident in a Bullfight*
and a popular print of the battle of Puebla, showing
a fallen general in the foreground, is not intended
to suggest that this painting, or the reworked *Dead*

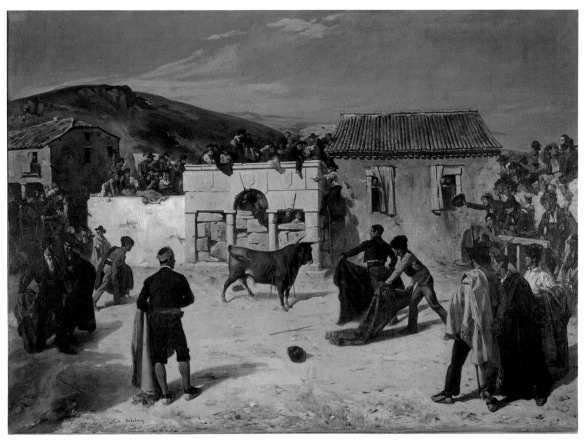

Fig. 35 (cat. 27)
Alfred Dehodencq,
*Bullfight in Spain. Novillada
at the Escorial*, Salon of
1850–1. Oil on canvas,
149 x 208 cm.
Pau, Musée des
Beaux-Arts.

Dehodencq's canvas was
commissioned by the state
in 1849 and was admired
by Manet in the Musée du
Luxembourg.

Man, is a 'true allegory' of the Mexican intervention. But it serves to highlight again the possibility
that Manet's compositions may contain unsuspec-
ted references to contemporary events. The Mexican expedition, like the Russian oppression of
Poland (see fig. 105) or Prussian expansion within
the German states, formed a permanent background to life in France in the 1860s. It would be
very remarkable if such a politically alert
and independent artist did not take account of
these events.

Dehodencq and Spain

Apart from the possibility of any broader significance in Manet's *Incident in a Bullfight*, the subject
itself was one which evidently interested and
excited him. A bullfight scene by Alfred Dehodencq (fig. 35) is known to have made a deep
impression on him in his student years.[33] Painted in
1849–50 as a state commission, it was shown at the
Salon of 1850–1 and then hung in the Musée du
Luxembourg, France's national collection of con-

temporary art. A quality reflected in one of Manet's
own later bullfight pictures (fig. 36) is its impressive stillness. Dehodencq referred to the difficulty of
painting such a 'celebrated, moving, terrible' subject without falling into all the horrors associated
with the spectacle, and explained how he found the
answer in a village bullfight at the Escorial. This
was a *novillada*, a fight in which there were no
victims, no disembowelled horses, and which
seemed to him 'an almost antique scene in modern
dress'.[34] Dehodencq's painting has a clarity and
strength that sets it apart from the turbulent and
romantic vision of Spain conveyed by Théophile
Gautier's picturesque *Voyage en Espagne*, by
Baudelaire's sinister and sensual evocations of
Goya's *Caprichos* prints, or Doré's book illustrations on Spanish themes.[35]

When Manet finally visited Spain in 1865, he
was bowled over by the works of Velázquez in the
Prado and by what was evidently his first visit to a
bullfight, describing it in a letter to Baudelaire as
'one of the finest, most curious and most terrifying
sights to be seen'.[36] On his return to Paris, he pain-

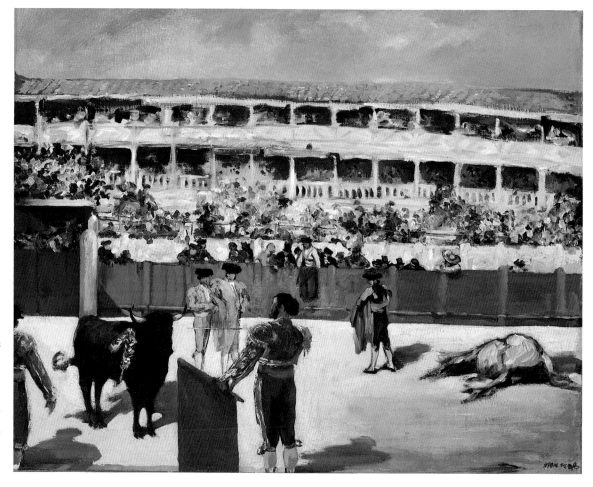

Fig. 36 (cat. 28)
Edouard Manet,
Bullfight, 1865–6. Oil on
canvas, 48 x 60.4 cm.
Art Institute of Chicago.

Painted on Manet's return
to Paris from Spain in the
autumn of 1865.

Fig. 37 (cat. 31)
Francisco Goya,
*Pedro Romero killing the
Halted Bull*, plate 30 of *La
Tauromaquia*, Madrid
1816. Etching and
aquatint, 24.5 x 35.5 cm.
London, British Museum.

Goya shows the celebrated
bullfighter preparing to
deliver the fatal thrust; the
final plate depicts a *torero*
fatally gored in the arena
(cat. 32).

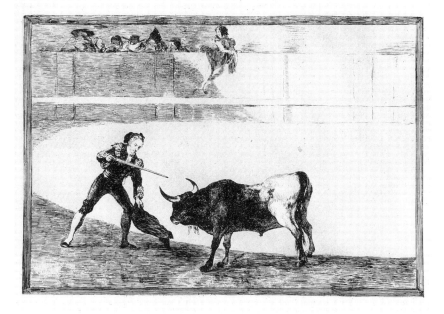

ted two bullfight pictures, one of the dramatic, violent scene he described to Zacharie Astruc (Paris, Musée d'Orsay),[37] the other a much quieter, more static composition, showing the moment of confrontation as the *espada* stands poised before the stationary bull (fig. 36). If the stillness recalls Dehodencq's bullfight, Manet's off-centre composition is related to those prints from Goya's *Tauromaquia* that exploit the dramatic effect of a few figures in the ring (fig. 37).[38]

Manet and Goya

Manet's relationship with Goya has been the subject of much discussion. His letters to friends during and after the visit to Spain expressed less enthusiasm for Goya than for Velázquez, but relatively few of Goya's works were then on public display, even in the Prado, where the paintings commemorating the uprising and executions of 2

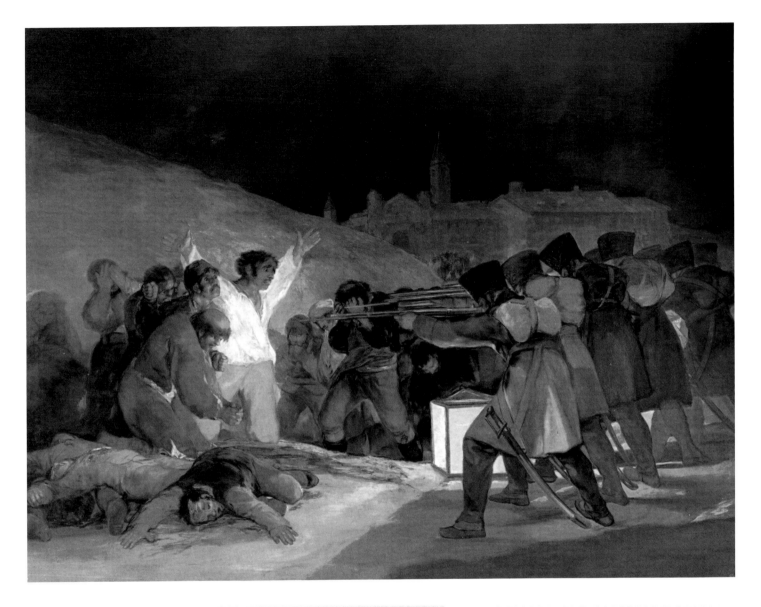

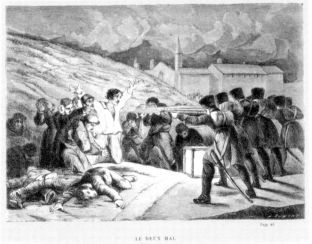

LE DEUX MAI

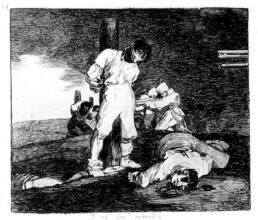

Y no hai remedio

Fig. 38
Francisco Goya,
The Executions of the Third of May 1808, 1814. Oil on canvas, 266 x 345 cm. Madrid, Museo del Prado.

In 1814, Goya asked to be commissioned to paint two scenes of the uprising in Madrid in May 1808 against Napoleon Bonaparte's intervention in Spain. Here a French army firing squad executes many civilians including a monk.

Fig. 39
After Francisco Goya,
The Third of May 1808. Wood engraving from a drawing by Bocourt, in C. Yriarte, *Goya*, Paris 1867.

This print, the first published reproduction of Goya's painting, appeared in Yriarte's book in April 1867.

Fig. 40 (cat. 33)
Francisco Goya,
Y no hai remedio (And it can't be helped), c. 1810–11, plate 15 of *The Disasters of War*, Madrid 1863. Etching, 14.1 x 16.8 cm. London, British Museum.

Fig. 41, right
Edouard Manet,
The Execution of Maximilian (detail of fig. 76:III).

Detail of the victims – Mejía, Maximilian and Miramón (from left to right) – in the final version of Manet's composition.

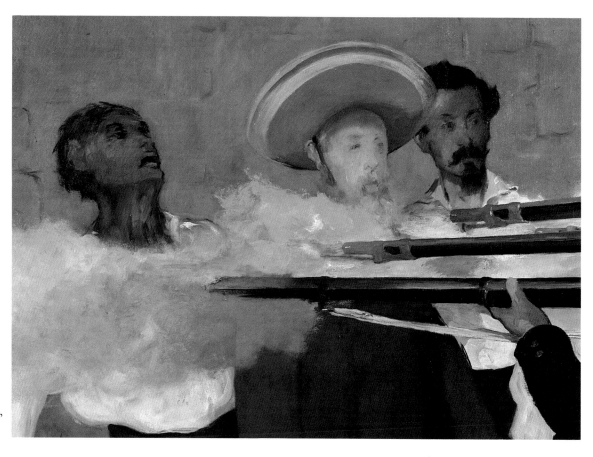

and 3 May 1808 were hanging in the corridors, uncatalogued and barely mentioned in guidebooks of the day. Manet spent much of his brief visit to Madrid in the Prado, where he signed the visitors' book on 1 September 1865. If he did see Goya's great history paintings, he never mentioned it.[39] Goya's heroic *Third of May* (fig. 38) has always been cited as a direct inspiration for *The Execution of Maximilian*. It is, however, almost the antithesis of Manet's composition, at least in the second and final versions (figs. 73:II and 76:III). Goya's interpretation is passionate and dynamic, built on diagonal tensions, with the confrontation between Spanish civilians and French army executioners dramatised by the glare from a huge lamp. He shows the victims advancing, facing the firing squad, then falling to the ground, in a time–space continuum that heightens the pathos of their fate and emphasises its universality. While Manet's first version (fig. 70:I) suggests something of the emotional charge of Goya's painting, and even its spatial organisation, he soon shifted towards a more

detached, apparently dispassionate presentation.

Goya's picture, now a universal icon of revolutionary heroism and patriotic fervour, was then virtually unknown in France. But in April 1867 it was reproduced, for the very first time, in an important publication by Charles Yriarte, an influential writer and critic whom Manet certainly knew.[40] A crude wood engraving (fig. 39) flattens the perspective effect of the original and in some ways brings it closer to Manet's composition. But while the *Third of May* undoubtedly played a role in Manet's *Execution of Maximilian*, the original etchings from Goya's war and bullfighting series (figs. 37 and 40) were probably a more immediate source and certainly inspired elements of Manet's first composition and his treatment of the spectators crowding over the wall in the final version. Although Manet adopted a different artistic stance from Goya, he was addressing a similar theme. This time, however, the successor of Napoleon I was fighting his Spanish war across the ocean in Mexico.[41]

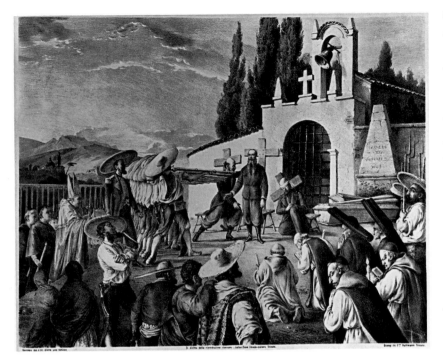

Fig. 42
The Execution of Emperor Maximilian, by Goineau. Lithograph, 40 x 50.5 cm, published by E. Guttmann and J. Dase, Trieste 1867. Vienna, Graphische Sammlung Albertina.

The lithograph, lettered in Italian, German, Hungarian and Slovenian, was also distributed as a carte de visite photograph.

Fig. 43
Apotheosis of H.M. Ferdinand Maximilian Emperor of Mexico, assassinated at Querétaro on 19 June 1867.
Anonymous lithograph, 51.2 x 36.2 cm, published by E. Guttmann and Della Baba, Trieste 1867. Vienna, Graphische Sammlung Albertina.

The scenes show the 'Arrival in Mexico City', 'The Betrayal' and the 'Departure from Miramare'.

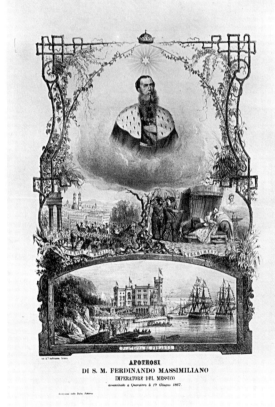

APOTEOSI
DI S. M. FERDINANDO MASSIMILIANO
IMPERATORE DEL MESSICO
assassinato a Querétaro li 19 Giugno 1867.

The origin and development of Manet's 'Execution' paintings

Although all three of Manet's *Execution* paintings, as well as his preparatory oil sketch (fig. 74) and lithograph (fig. 77), differ from one another to a greater or lesser degree, the basic composition altered little once it had been established in the first version of the picture. An account of how they were painted was later given by Théodore Duret, whom Manet had met in Spain in 1865 and whose portrait he painted in 1868 (Paris, Musée du Petit Palais).[42] Although Duret's description may not be strictly accurate, he was in a position to watch the paintings develop and to discuss them with Manet, and he gives a convincing impression of the way Manet approached his subject.

In 1867 and 1868, [Manet] painted *The Execution of Maximilian*. . . . Its composition occupied him for many months. He first tried to discover the circumstances and details of the drama. This is why the three victims are placed so close to the execution squad, to accord with what actually occurred. When he was satisfied with the effect he intended, he began to paint his picture, with the help of an infantry platoon lent to him from a barracks, as models for the firing squad. He also asked two friends to pose for Generals Mejía and Miramón, although he altered their heads. Only Maximilian's head was painted in the conventional way, from a photograph. When a first composition and even a second appeared not to match the detailed information he was finally able to obtain, he painted the work again, for the third time, in its final and definitive form.[43]

There is no record of exactly when or in what circumstances Manet began the first of his three large canvases representing *The Execution of Maximilian*. The energy and roughness of its handling and its much altered, unfinished appearance suggest that it was an immediate response to the event, painted without the careful preparation that a preliminary sketch might have afforded. Interest in the dramatic events in Mexico was inevitably intense after the news was confirmed via the Atlantic cable. Wild rumours, deplored by the responsible press, circulated in the early days and the first detailed account of the execution was in fact a fabrication.

On 8 July, just a week after the cabled announcement of Maximilian's death, *Le Figaro* reproduced an article purporting to be a transcription from a Querétaro newspaper made by a New Orleans journal. It described Maximilian's final moments – his last words, his last glance at a miniature of Charlotte, the scene in front of the cemetery wall,

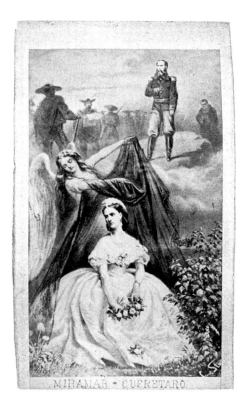

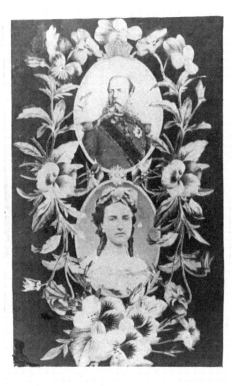

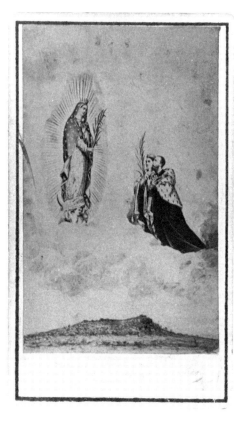

Fig. 44
Miramar – Querétaro.
Carte de visite photograph
by Jägern after Karl von
Stur, published by P.
Kaeser, Vienna *c.* 1867–8.
Brussels, Musée Royal de
l'Armée.

Fig. 45
*Memorial Portraits of the
Emperor and Empress of
Mexico.* Carte de visite
photograph by Aubert,
1867.
Commandant Spitzer
Collection.

Fig. 46
*Our Lady of Guadalupe ap-
pearing to the Emperor and
Empress in the Clouds above
the Cerro de las Campanas.*
Carte de visite photograph
by Aubert, 1867.
Commandant Spitzer
Collection.

Many souvenir portraits
and symbolic images of the
imperial couple were pub-
lished after Maximilian's
death (see cat. 22).

with crosses and coffins and muffled bells – and even gave the text of a touching farewell letter to his wife. An editorial caveat pointed out that the article could not possibly have reached France via the New Orleans newspaper office in less than a month and that *Le Figaro* could certainly not afford the 30,000 francs it would have cost to send it by the Atlantic cable. Nevertheless, papers in France and other countries printed the article without question, and it seems to have served as the basis for many souvenir prints published in Brussels, Trieste and Vienna (fig. 42), and also widely circulated in the popular form of small 'carte de visite' photographs.[44] On the following day, 9 July, *L'Indépendance belge* denounced this 'obviously apocryphal' account, pointing out that the most recent despatches from Mexico were dated 13 June, before Maximilian's death. Although it is unlikely to have deceived Manet, it may have served to spark his imagination, particularly since it fol-lowed a feature, also in *Le Figaro*, describing the way in which executions were carried out in Mex-ico.[45] They took place at very close range, with the victim seated on a stool and the soldiers only four paces away, while the large crowds that flocked to

witness the drama would scale the wall against which the execution took place. This account, together with a few details from the spurious story, may have enabled Manet to start planning his com-position while waiting for an authoritative report.

Souvenir prints and photographs were soon in circulation, with pious and sentimental images of the imperial couple (figs. 43–6).[6] Prints and carte photographs relating to the execution (see fig. 42) were published in Europe probably soon after the first reports were received and, in spite of strict censorship, examples may have reached Paris and provided Manet with a further stimulus. Many of these fanciful representations show the execution squad in the *charro* costume worn by Juárez's guer-rilla forces, with sombreros and leather suits with flared trousers. These elements appear in the first version of Manet's execution composition, re-inforcing the suggestion that he began it at the time of the very earliest reports and before any eye-witness accounts reached Paris.

The first brief, official details, reported in the London *Express* on 16 July, and repeated four days later in *Le Mémorial diplomatique*, stated that 'Max [*sic*] was shot faced to the front. . . . Miramón and

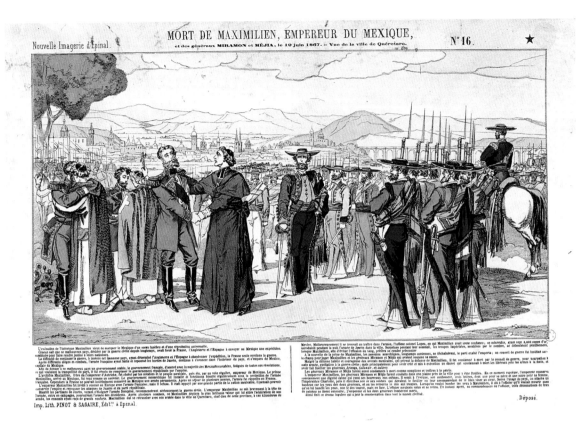

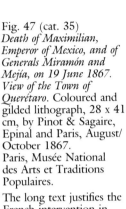

Fig. 47 (cat. 35)
*Death of Maximilian,
Emperor of Mexico, and of
Generals Miramón and
Mejía, on 19 June 1867.
View of the Town of
Querétaro.* Coloured and
gilded lithograph, 28 x 41
cm, by Pinot & Sagaire,
Epinal and Paris, August/
October 1867.
Paris, Musée National
des Arts et Traditions
Populaires.

The long text justifies the
French intervention in
Mexico and emphasises
that Maximilian had been
invited to return to Europe
when the French troops
were withdrawn. Contrary
to all eyewitness accounts,
Maximilian and his generals
are wearing full military
uniform, while the firing
squad is in guerrilla
costume.

Mejía were reduced from their rank, and shot in the back.' On 22 July, *L'Indépendance belge* carried a substantial account, taken from the *New Orleans Times*, by a Mexican officer said to have been present at the execution. Some of the information agrees with later reports, most importantly that the condemned men were in civilian dress; other details, such as the fact that there was more than one officer (and therefore more than a single execution squad), remained unsubstantiated or were contradicted by further eyewitness accounts. Indeed, no single, official report – not even the certified deposition made at the time of the execution[47] – has established an entirely authoritative version of the events.

A further report was published on 31 July in *L'Indépendance belge*, from a correspondent in Mexico City. He commented that the execution was bound to be condemned in Europe but that Juárez was widely regarded in Mexico as an honourable, upright man and would only have ordered the execution under extreme pressure and certainly not in a spirit of hatred and revenge. The writer pointed out that communications had not yet been

restored and that the information circulating in the city was unconfirmed, but his account agrees with the 22 July and later reports. The place of execution is named in it for the first time, as the summit of the 'Cerro de la Campana' (*sic*, for 'las Campanas', the Hill of Bells),[48] and the description of the execution is brief but specific. It repeats the earlier statement that Miramón and Mejía were shot in the back, as traitors, while Maximilian faced 'the company detailed to carry out the execution', and was allowed to die between his generals, holding their hands, with Miramón on his right and Mejía on his left. The Emperor, being taller, dominated the other two, and was described as dressed in black from head to foot, in a buttoned coat and wearing a broad-brimmed Mexican hat with the brim down to shade his face. The number of shots is not mentioned but a *coup de grâce* from the NCO failed to end his movements and a second shot was necessary. The writer ended by alluding to the universal mourning with which the largely republican city of Mexico had responded to the death of the Emperor, whose charm and personality had won the sympathy even of his enemies.[49] On the same day, *Le Mémorial diplomatique*, giving similar information on the execution, noted that there were contradictory accounts as to whether the Emperor or Miramón stood in the centre.

The first version of 'The Execution'

By this time, Manet had almost certainly begun his picture and may already have started adapting it to take account of changes in the reports received in Paris. The painting was evidently carried out at considerable speed and the canvas shows signs of extensive scraping and repainting in many areas, with underlying paint layers that are unrelated to the present composition: white areas visible in the background suggest architectural features, while a sizeable area of bright yellow pigment, obscured by overpainting near the right edge, is so far unexplained. The two figures on the right, the soldier waiting to give the *coup de grâce* and the officer with a sword, were added after the painting of the execution squad, since the soldiers' jackets are still perceptible beneath the figure facing front. As to the firing squad's costume, an underlying layer of orange-ochre pigment reveals that the soldiers were originally dressed in short jackets and flared trousers of light-brown leather, and it is clear that they were wearing sombreros.[50]

This guerrilla costume – as opposed to the uniform of Juárez's regular Liberal army[51] – is seen in many souvenir prints, including the only two

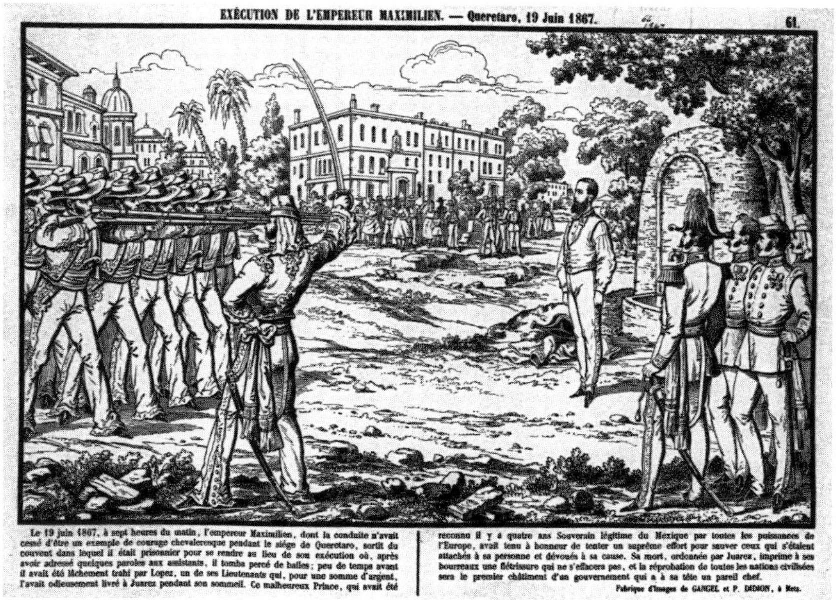

Fig. 48 (cat. 36)
Execution of the Emperor Maximilian – Querétaro, 19 June 1867. Lithograph, 26.9 x 38.9 cm, by Gangel and Didion, Metz, September 1867; Paris, June 1868. Paris, Bibliothèque Nationale.

Maximilian faces the firing squad alone, in shirtsleeves and waistcoat, with his hat and coat on the ground beside him. This print was withheld for nine months from publication in Paris.

images known to have been authorised in France (figs. 47 and 48). The first was issued at Epinal in the Vosges, famous for its print workshops, on 23 August and its publication in Paris was announced on 5 October 1867; the second was issued in Metz on 17 September but not released for sale in Paris until June the following year.[52] Their sobriety, compared with images produced in other countries, no doubt reflects the stringent censorship in force in France, and only the Epinal print, which does not even show the actual execution, was immediately allowed past the censors.

When Manet first sketched out his composition, it may have looked rather different from the way it does now. A vertical element behind the figure of Mejía, whose head falls forward, suggests that his body may have been tied to a cross or post, as in one of Goya's etchings or the Goineau lithograph (see figs. 40 and 42). The central figure of the Emperor is barely indicated, and rough outlines over his left shoulder probably correspond with the head of Miramón. The background is also unclear, with white elements showing through above the victims and the firing squad, while stabbing black and white accents in the upper right corner suggest bayonets and lances and recall the rhythms of Velázquez's *Surrender of Breda* (Madrid, Museo del Prado) as well as the Epinal print (fig. 47).

Although the X-ray of the thinly painted canvas does not afford a clear reading of its underlying layers, it is possible that the original design may even have incorporated some of the anecdotal motifs – coffins and crosses, chapel bells and cemetery wall – described in the earliest, fanciful accounts of the execution and recalled by Manet in the final picture. The visible reworking of the canvas conveys the urgency and inventiveness that Manet brought to his picture making, but also suggests that in the early stages the event remained elusive, outside his grasp. Conceived initially as an imaginative, even 'exotic', Mexican drama, expressed through costume and brilliant touches of colour, Manet worked at his composition until he had established the pattern of confrontation between the two groups that was to remain the basic design for all the other versions, large and small.

The final alterations to this first canvas indicate a crucial and far-reaching change. Manet began to transform the sombreros of the execution squad into something resembling the peaked caps of regular army troops (fig. 55), straightened flared

EXÉCUTION DE L'EMPEREUR MAXIMILIEN. — Queretaro, 19 Juin 1867. 61.

Le 19 juin 1867, à sept heures du matin, l'empereur Maximilien, dont la conduite n'avait cessé d'être un exemple de courage chevaleresque pendant le siège de Queretaro, sortit du couvent dans lequel il était prisonnier pour se rendre au lieu de son exécution où, après avoir adressé quelques paroles aux assistants, il tombe percé de balles; peu de temps avant il avait été lâchement trahi par Lopez, un de ses Lieutenants qui, pour une somme d'argent, l'avait odieusement livré à Juarez pendant son sommeil. Ce malheureux Prince, qui avait été

reconnu il y a quatre ans Souverain légitime du Mexique par toutes les puissances de l'Europe, avait tenu à honneur de tenter un suprême effort pour sauver ceux qui s'étaient attachés à sa personne et dévoués à sa cause. Sa mort, ordonnée par Juarez, imprime à son bourreaux une flétrissure qui ne s'efface pas, et la réprobation de toutes les nations civilisées sera le premier châtiment d'un gouvernement qui a à sa tête un pareil chef.

Fabrique d'images de GANGEL et P. DIDION, à Metz.

trousers, and overpainted the original warm brownish tones of the leather costumes in blue-black. What prompted him to make these changes is revealed by another account of the Mexican drama, accompanied this time by authentic visual documentation.

Detailed accounts and photographs reach Paris

On 11 August 1867 *Le Figaro* carried three columns by the redoubtable journalist Albert Wolff.[53] Under the title 'Gazette du Mexique', Wolff quoted the text of a letter brought to France by a courier who had managed to evade the Mexican – and by implication French – censors. The letter, which was addressed to one of Wolff's friends, described the events in Querétaro leading up to Maximilian's capture and trial, and gave gruesome details of the execution itself and three failed attempts to end the Emperor's death agony. Wolff's account of the letter was followed by this comment:

With the letter were four photographs, which I have in front of me. The first is of the church where Maximilian's body was taken. The second shows the squad responsible for the Emperor's execution [fig. 49 or 51]. It consists of six soldiers, a corporal and an officer. The soldiers have horribly sinister expressions. The uniform looks like the French uniform: the kepi and tunic appear to be of grey canvas; the belt of white leather; the trousers, reaching down to the feet, are of darker material. The corporal, the

one who finally killed Maximilian, is a very handsome young fellow whose friendly appearance is in marked contrast to the gruesome task he had to perform. The most bizarre of the seven [*sic*] is the officer commanding the squad who appears to be under eighteen.

The third photograph shows the Emperor's frock coat [fig. 53], seen from the back. It clearly shows the holes made by the bullets that struck Maximilian's chest and passed through his back. . . . The fourth photograph . . . shows Maximilian's waistcoat, or rather the waistcoat lent to him by his servant [fig. 54]. One can clearly see the traces of the three bullets which struck the Emperor in the area of his stomach, [and] the trace left by the last bullet, which ended the unhappy sovereign's suffering.

Wolff vouched personally for the authenticity of the letter, which generally corresponds with other, evidently authoritative accounts. The writer of the letter referred to photographs of 'the squad that shot Maximilian' and 'the place where Mejía, Miramón and the Emperor died' (see fig. 64), as well as of Maximilian's frock coat and waistcoat (figs. 53 and 54), saying that he had received them from the chief army medical officer 'who embalmed Max or rather who stuffed him, since he gave him black glass eyes when he couldn't find any blue ones' (see fig. 24). He added that the photographs had been made in secret.

All the photographs were taken by François Aubert who may or may not have been present at the execution (see fig. 21) but made many striking images immediately after the event (figs. 22, 24 and 69). Distributed by Aubert in carte de visite form, they were widely copied by other photographic firms in Mexico and Europe.[54] The four subjects described by Wolff were reproduced in France by Disderi, both individually and as a combined four-in-one print (figs. 51, 53 and 54), and distributed under the name of the Viennese firm Klein, from their shop on the boulevard des Capucines, thus providing cover for images that would have been – and indeed were – banned in France. The London *Times* of 27 September announced that 'The sale of photographs of Maximilian's coat, the firing party, &, has been interdicted in Paris', and a month later the photographic dealer Alphonse Liébert was condemned to two months in prison and a 200 franc fine for possessing photographs of Maximilian's clothes with intent to exhibit or sell them, although he contended that these were neither morally nor politically offensive.[55]

There are two different views of the execution squad. In one the squad stands at ease, on wooden

Fig. 49
The Execution Squad standing at Ease. Contact print from the original glass negative by François Aubert, June 1867. Brussels, Musée Royal de l'Armée.

In this print recently taken from Aubert's negative, the squad is seen in the same setting as in fig. 23, but with the soldiers in slightly different positions.

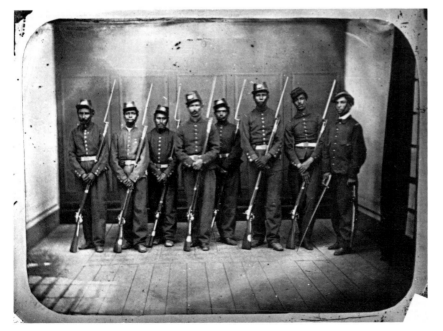

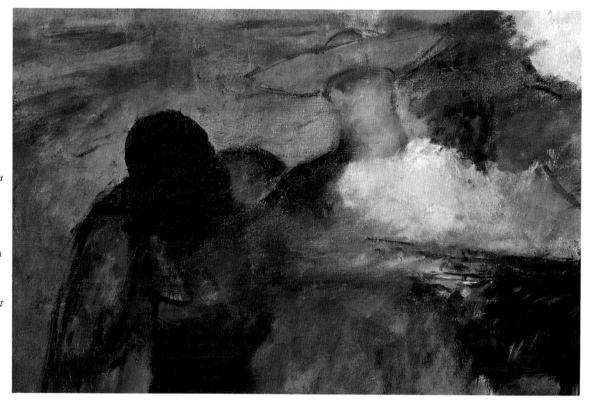

Fig. 50
Edouard Manet,
The Execution of Maximilian
(detail of fig. 70:I).

Detail of the victims in the
first version of the com-
position. The handling is
very free and sketchy compared with the final version
(fig. 41).

Fig. 51
*The Execution Squad against
a Painted Background.*
Carte de visite photograph
(slightly enlarged) by Dis-
déri (after Aubert), 1867.
Paris, Bibliothèque
Nationale.

This reproduction by Dis-
déri of a retouched photograph (see fig. 23) was distributed by the Viennese
firm of Auguste Klein, together with carte photo-
graphs of Maximilian's
frock coat and waistcoat
(figs. 53 and 54, see cats.
22 and 37). They were
banned by the authorities
in France.

floorboards and against a panelled wall or screen (fig. 49).[56] In the other the same figures in slightly different positions are standing to attention (fig. 23). Most cartes reproduce this photograph in a heavily retouched version, with a painted setting that gives the fixed bayonets a particularly sharp and steely appearance, and alters the heads of the soldiers (fig. 51). In both versions, six soldiers wearing shakos are accompanied by an NCO and an officer wearing kepis.[57]

Wolff's article in *Le Figaro* probably marks the point at which Manet began making final alter-ations to his first canvas. Even the belated addition of the NCO and the officer on the right of his canvas may have been an initial response to the photograph, before he grasped the idea of altering the uniforms. The new information would have provided Manet with the opportunity to paint a more factual picture of the execution, one that would appear authentic to a well-informed public. The 'facts' had changed with every fresh report, and by placing Maximilian in the centre, Manet had already elected to follow a particular (in fact erroneous) version. If he still intended to show the picture in his temporary exhibition, he would, as Duret pointed out, have wanted to recast it to take account of important new information published in an influential Paris paper. After a visit to Trouville, Manet returned to Paris for the funeral of Baude-laire on 2 September. His exhibition closed on 10 October, and the following months were spent working on his new canvas for the Salon of 1868.

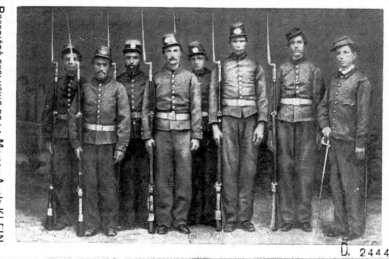

PROPRIÉTÉ EXCLUSIVE DE LA MAISON AUG^te KLEIN

REPROD. PAR DISDÉRI.

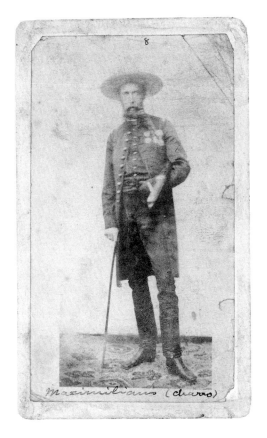

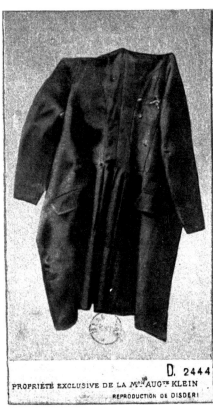

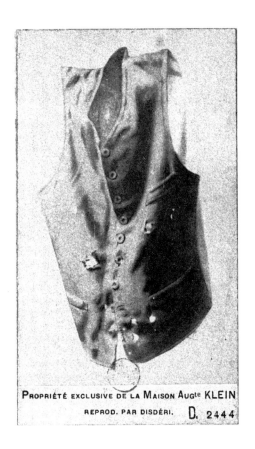

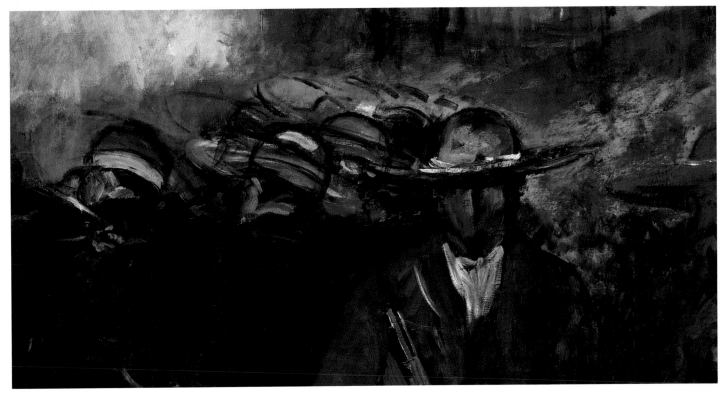

The second version. On the summit of the Cerro de las Campanas

Keeping to the basic design established in his first painting, Manet set out to create a much grander and simpler presentation of his composition on a new canvas. Any discussion of this picture is affected by its present fragmentary state (fig. 73:II), due to severe damage caused before and after the artist's death (see page 112). A photograph taken in Manet's studio in 1883 shows the canvas without two figures on the left (fig. 71), but the surviving fragments give a clear idea of the complete work, and recent restoration has revealed the quality of Manet's brushwork and colour. The setting is a wide landscape, suggesting the 'platform at the top of the Cerro de las Campanas', described in the 31 July account in *L'Indépendance belge* (see page 50), while the intense blue of the sky over the distant hills evokes Maximilian's exclamation, 'Ah, what a splendid day! I always hoped to die on such a day.'[58] Besides simplifying the setting, Manet brought the victims forward, so that they stand on a level with the squad. The figures, defined with great energy and precision, are now very close to the spectator and even in its present condition the effect of the painting is very powerful.

It was for this version that Commandant Lejosne is said to have arranged for a squad of soldiers to come to Manet's studio.[59] The photographic evidence concerning the Mexican firing squad – the largest element in his composition – enabled Manet to engage with his picture in a much more direct way. The fact that their 'uniform looks like the French uniform', as Wolff stated in his article, was not simply political and anti-imperial in its implications. The documentary evidence of the photograph allowed Manet to see the tragedy at Querétaro in terms of his own, familiar, French environment, with real soldiers standing in as models for the Mexican firing squad.

It has often been suggested that Manet looked to illustrated journals for information and motifs, making use of individual figures or whole scenes, such as the engraving of a military execution in Mexico, published in Paris in 1863.[60] However, while such imagery may have formed part of his general mental picture of Mexico, Manet always sought first-hand documentary material and the presence of live models. In February 1868, when he was presumably working on this picture of *The*

Execution, he told Zola, who was sitting for his portrait (fig. 106), 'I can't do anything without a model. I don't know how to invent.'[61]

In this second version of *The Execution of Maximilian*, Manet painted a remarkable 'live' study of the event that had taken place in Mexico. If Duret and Tabarant are to be believed, an infantry squad from the Pépinière barracks marched up the boulevard Malesherbes to the artist's studio on the rue Guyot (now rue Fortuny), where the soldiers raised their muskets to the firing position. However, the soldiers in this second version are in almost exactly the same positions as those in the earlier picture, where the squad is already standing in close order, the front line to attention, feet together, and the second line with feet apart, having taken the regulation half-step to the left in order to fire between the men in front. This suggests that Manet may already have used a model or models when he was sketching his leather-clad guerrillas, and that the story of the squad from the barracks may have been a picturesque invention of the kind often used to catch the imagination of the public and enhance the 'veracity' of a history painting.

As far as they can be identified from Aubert's photographs, the arms held by the Mexican squad are US Springfield muskets model 1842, whereas the execution squad in Manet's second painting is armed with standard French infantry muskets.[62] These are shown at the moment of detonation, as the sword swings down and an oral command is given by the unseen officer, the young man whom the Emperor had to encourage to carry out his duty.[63] On the right, the NCO, replacing the blank-faced figure who confronts the spectator in the first version, holds his musket firmly for the *coup de grâce*. The X-ray of this fragment (fig. 61) reveals that the NCO was originally in a more active pose, readying his weapon, with his head bent farther forward and his right hand cocking the hammer, in a gesture to which Manet returns later.

Compared with the distinctly rumpled soldiers of the real firing squad in the field (figs. 23 and 49), Manet's urban executioners show evidence of a proper application of spit, polish and pipe-clay, and would certainly have created an impression of authenticity for the Parisian public. However, these smartly turned out soldiers are in many ways inauthentic. Their uniform most closely approximates to that of the Imperial Guard light infantry,

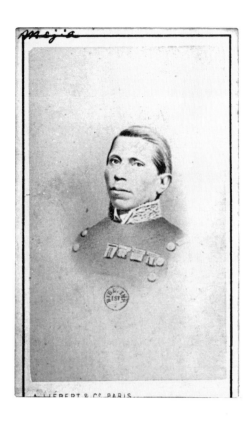

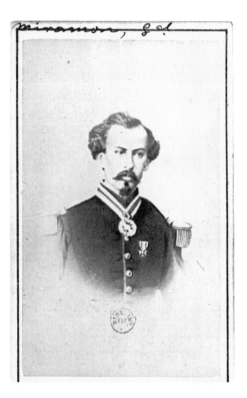

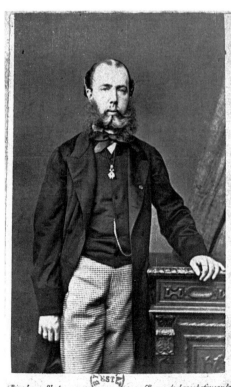

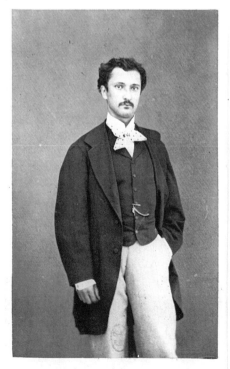

Fig. 56
General Tomás Mejía.
Carte de visite photograph
by Liébert (after Aubert),
September/October 1867.
Paris, Bibliothèque
Nationale.

Fig. 57, upper right
General Miguel Miramón.
Carte de visite photograph
by Liébert (after Aubert),
September/October 1867.
Paris, Bibliothèque
Nationale.

Liébert's reproductions of
Aubert's portraits of Mejía
and Miramón were
authorised for publication
by 5 October 1867.

Fig. 58
The Archduke Maximilian.
Carte de visite photograph
by Bingham, published
1864.
Paris, Bibliothèque
Nationale.

This was the most widely
circulated image of Max-
imilian, taken by Bingham
in Paris when Maximilian
and Charlotte visited
Napoleon III in the
Tuileries in March 1864,
before accepting the crown
of Mexico (see cat. 22).

Fig. 59, lower right
The Violinist Damourette.
Carte de visite photograph
by Lebrun-Hervé,
c. 1865–8.
Paris, Bibliothèque
Nationale.

This violinist friend of
Manet posed in the artist's
studio for the figure of
General Miramón in the
second version of his
Execution of Maximilian
(figs. 71 and 73:II).

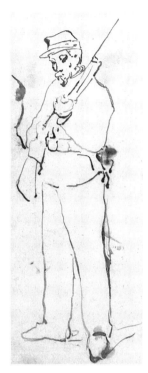

Fig. 60 (cat. 38)
Edouard Manet,
Sergeant holding his Musket,
1868. Pen and sepia ink on
tracing paper, laid on card,
26.6 x 9.8 cm.
Mannheim, Städtische
Kunsthalle.

This traced drawing may
have served to transfer the
composition of the second
Execution painting to the
third and final canvas (fig.
76: III).

Fig. 61
Composite X-ray of the
fragment with the NCO
from *The Execution of
Maximilian* (II, detail of
fig. 72).

Fig. 62
Edouard Manet,
The Execution of Maximilian
(detail of fig. 73:II).

The X-ray of this fragment
of the second version of
Manet's composition reveals
several alterations to the
pose: the NCO's head was
lower, showing more of the
top of his kepi, and his
right hand was cocking the
hammer of his musket, as in
the final version (fig. 67).

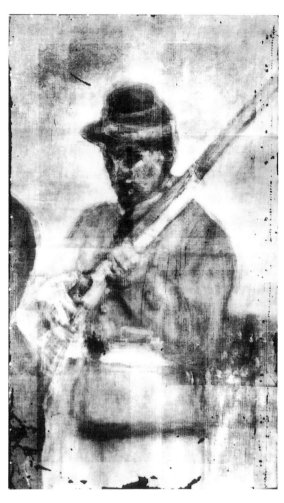

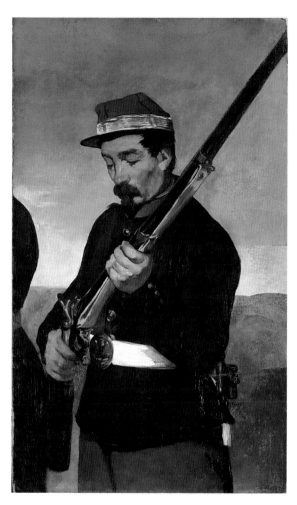

or *chasseurs à pied*, but Manet chose not to paint the dark green epaulettes and the pompoms on their shakos, or the *chasseurs'* distinctive yellow collars. He did, however, paint the spats that were clearly no part of the Mexican uniform but provided a perfect counterpoint to the white belts of the Mexican soldiers, which replace the regulation French black leather belt. He also replaced the yellow piping on the *chasseurs'* dark blue jackets with vivid green, applied in lively, fluid touches. Departing from both French and Mexican reality, Manet brought a swashbuckling touch to his Mexican firing squad by adding yatagan swords, long since abandoned except by the gendarmerie in France, and he eliminated the bayonet scabbards that are visible in the photographs of the Mexican squad. If the troops stationed at the Pépinière barracks in 1867–8 were indeed *chasseurs à pied de la Garde*

impériale, one may give credence to the story of the studio visit and note Manet's fine disregard for the details of their uniform, but it seems equally possible that he used a model or models from the start, and concocted both the guerrilla and 'regular' uniforms from elements that seemed appropriate to his theme.

Although two of the three victims are missing from the damaged canvas, they all appear to have been brought forward largely unchanged from the first version. A slight curve at the edge of the canvas, cutting into Miramón's forehead, was filled in at an early date with a strip of canvas cut from an area of sky, already visible in the photograph taken in 1883 (figs. 71 and 72). This suggests that Maximilian's sombrero was in the position it occupies in the lithograph (fig. 77), where it overlaps Miramón's head. The Emperor was therefore still

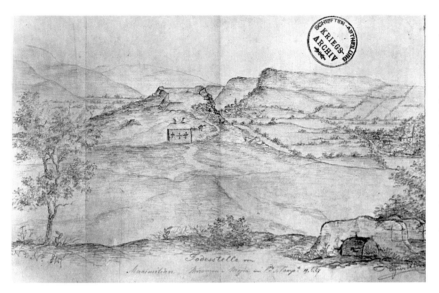

Fig. 63
Johann Nepomuk von
Fürstenwärther,
*The Place of Death of Max-
imilian, Miramón and
Mejía,* 1867. Graphite,
17 x 24 cm.
Vienna, Österreichisches
Kriegsarchiv.

The sketch is in a manu-
script diary by Maximilian's
Austrian topographer, who
was present in Querétaro
during the siege.

Fig. 64
*The Adobe Wall on the
Cerro de las Campanas.*
Contact print from the
original glass negative by
François Aubert, June
1867.
Brussels, Musée Royal de
l'Armée.

Fig. 65
*Souvenir of the Execution of
Maximilian.* Carte de visite
photograph by Cordiglia,
1867.
Washington DC, Library
of Congress

Onto a frontal view of the
wall (fig. 64), the two
halves of the execution
squad (see fig. 49) have
been superimposed to-
gether with the victims –
whose heads are placed on
'borrowed' bodies. Max-
imilian's last words appear
below.

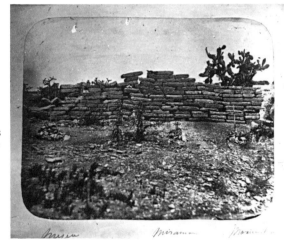

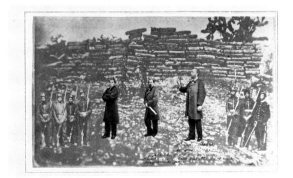

in the centre, with Miramón on his left and Mejía
on his right. A glimpse of the Emperor's left arm
reveals that he was dressed in black, as indicated in
the eyewitness reports, and held General Miramón's hand. However, Manet made a selective
choice from information concerning the generals.
Neither 'shot in the back as traitors', nor in civilian
dress, Miramón in this picture and both generals in
the later versions are shown in shirtsleeves, without
their uniform jackets.

The generals' heads were painted from photographs available in Paris. The firm of Liébert, soon
to be condemned for possessing photographs of
Maximilian's clothes (see page 52), was authorised
by early October to publish carte portraits of Mejía
and Miramón, which Manet almost certainly used
(figs. 56 and 57).[64] Miramón, seen intact in the
1883 photograph of the canvas (fig. 71), was
apparently modelled by a violinist named
Damourette, who attended the Manet family's
soirées and appears in Manet's photograph album
(fig. 59).[65] As for Maximilian, there were many
photographic portraits from which to choose,
including one by Bingham on which Manet may
well have based his painting of the head (fig. 58).

As far as can be judged from its present state, this
picture was 'finished' by the artist. The figures,
painted with great boldness, are full of subtle
details such as the touches of emerald green piping
on the soldiers' uniform. The decision to abandon
this canvas like the first one, and start all over again,
may reflect Manet's dissatisfaction with the composition, since the X-ray reveals he had played
around with the position of Miramón (see figs. 71
and 72) and pigment sections show that he tried
out several solutions for the setting, altering the
horizon line and the colour of the ground. Alter-
natively, it may indicate a fresh attempt to keep
abreast of the latest information on the execution,
or a further rethinking of the significance and
meaning of his picture. All that seems certain is that
Manet intended to exhibit this canvas in 1868. The
May issue of *L'Artiste* announced that his 'Death of
Maximilian' would be among the pictures presented in the Salon,[66] and the chronology of Manet's
project suggests that this must have been a
reference to the second version rather than the
third, which he completed for exhibition the following year. *The Execution* did not appear in the
Salon of 1868, to which the artist sent an earlier
figure study and his portrait *Emile Zola* (fig. 106).

The third and final version of Manet's 'Execution'

Over the next twelve months, Manet worked on his third and final composition, only to be dissuaded from submitting it to the Salon of 1869 as a result of pressure from the authorities. The development of this third version was carried out in several stages, starting with the making of an oil sketch (fig. 74), a traditional academic practice (see fig. 12). However, the sketch itself was subject to extensive alterations while Manet was painting his final canvas (fig. 76:III). He also made a lithograph (fig. 77), which differs from the paintings in several important respects.

The most striking difference between the two earlier versions of Manet's composition and the final one is the introduction of a wall behind the figures. One of the most substantial accounts of the execution, published in London and Stuttgart towards the end of 1868, was transcribed by Maximilian's aide-de-camp (who was not present) from what 'eight or ten Liberal officers . . . concurred in stating'. It described the place of execution on the Cerro, with troops drawn up on three sides of a square: 'Where the square was open, a kind of wall of adobes had been erected. In the middle, where the Emperor was to stand, who was taller than his two companions, the wall was somewhat higher.'[67]

The description of the execution and its site is confirmed by Aubert's photographs taken shortly afterwards, and by his drawing (figs. 21, 22 and 64). Another drawing, by Baron von Fürstenwärther (fig. 63), provides the only detailed view of the site as a whole, showing the Cerro de las Campanas rising up in the distance, crowned by the remains of an old walled fort, and with the *Todesstelle*, or 'place of death', marked by a symbolic wall with three crosses half-way up the hill.[68] Aubert's photograph of the adobe wall (fig. 64) shows the extra bricks in the centre, with three small crosses – later replaced by more substantial mounds of rock and larger wooden crosses (fig. 22) – marking the spot where the victims fell. These photographs were marketed as cartes by Aubert and Peraire, and the first was used by Cordiglia, another photographer in Mexico City, for a photomontage of the execution (fig. 65). In this bizarre memorial image, the soldiers were cut from the photograph of the squad (fig. 49) and applied to the view of the wall, on either side of the three victims, who were made up from portrait heads mounted on other bodies. Maximilian's 'last words' were written below the rhetorical, gesturing figure, here correctly placed on the right. The Emperor's final speech was variously reported, one version ending in the words inscribed on this photograph: *Mexicanos, que mi sangre sea la última que se derrame y que esta regenere este desgraciada pays* (*sic*) – 'Mexicans, may my blood be the last that is shed and may it revive this unhappy country.' Another, perhaps more authoritative, version was given by the Emperor's servant Tüdös and reports the Emperor as saying 'I forgive everyone, and beg everyone to forgive me. I pray that my blood which is about to be shed will be shed for the good of this country. Long live Mexico! Long live Independence!'[69]

The carte photographs and the later accounts of Maximilian's last moments, including his tribute to the young officer and his moving and dignified farewell speech, may all have played a role in Manet's definitive version of the execution at Querétaro. Trustworthy reports and authentic images from Mexico had clarified many details, although some areas of doubt concerning the actual event remained. Tüdös's account, published in Paris on 10 October 1867, referred to an execution squad under a single commander, with four soldiers and one reserve for each prisoner. Other reports had spoken of three separate squads, and these were 'illustrated' by another widely circulated carte photograph (fig. 66), in which the three victims, correctly positioned in front of a wall reminiscent of that in Aubert's photograph, are confronted by three separate squads commanded

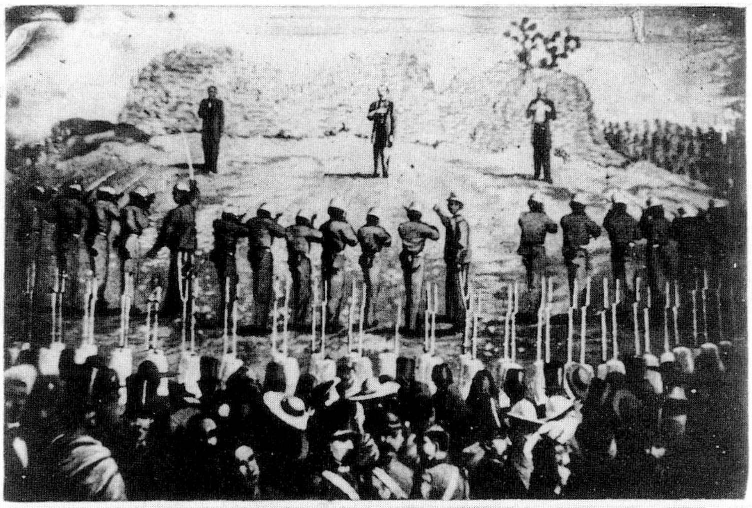

Fig. 66
The Execution of Mejía, Miramón and Maximilian by Three Firing Squads. Carte de visite photograph (slightly enlarged) by Aubert, 1867. Commandant Spitzer Collection.

This painted reconstruction of the execution is based on Aubert's drawing and photographs (figs. 21, 22 and 64). The image shows the open square of soldiers around the site and three firing squads in action.

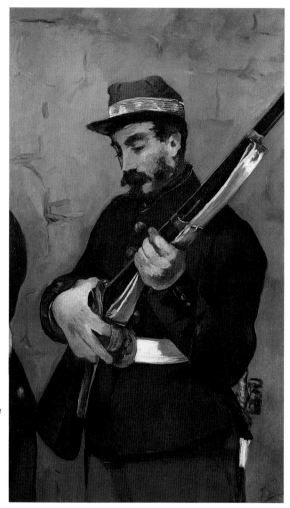

Fig. 67
Edouard Manet,
The Execution of Maximilian
(detail of fig. 76:III).

In Manet's final version, the NCO's features are softened and the brushwork is swifter and more impressionistic than in the previous version (fig. 62).

graph taken shortly before his death (fig. 52)[71] – rather than being turned up to form a circular, halo-like shape.

The earlier, underlying composition of the sketch was squared for transfer in the normal way. The grid lines, whose numbering is still visible at the edge of the canvas,[72] correspond with the format of the lithograph (fig. 77), which in its turn seems to have served as a stage in the development of the composition. In the lithograph, the wall is in two planes and extends across the background, and Mejía's head is raised and thrown back in a dramatic gesture that greatly increases the sense of tension and violence in the otherwise static scene. It seems probable that Manet began by following the earlier stage of the sketch, although an X-ray (fig. 78) shows only the faintest traces of an original design.

One of the artist's concerns was evidently to find satisfactory rhythms and relationships between the figures and to dramatise the confrontation between the two groups in his composition. An innovation in both sketch and print is the placing of the officer, now fully visible between the squad and the NCO, and picked out in the oil sketch by his red kepi and trousers. In the second, large version of the painting (fig. 73) only the barrels of the muskets act as a link between victims and squad, and the NCO stands detached from the other soldiers, while in the X-ray of the sketch and in the lithograph the figures are all in close contact with each other. Even after the oil sketch was revised, squared up a second time and transferred to the final, large canvas,[73] Manet made further alterations to the definitive version of his picture. The most important of these was the painting out of the figure of the officer, whose shape is still apparent under the paint on the wall and is clearly seen in the X-ray (fig. 78).

It remains a matter of speculation as to whether this figure was obliterated for aesthetic reasons, on grounds of military practicality – because technically the officer is standing too far back to give the sword command–or for political reasons, since the figure in red trousers may have been too clearly identifiable as a French officer. Whatever Manet's motives, this alteration could have been carried out at any time from the completion of the painting in the early months of 1869 to its shipment to America in late 1879 (see page 69). A photograph made in New York shows the picture in its present, final state (fig. 80).

by three officers. Although this is one of many painted rather than photographic souvenir images, it may also have played a role in Manet's final conception of his scene.[70]

The first indication of a wall in Manet's composition appears in the X-ray of the oil sketch (fig. 75). It shows as a light shape on the left, and apparently extends only a short way beyond the victims. The X-ray image also reveals changes in the placing of the three figures and the shape of the Emperor's hat. In the final, repainted design of the oil sketch (fig. 74), the prisoners are set back from the firing squad, with Miramón's left leg almost touching the wall, which now runs the full width of the composition. But the X-ray shows that they were originally much farther forward, and also that, as in the earliest version of the composition, Mejía's head fell forward, while the brim of the Emperor's sombrero was set straight on his head – recalling the photo-

Manet's three versions of the 'Execution' pictures

Over the months from July 1867 to early 1869, Manet wrestled with his 'history' paintings, picking his way through often conflicting evidence in order to sharpen the impact and meaning of his image. The first version of the painting is sketchy, and the second now incomplete, but the 1883 studio photograph (fig. 71), the X-ray of the oil sketch (fig. 75) and the lithograph (fig. 77) reveal the development of Manet's composition.

The first, unfinished version was an immediate response to the event, a 'romantic', largely imaginative construction. Manet left it at the point where he had settled the basic composition and decided on the placing of the victims. Maximilian, as hero and martyr, stands between and slightly in front of his generals. Mejía appears always to have been on the Emperor's right and Miramón on his left.

The second version was an impressive, more bluntly 'realist' statement, based on documentary evidence and painted with the help of live models. A powerful handclasp[74] links Miramón to the Emperor, as in all the later versions, although in no version of the composition does the Emperor appear to hold Mejía by the hand. In the later images Maximilian grasps in his right hand the handkerchief he was reported to have passed, with his hat, to his servant Tudos.[75] The Mexican Indian general is nevertheless visually and physically linked to the fair-haired, blue-eyed Habsburg Emperor and through him to his creole brother officer, General Miramón. Mejía himself becomes progressively more dramatic and expressive, from the figure with outflung arm and bowed head in the first canvas to his transformation in the lithograph and later painted versions where he comes to resemble the central figure in Goya's *Third of May* (fig. 38).[76] The head is retouched on the final canvas, giving it an even greater nobility, while Maximilian's face and beard almost dissolve in a flurry of soft brushstokes. Miramón alone remains alert, gazing at the squad as he leans towards the Emperor.

In this third and final canvas, Manet restates the dramatic compositional device of the repainted sketch (fig. 74), emphasising the recession of the

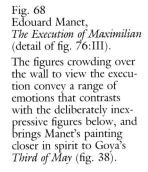

Fig. 68
Edouard Manet,
The Execution of Maximilian
(detail of fig. 76:III).

The figures crowding over the wall to view the execution convey a range of emotions that contrasts with the deliberately inexpressive figures below, and brings Manet's painting closer in spirit to Goya's *Third of May* (fig. 38).

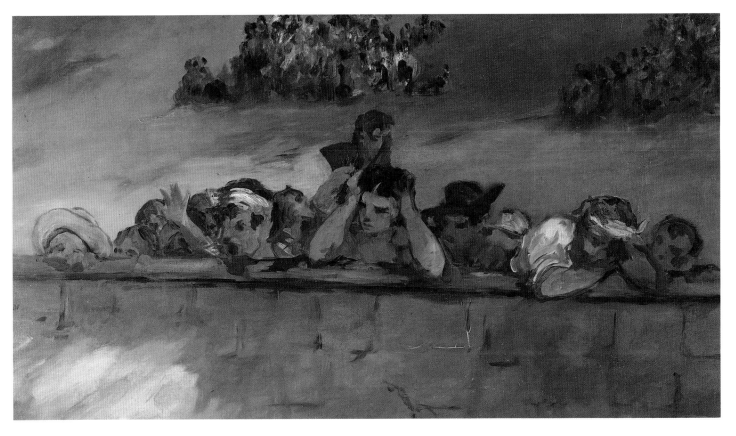

victims in space. The process of transfer from the second canvas to the third was almost certainly a purely painterly operation, without the further use of models. That most of his working material has been lost is suggested by the fact that in the final version of the painting, Manet reverted to the active position of the NCO's right hand, as seen in the X-ray of the second version (figs. 61 and 67). Although the picture's documentary realism is in one sense increased through the introduction of the wall in this final version, Manet manipulated the pictorial elements with a free hand. The muskets, still lying parallel to the picture plane as in the second painting, are no longer pointing at the victims, while for compositional reasons the soldier in the centre has been reduced in size, and the officer has been eliminated altogether.

The setting in the final version emphasises the simple grandeur of the figures. The modest adobe wall on the Cerro de las Campanas has been transformed into a barrier suggesting a prison compound (particularly in the lithograph) or the exterior wall of La Cruz, the convent headquarters where Maximilian was betrayed (fig. 20). In a return to some of the more fanciful early accounts, Manet combined the high wall with the suggestion of a cemetery. Funeral monuments and cypress trees are glimpsed under a bright blue sky, as if to recall the Emperor's words on his way to the place of execution and suggest the heavens above the martyrs' heads, while an impression of mystic witnesses is conveyed in the blurred brushing in of the crowds 'higher up the hill, the people . . . almost all of them poor Indians' (fig. 68).[77] The Mexican people on the wall, the only overtly emotional note in the picture, express horror and dismay like the victims in the *Third of May*. Over the months following Maximilian's execution, Manet's picture slowly acquired the striking, 'naïve' qualities that he sought, as its symbolism became more complex and more powerful. He was finally ready to send his *Execution* to the Salon. But the authorities in France were determined that such an image should remain unseen.

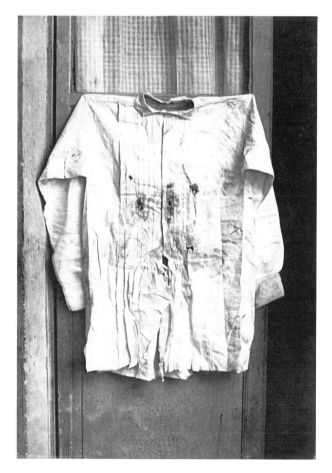

Fig. 69 (cat. 20)
The Emperor's Shirt after the Execution, photograph by François Aubert, June 1867. Albumen print, 22.5 x 16 cm.
Brussels, Musée Royal de l'Armée.

Aubert made several photographs of the Emperor's bullet-riddled and bloodstained clothes (see figs. 53 and 54). This moving image was also reproduced as a carte de visite photograph.

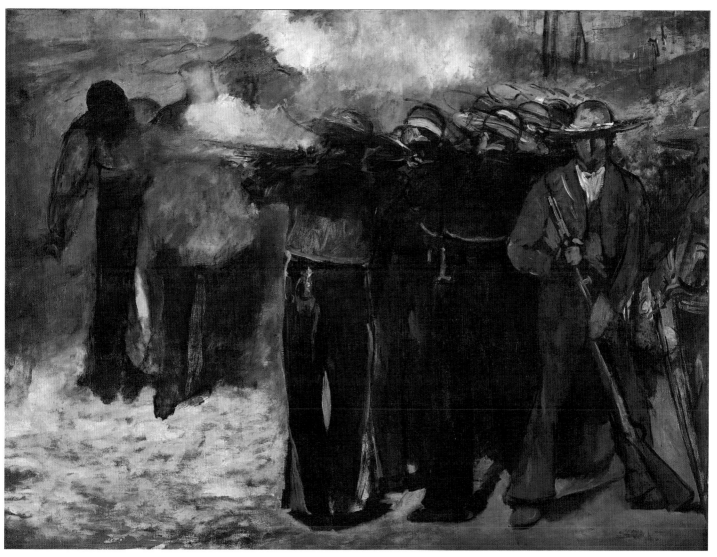

Fig. 70 (cat. 1)
Edouard Manet,
The Execution of Maximilian (I), *c*. July–September 1867.
Oil on canvas, 196 x 259.8 cm.
Boston, Museum of Fine Arts.

Fig. 71
Edouard Manet,
*The Execution of
Maximilian* (II),
photograph by Fernand
Lochard, December 1883.
Albumen print,
7.2 x 9.5 cm.
Paris, Bibliothèque
Nationale.

The earliest known photograph of the second version (fig. 73:II), taken in Manet's studio soon after his death, shows the picture without the two figures on the left. The photograph shows a diagonal tear over Miramón's right leg, also visible in the X-ray (fig. 72), and a row of nail holes along the left edge. This suggests that the canvas had once been attached to a stretcher. Since all the known photographic prints are masked or trimmed on the left, they do not reveal whether Mejía and the Emperor had already been cut from the canvas.

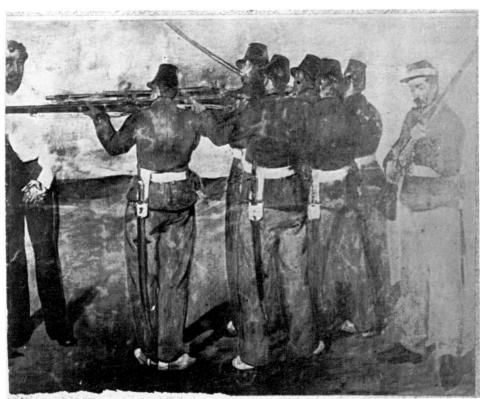

Fig. 72
Composite X-ray of
*The Execution of
Maximilian* (II).

The X-ray of the four fragments reveals the extent of the damage to the canvas, particularly the paint losses that occurred where it must have been folded across the centre. However, the X-ray image also emphasises the boldness with which Manet attacked this second version, laying in the figures very directly, with a minimum of revision on the canvas. The position of Miramón was shifted, probably more than once, and Manet also altered the figure of the NCO (see fig. 61). Alterations to the background, suggested by an analysis of pigment samples, are barely appreciable in the X-ray, which nevertheless shows some 'dappling' over the distant background that is not related to the present line of hills.

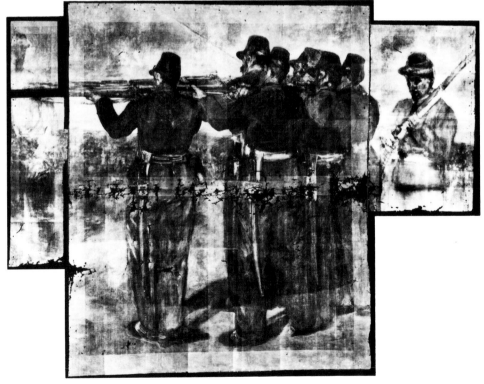

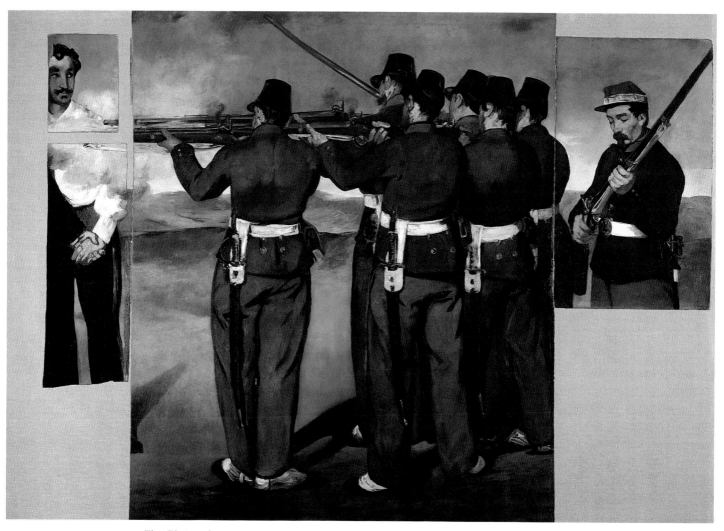

Fig. 73 (cat. 2)
Edouard Manet,
The Execution of Maximilian (II), *c.* September 1867–March 1868.
Oil on canvas, four fragments on a single support, 193 x 284 cm.
London, National Gallery.

No reproduction of the complete painting is known (see figs. 71 and 116).

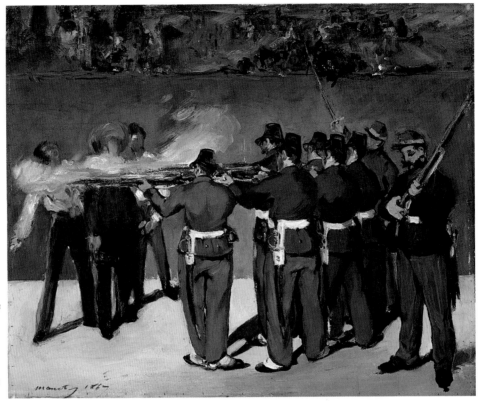

Fig. 74 (cat. 40)
Edouard Manet,
The Execution of Maximilian
(sketch), 1868–9. Oil on
canvas, 50 x 60 cm.
Copenhagen, Ny Carls-
berg Glyptotek.

Preparatory sketch for the
third and final large picture
(fig. 76:III).

Fig. 75
Composite X-ray of
Manet's oil sketch for
The Execution of Maximilian
(fig. 74).

The alterations made to the
painting are clearly visible
in the X-ray and through
comparison with the
lithograph (fig. 77).

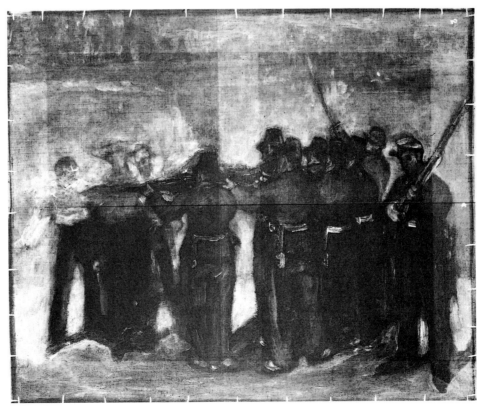

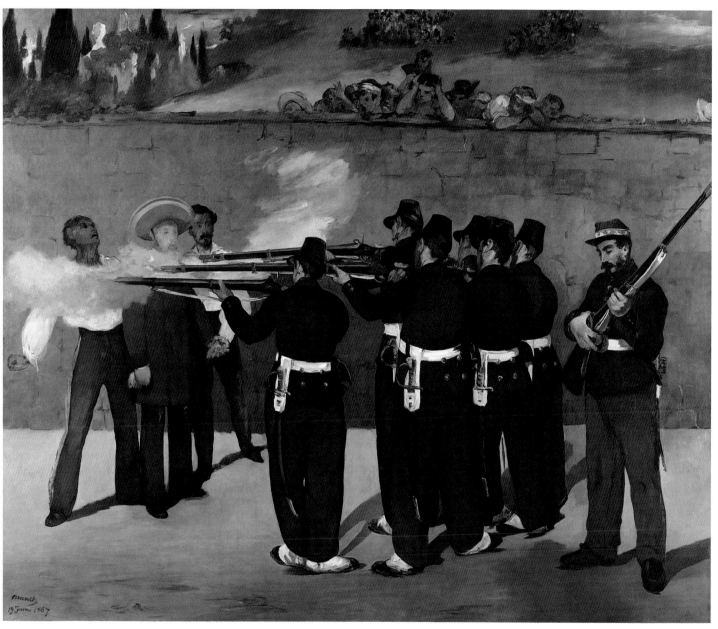

Fig. 76 (cat. 3)
Edouard Manet,
The Execution of Maximilian (III), 1868–9.
Oil on canvas, 252 x 302 cm.
Mannheim, Städtische Kunsthalle.

The painting is signed and inscribed with the date of the execution, 19 June 1867.

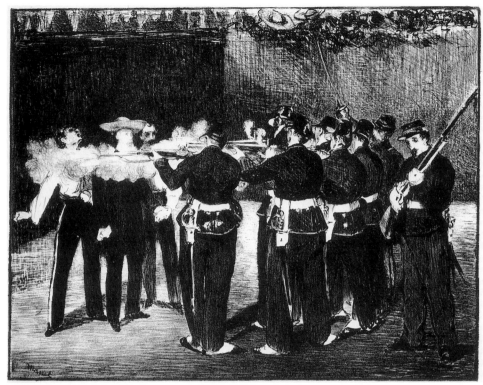

Fig. 77 (cat. 39)
Edouard Manet,
The Execution of Maximilian,
1868. Lithograph,
33.3 x 43.3 cm.
Amsterdam, Rijksmuseum.

The composition of the
lithograph appears to lie
between the earlier and
final stages of the oil sketch
(see figs. 74 and 75). It
bears no title, and was
never published in Manet's
lifetime.

Fig. 78
Composite X-ray of
*The Execution of
Maximilian* (III).

The earlier position of the
three victims, as seen in the
lithograph (fig. 77) and in
the X-ray of the oil sketch
(fig. 75), is not apparent in
the X-ray image of the
thinly painted large canvas
(fig. 76:III). However, the
officer standing between
the squad and the NCO is
clearly visible, in a slightly
different relationship to the
NCO who has been moved
farther to the right. The
head of Mejía corresponds
with the final state of the
oil sketch (fig. 74), as does
Maximilian's upturned
sombrero.

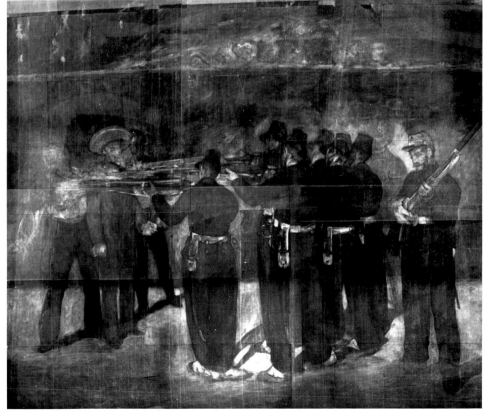

The banning of Manet's 'Execution of Maximilian'

On 7 February 1869, a Paris art journal carried the following announcement:

M. Edouard Manet has painted the tragic episode that brought our intervention in Mexico to a close, the 'Death of Maximilian'. It would appear that this lamentable event has still not become accepted history, since M. Edouard Manet has been unofficially informed that there is every likelihood that his picture, which is in fact excellent, would be rejected at the next Salon if he insisted on presenting it. This is strange, but what is even stranger is that when M. Edouard Manet executed a sketch of this picture on a lithographic stone, and the printer Lemercier presented it for registration, an order was immediately given that the image should not be authorised for sale, even though it bears no title.[78]

The threat to prevent the exhibition of Manet's picture and the banning of his lithograph (fig. 77) were issues that surfaced at the beginning of the year and turned into something of a crusade against censorship when they were aired in the press.[79] In January, the artist had written to Zola about the interdiction of his lithograph and asked for his advice. This produced a brief unsigned note in *La Tribune*, a paper to which Zola regularly contributed, announcing that:

M. Manet has just been refused permission to print a lithograph representing the execution of Maximilian. M. Manet having treated this subject from a purely artistic point of view, it is to be supposed that before long the government will be led to pursue people who simply dare to maintain that Maximilian was shot.

Four days later, on 4 February, in a signed article in the same paper, Zola expressed his contempt for the government and its censors who were trying to put the ghost of Maximilian behind bars. He feigned not to understand their severity, recalling 'in all the stationers' windows, a penny print that came, I believe, from the presses at Epinal, and depicted with terrifying *naïveté* the last moments of Maximilian' (fig. 47). Asking why an accomplished artist should be refused what was permitted in a commercial artisan, he found the answer in the fact that the soldiers in Manet's lithograph 'were wearing a uniform almost identical to that of our own troops,' and his conclusion was that the censors had reacted to the 'cruel irony' depicted by Manet, who was effectively showing 'France shooting Maximilian'.

When the censors refused to authorise the sale of his lithograph, Manet was obliged to take legal action against his printer to prevent the design being effaced and to recover the stone. In the end, the lithograph was not published until after Manet's death. As to the painting, the history of all three versions was a complex one (see pages 112–13).

The fate of Manet's painting

The Second Empire was indeed haunted by the ghost of Maximilian, as Zola implied. Apart from comment and criticism in the press, by 1869 dozens of books and pamphlets had been published on the French intervention in Mexico and Maximilian's fate, and many of them did not hesitate to condemn Napoleon and his fatal policies. In this climate, the painting of Maximilian's execution could not be shown. Manet considered it one of his two or three most important paintings, and in a list of works made in 1872 he valued it at 25,000 francs, alongside *Le Déjeuner sur l'Herbe*.[80] He evidently continued to think of exhibiting the picture, as appears from a letter from his wife to Mme Jules Michelet, wife of the celebrated historian. In June 1873, Suzanne Manet wrote that 'my husband . . . thinks that he will probably have to give up the idea of exhibiting Maximilian, it was an impossible project.' She goes on to mention one of his pictures then in the Viennese Universal Exhibition, and it may be that Manet had planned to exhibit the *Execution* in Vienna rather than Paris.[81] No more is heard of the picture until the young poet and critic Arthur O'Shaughnessy wrote to Manet from London, recalling his visit to the artist's studio in December 1875, and adding: 'I have told all my friends about the big painting of the execution of Maximilian, which even from my description always arouses great interest and the most lively curiosity.'[82] In April 1876 it was Manet's turn to hide the picture from view. He had opened his studio to the public after his two Salon entries were rejected by the jury,[83] and when asked by a critic from *L'Evénement* about a canvas with its face to the wall, he replied: 'Well, that intrigues all the visitors – it's an unfinished canvas of *The Execution of Maximilian*. I'll reveal it in due course.'[84]

The picture was finally revealed not to a French public but when it was 'paraded round America', as Manet put it, by the operatic diva Emilie Ambre and her manager Gaston de Beauplan.[85] They took

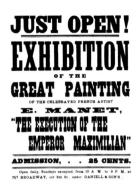

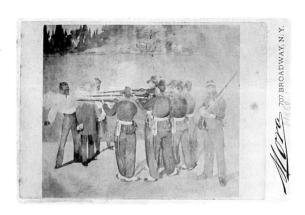

the huge canvas to New York in December 1879 and arranged for its exhibition in a hall on the corner of Broadway and Eighth Street. In spite of handbills, press announcements, photographs and invitations to critics (figs. 79 and 80), the show met with little success. It was more widely noticed and better received in Boston,[86] where the picture was on view for a week in the Studio Building gallery, but any hopes of continuing the tour to Chicago and beyond were abandoned in view of the poor public response and the expense involved.[87] The picture was shipped back to Paris and remained unseen by any but a few friends.

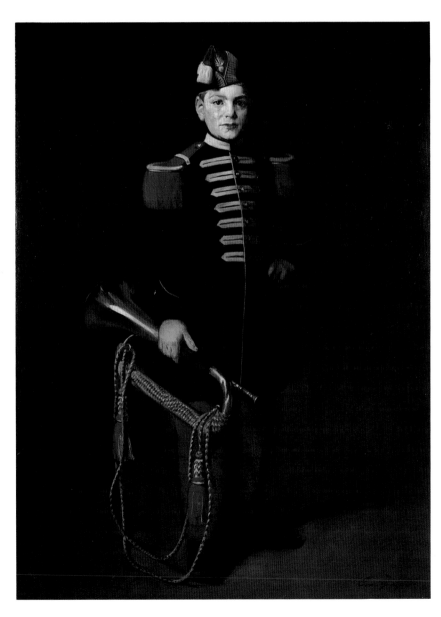

From the end of the Second Empire to the Commune

The execution of Maximilian dealt an irreparable blow to France's power and prestige, and the troops withdrawn from Mexico were unable to save the country from defeat in Europe. In the summer of 1870 the question of a Hohenzollern succession to the throne of Spain suddenly precipitated a crisis (see page 31), and France declared war on Prussia on 19 July. In August the Prussian army advanced into Alsace and Lorraine and one after another the French defeats were announced in Paris.

Manet's attitude to the military had always been one of respect. This was expressed in his poised and crisply concentrated boy *Fifer* of 1865–6 (fig. 82), and is also felt in the stolid young *Bugler* (fig. 81) painted by his pupil Eva Gonzalès in his studio, some months before the outbreak of the Franco–Prussian War. Antonin Proust recorded Manet's increasingly sombre and taciturn mood at this time, and an emotional outburst when he refused to accept any criticism of the army. He insisted that common soldiers, in particular, were victims deserving of respect, and that if the ill-advised policies of the Empire were to blame, then the Empire should be dispensed with, but no blame should attach to the army.[88]

The Second Empire collapsed when Napoleon III surrendered to Bismarck's troops at Sedan and the Third Republic was proclaimed in Paris on 4 September 1870. When the provisional government of National Defence committed itself to all-out war against the Prussian invasion, Manet sent his family to safety in the Pyrenees. He closed his studio, depositing his most important pictures with Théodore Duret and a lawyer cousin, just before

Fig. 79
Handbill for the exhibition
of Manet's *Execution of
Maximilian* (fig. 76:III) in
New York in December
1879.
Paris, Huguette Berès
Collection.

Fig. 80
Edouard Manet,
*The Execution of
Maximilian* (III). Cabinet
print by the Mora Photo-
graphic Studio, New York,
1879.
New York, Pierpont
Morgan Library, Tabarant
archive.

A reproduction of Manet's
painting at the time of its
exhibitions in America in
the winter of 1879–80.

Fig. 81 (cat. 30)
Eva Gonzalès,
The Bugler, Salon of 1870.
Oil on canvas, 130 x 98 cm.
Villeneuve-sur-Lot, Musée
Gaston-Rapin.

The boy bugler, from the
same regiment as Manet's
fifer, is in full dress
uniform. The picture was
acquired by the state at the
Salon of 1870.

Fig. 82 (cat. 29), right
Edouard Manet,
The Fifer, 1865-6. Oil on
canvas, 161 x 97 cm.
Paris, Musée d'Orsay.

The fifer is wearing the
service dress uniform of the
Imperial Guard infantry.
Manet's friend Comman-
dant Lejosne is said to have
brought the boy to Manet's
studio. The painting was
rejected by the jury for the
Salon of 1866.

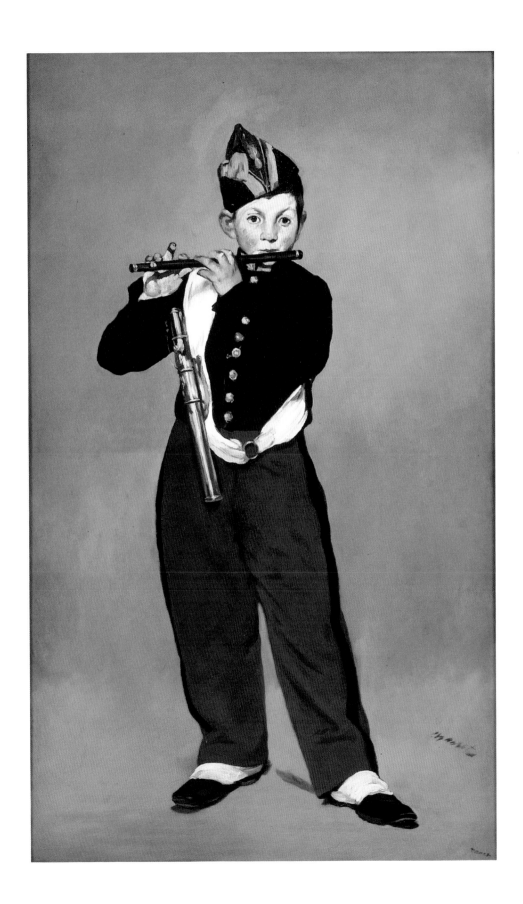

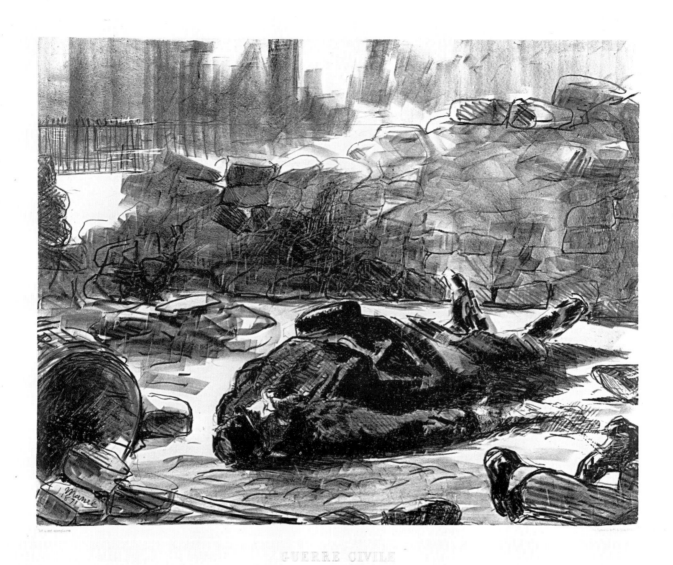

GUERRE CIVILE

Fig. 83 (cat. 43)
Edouard Manet,
Civil War, 1871–4.
Lithograph,
39.9 x 58 cm.
London, British Museum.

Possibly drawn on the
lithographic stone on
Manet's return to Paris in
1871, it was published in
1874 with the title *Guerre
Civile*. The lithograph was
printed by Lemercier, who
had refused to cooperate
with Manet over his *Execution of Maximilian* (fig. 77).

the Prussian troops surrounded Paris on 18
September.[89] Léon Gambetta, Minister of the
Interior in the provisional government, escaped
from the besieged city by balloon to raise an army
for the defence of Paris. Marshal Bazaine, who had
been blockaded at Metz, surrendered to the Prus-
sians on 27 October, and in November Manet and
Degas enrolled, with many other volunteers, in the
National Guard. The hardships and privations of
the bitter winter siege are vividly evoked in Manet's
letters to his wife,[90] and when Paris finally
capitulated in January 1871 he rejoined his family
in the west of France.

After the signing of the armistice, the provisional
government was succeeded by an elected National
Assembly, which met in the Grand Théâtre in
Bordeaux. On a visit there in February, Manet
attended a session of the Assembly, commenting on
the 'doddering old fools', led by that 'little twit
Thiers', who were now in charge of France's
destiny.[91] In March Thiers moved the Assembly
not to Paris but to Versailles, and failed in an
attempt to take control of the rebellious capital.
The provisional government's capitulation and the
humiliating peace terms agreed with Prussia led the
Paris Commune to defy the Versailles government

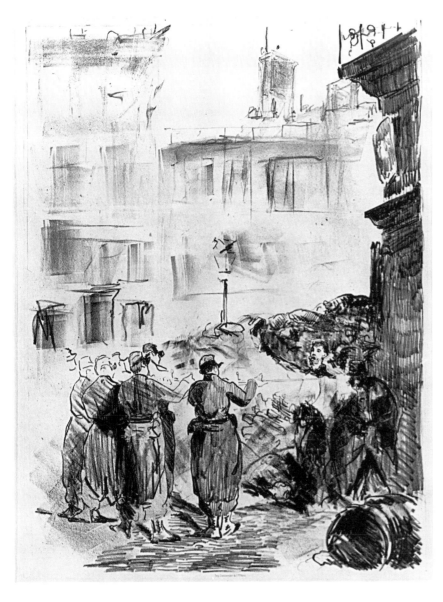

Fig. 84 (cat. 42)
Edouard Manet,
The Barricade, c. 1871–3.
Lithograph,
46.5 x 33.4 cm.
Mannheim, Städtische
Kunsthalle.

Manet's lithograph, which
reverses the composition of
a gouache drawing (fig.
85), remained unpublished
in his lifetime.

had met 'two Communards, just when they are all being shot . . . Manet and Degas! Even at this stage they are speaking out against the drastic measures of the repression.'[93]

Manet himself wrote in a letter to Berthe a few days later: 'Everyone blames his neighbour but the fact is that we're all responsible for what happened.'[94] He expressed his feelings in two powerful works. In one of them (fig. 83), he transposed *The Dead Man* from an earlier period (fig. 31) into a new, more immediately tragic and political context. An unknown soldier lies beside a barricade, with the shoes and striped trousers of an anonymous civilian intruding into the picture. Signed and dated 1871 on a *pavé* from the barricade, the lithograph was published three years later with the title *Guerre civile*,[95] the reprise of his motif supporting the suggestion of a wider political significance in the earlier work.

The other work, *The Barricade*, involved a transformation of Manet's banned Maximilian composition, and may have been made as a study for a Salon painting. The artist began by tracing the outlines of *The Execution of Maximilian* from his lithograph (figs. 77 and 86), then reworked the design in pencil, watercolour and gouache on the other side of the sheet, extending it to form a vertical street scene (fig. 85). There is no ambiguity here. Manet altered the uniforms to show a squad of government troops dispatching Communards beside a piled-up barricade, a wall built of Parisian *pavés* rather than Mexican adobe bricks. A stocky figure in greatcoat and kepi on the left recalls the earlier representations of Mejía (figs. 70:I and 75). Beside him, a revolutionary with a moustache and goatee beard – surely a portrait – waves his arm defiantly above the smoke from the muskets. The work has a freedom that recalls the first *Execution of Maximilian* and evidently had the makings of a superbly effective painting. It may have been inspired by a triple execution that Manet is known to have witnessed. On 28 November 1871, Louis Rossel, a patriotic army officer who went over to the Commune, was shot with two other Communards at a military camp near Versailles, and Manet went to see the dawn execution with three friends.[96] The precise date of *The Barricade* is not known, nor is there any record of a version in oils. In the end it served only as the basis for a lithograph (fig. 84) which, like that of *The Execution of Maximilian*, remained un-published until after the artist's death.

and call for a national insurrection. But on 21 May the Versailles troops entered the city and crushed the Commune with extreme brutality in the course of the notorious 'bloody week'. Some 20–30,000 Parisians were killed – Communards and innocent civilians – and many more arrested. Thousands were later deported to New Caledonia, including Henri Rochefort – whose portrait Manet painted in 1881 (fig. 88). Manet probably returned to Paris just after the *semaine sanglante* ended on 28 May, and Antonin Proust claimed that they both witnessed some part of its horrors.[92] On 5 June Berthe Morisot's mother wrote to tell her that her brother

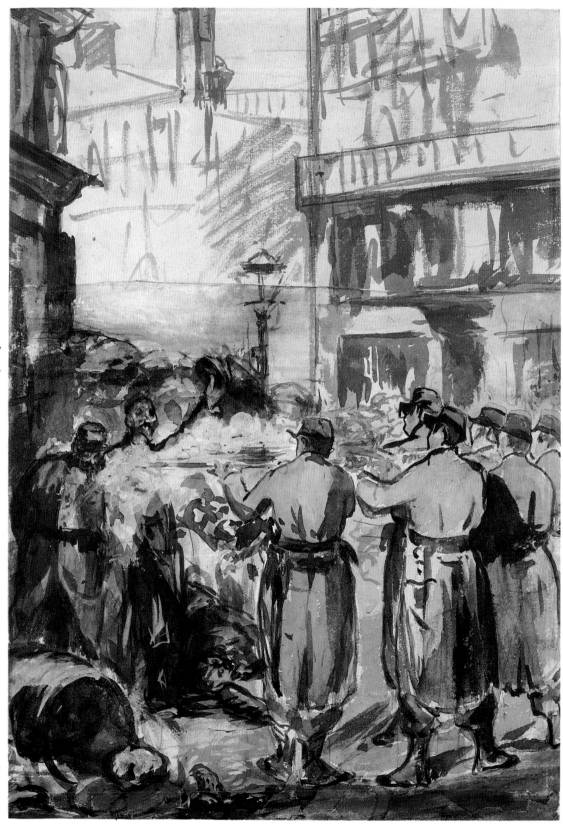

Fig. 85 (cat. 41)
Edouard Manet,
The Barricade, c. 1871.
Graphite, watercolour and
gouache on two joined
sheets of paper, 46.2 x
32.5 cm.
Budapest, Museum of Fine
Arts.

Manet's Mexican execution
(figs. 77 and 86) has been
transformed into an execution during the Paris
Commune.

Fig. 86 (cat. 41)
Edouard Manet,
The Execution of Maximilian,
tracing on the verso of
The Barricade (detail), 1871.
Black chalk and stylus
(see fig. 85).

This tracing (in reverse) of
Manet's *Execution of Maximilian* lithograph (fig. 77)
served as a basis for *The
Barricade*.

Opposite, upper left and
right
Fig. 87 (cat. 47)
Edouard Manet,
Georges Clemenceau,
1879–80. Oil on canvas,
115.9 x 88.2 cm.
Fort Worth, Texas,
Kimbell Art Museum.

Photographs taken in
Manet's studio in 1883
show two unfinished
portraits of Clemenceau;
this one appears to have
remained untouched.

Fig. 88 (cat. 48)
Edouard Manet,
Henri Rochefort, Salon of
1881. Oil on canvas,
81.5 x 66.5 cm.
Hamburg, Kunsthalle.

Manet sent his 'Portrait of
M. Henri Rochefort' to the
Salon in place of a picture
of Rochefort's escape from
Nouméa (see figs. 94 and
95).

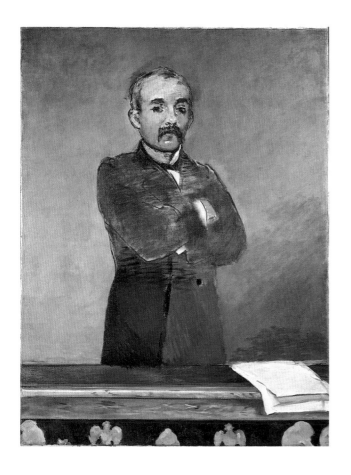

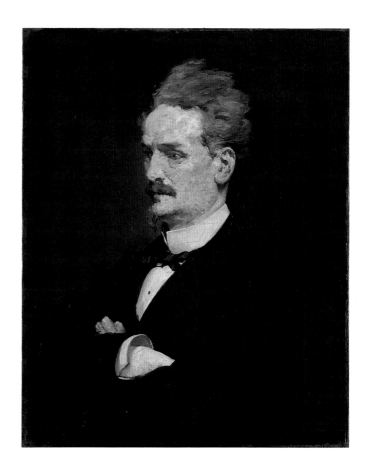

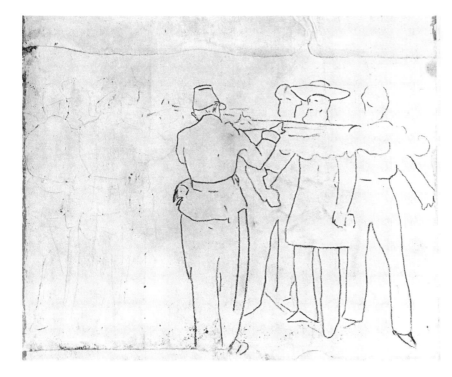

Manet's politics and portraits of politicians

The collapse of France and the Second Empire, followed by the violence of the Commune, forced Frenchmen to take sides in the political debate. Even the most liberal members of the bourgeoisie could not condone the excesses of the revolutionary Commune, and by 1 March 1871 Manet was bitterly regretting that its leaders – political opportunists, 'party hacks' and 'cowardly assassins' – were going to 'kill off . . . the sound idea that was beginning to gain ground, that the only government for honest, peaceful, intelligent people is a republic. . . .'[97]

It was not until the end of the decade that the Third Republic, officially confirmed in March 1871, became a more truly democratic, parliamentary regime. In the early years, the competing claims of Bonapartists, monarchists and republicans of every hue led to the authoritarian rule of 'law and order' established under the presidency of

Fig. 90 (cat. 45), opposite
Edouard Manet,
*The Battle of the Kearsarge
and the Alabama*, 1864,
Salon of 1872. Oil on
canvas, 134 x 127 cm.
Philadelphia Museum of
Art.

As the Confederate steamer
Alabama sinks under fire
from the Union corvette
Kearsarge near Cherbourg,
a small boat heads out to
pick up survivors, one of
whom is clinging to a spar.

Fig. 89 (cat. 46)
Edouard Manet,
*The Trial of Marshal
Bazaine*, 1873. Graphite,
18.5 x 23.8 cm.
Rotterdam, Boymans-van
Beuningen Museum.

Manet sketched Bazaine sitting at a table, confronting
the military tribunal which
condemned him to death
for treason during the
Franco-Prussian War. The
sentence was commuted to
imprisonment, and he later
escaped to Spain.

the elderly, conservative Marshal Mac-Mahon, from 1873 until he was forced to resign in 1879. During these years, Manet was more overtly engaged in political issues than in the 1860s. His younger brother Gustave was a radical city council-lor, and the guests at the family's weekly soirées included the politicians and statesmen Georges Clemenceau, Léon Gambetta and Emile Ollivier.[98]

Ollivier was an old family friend and a lawyer like Manet's father, who became an opposition Deputy in 1857.[99] Manet's very first published print was a shrewd and sensitive caricature portrait of Ollivier, which appeared in a satirical journal in 1860.[100] The republican politician later rallied to Napoleon III's 'Liberal Empire' and voted to declare war on Prussia. Léon Gambetta, on the other hand, came out against the imperial regime in 1868 and was elected a Deputy the following year on a radical programme. Manet came to know and admire him at this time, and between 1871 and the end of the decade made several abortive attempts to paint his portrait.[101] Plagued as always by his need for end-less sittings, he left incomplete two striking portraits of Georges Clemenceau (fig. 87), Gam-betta's colleague and rival,[102] but succeeded in finishing and showing in the Salon a later portrait of the radical Henri Rochefort (fig. 88).

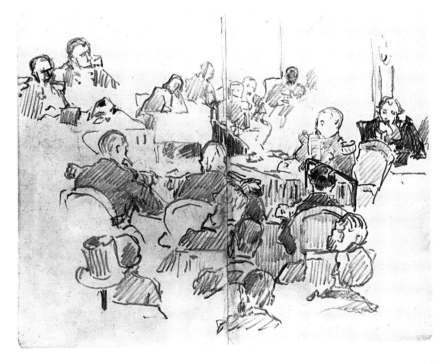

History painting under the Third Republic

Manet's first Salon entry under the Republic, in 1872, was not a scene of the execution of Max-imilian or of Paris Communards. Such subjects were taboo and battle scenes had been banned alto-gether from this first post-war, post-Commune Salon, which in the event proved to be a pro-foundly backward-looking exhibition, crowded with inappropriate mythological, erotic and genre scenes.[103] Manet chose instead to present a picture from the 1860s, which though a battle scene could pass as a sea piece. This was his magnificent *Battle of the Kearsarge and the Alabama* (fig. 90), depicting a celebrated incident in the American Civil War that had taken place off the coast of France in 1864. Manet's motives for selecting it have been the sub-ject of speculation.

In February 1872, the *Alabama* incident had once again become topical. An Anglo–American commission in Washington had just agreed that the English and American claims arising out of the Civil War should be settled by arbitration in Geneva. The February–March issue of *Le Journal illustré* carried a front-page report that recalled the original incident and gave a detailed account of the *Alabama* and its end. Built in Liverpool, the ship was the most notorious of the Confederate raiders that harried Union merchant ships from British harbours. It was pursued by the Union corvette *Kearsarge* and forced into harbour at Cherbourg. The captain of the *Alabama* challenged his rival to a duel at sea and paid the price of his temerity. The 1872 article illustrated the battle – which at the time had been announced in the press and was witnessed by great crowds[104] – as well as a session of the commission in Washington. Manet was therefore presenting a work that was related to a current issue and into which could be read any number of political allusions, including that of the 'cost' of war.[105]

A contemporary issue to which Manet turned his attention in 1873 was the trial of Marshal Bazaine, the former commander-in-chief of the expedition-ary forces in Mexico (fig. 10). Manet attended the court martial, which was held in the Grand Trianon at Versailles from October to December. Bazaine's trial on charges of treason arising out of his con-duct during the Franco–Prussian War was exten-sively reported and illustrated in the press. But in

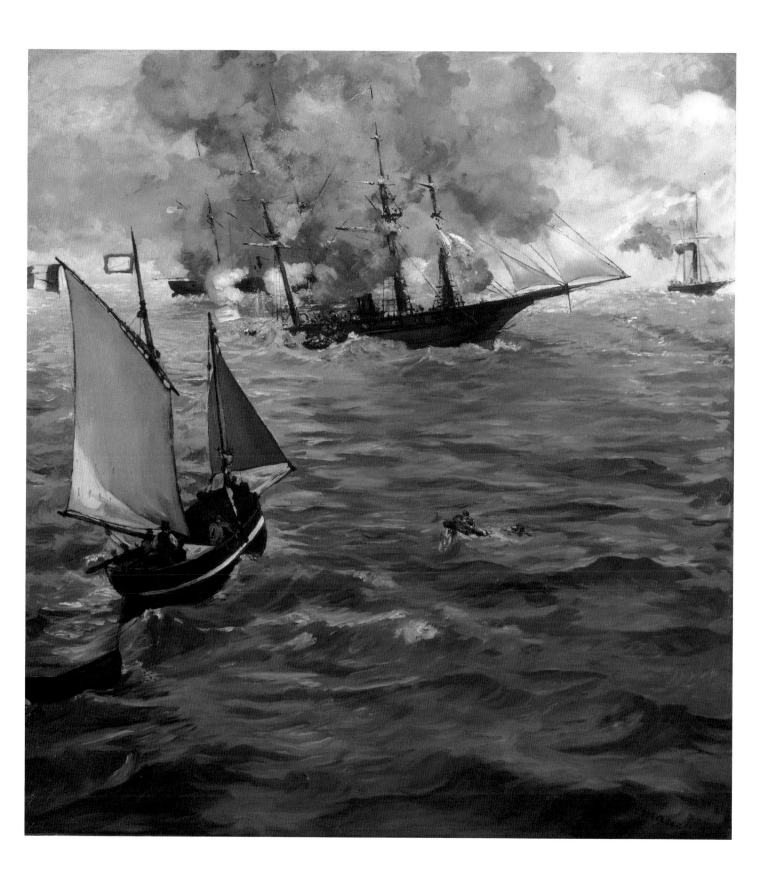

spite of Manet's interest in the subject, two or three pencil sketches and a tracing (fig. 89) are all that is known of a project for an ambitious courtroom composition, perhaps intended for publication as a lithograph or even for a large-scale history painting.[106] It is possible that Bazaine himself was responsible for the abandoning of this project. Antonin Proust attended the trial with Manet and recorded the artist's disgust at Bazaine's 'indifference', when he had hoped to see him boldly standing by his decisions and defying the prosecution.

Censorship, caricature and political comment

It is difficult to assess the effect of censorship or auto-censorship on Manet's work. In February 1874 he published a café scene in a radical Belgian journal that was banned in France.[107] Shortly afterwards he made a gaudy chromolithograph of *Polichinelle* (fig. 91), which he may have intended as a caricature of Marshal Mac-Mahon. It was seized by the police, but passed for publication in June 1874.[108] Censorship, feared or actually exercised,

may also have prevented the publication of a song entitled *The Beggars*, by the radical poet Jean Richepin. Manet's illustration for the songsheet (fig. 92) shows a one-legged man on crutches with his back to the spectator. Recalling the cripple in his lithograph of *The Balloon* (fig. 93), the figure also appears in a view of the rue Mosnier decked with flags (Malibu, J. Paul Getty Museum). Flags for the Fête de la Paix on 30 June 1878 fill two radiant canvases by Claude Monet,[109] but Manet's response to the event was evidently less enthusiastic. This first national celebration since the end of the war and the Commune was held while a new Exposition Universelle was in progress. The holiday became a delicate political issue in a republic still dominated by conservatives, since the radical municipal council – of which Gustave Manet was a member – wanted the fête to be held on 14 July, Bastille Day. Manet's songsheet design and the view from his studio window in June 1878 suggest his detachment from the official celebrations and his scepticism concerning a nation that was still far from truly republican and that neglected or repressed its working poor.[110]

Fig. 91
Edouard Manet,
Polichinelle, 1874.
Chromolithograph,
46 x 33.5 cm.
Paris, Bibliothèque
Nationale.

The image of a *polichinelle* suggests a caricature of Marshal Mac-Mahon, the President of France; the first edition of the lithograph was seized by the police.

Fig. 92
Edouard Manet,
The Beggars, 1878. Brush and ink over graphite,
34 x 26.5 cm.
Paris, Huguette Berès
Collection.

The cover design for a song with 'Music by Cabaner' to a 'Poem by J. Richepin', it is sketched on a sheet with the words and music printed on the other side.

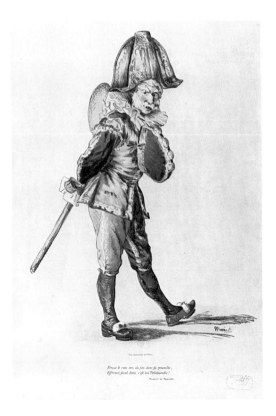

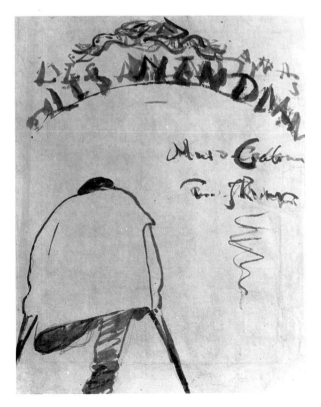

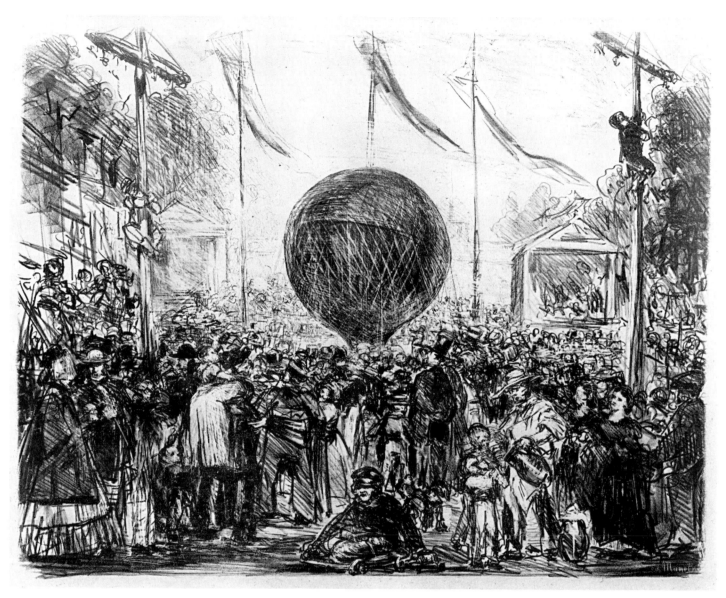

Fig. 93 (cat. 44)
Edouard Manet,
The Balloon, 1862. Litho-
graph, 40.3 x 51.5 cm.
London, British Museum.

This rare print is an ironic
illustration of the fête given
on the Esplanade des In-
valides on the Emperor's
official birthday, 15 August
1862. It was never pub-
lished.

The return of Rochefort – Manet's Legion of Honour nomination

Fig. 95 (cat. 49), opposite
Edouard Manet,
The Escape of Rochefort,
1880–1. Oil on canvas,
143 x 114 cm.
Zurich, Kunsthaus.

Two studies for the
painting Manet intended to
send to the Salon of 1881.
Although smaller, the
signed version (fig. 94) is
more highly finished.

Fig. 94 (cat. 50)
Edouard Manet,
The Escape of Rochefort,
1880–1. Oil on canvas,
80 x 73 cm.
Paris, Musée d'Orsay.

In January 1879 the Republicans gained control of the Senate as well as the Chamber of Deputies, and President Mac-Mahon was forced to resign. Bastille Day, 14 July, was finally chosen as France's official national holiday and celebrated for the first time in 1880. Manet decorated letters to friends with flags to salute both the holiday and the amnesty that had just been proclaimed,[111] which enabled exiled or deported Communards to return to France. One of the most celebrated of these was the radical politician and satirical journalist, Henri Rochefort (fig. 88). With the reform of the press laws in May 1868 (see page 100), the 'red' marquis de Rochefort-Luçay had launched his pocket-sized but virulently anti-imperial journal *La Lanterne* with the celebrated opening statement: 'According to the Imperial Almanach, France has thirty-six million subjects not counting subjects of discontent.'[112] After the collapse of the Commune, Rochefort was deported to the prison colony at Nouméa in New Caledonia. His escape in 1874 caused a sensation, and he became a hero of the Republican left.

Rochefort made a triumphal return to Paris just in time for the celebrations of 14 July 1880. When Manet returned from a summer cure at Bellevue, he contacted Rochefort who was enthusiastic about the artist's plan to paint a picture of his escape, with an '*Alabama* sea' (fig. 90).[113] After meeting him, Manet jotted down details of the boat for his poet friend, Stéphane Mallarmé, 'a whaleboat – the colour was dark grey – six people – two oars', and Monet wrote to Théodore Duret in December that Manet was 'reasonably well, very busy with a sensational picture for the Salon, the escape of Rochefort in a boat on the open sea; he is just waiting for Rochefort's permission before starting work.'[114]

Manet painted two versions of *The Escape of Rochefort*, one with the boat near enough for the heads to be recognisable (fig. 95) – Rochefort at the tiller and Olivier Pain in profile on the left, the other showing the boat farther away, almost lost in the huge expanse of water, but with Pain's profile still clearly recognisable (fig. 94).[115] Although this version is signed, both paintings should no doubt be regarded as *esquisses*, studies for a large-scale Salon work that he was unable to complete. This idea is born out by Manet's oil studies of Olivier Pain and of the boat.[116] In the end, he sent his portrait of Rochefort to the Salon of 1881, where it helped to win the medal, if only a second-class one, that finally put him beyond the reach of the jury. The portrait's bold brushwork evokes Rochefort's striking but heavily pockmarked features, and the picture was ungraciously refused by the sitter.[117]

When Gambetta's party came to power in November 1881, Manet's old friend Antonin Proust was appointed Minister of Fine Arts. One of the first acts of this short-lived government was to nominate Manet for the Legion of Honour. The Republic had finally, with an ironically old-fashioned gesture in the time-honoured tradition, kept faith with one of its most committed sons.

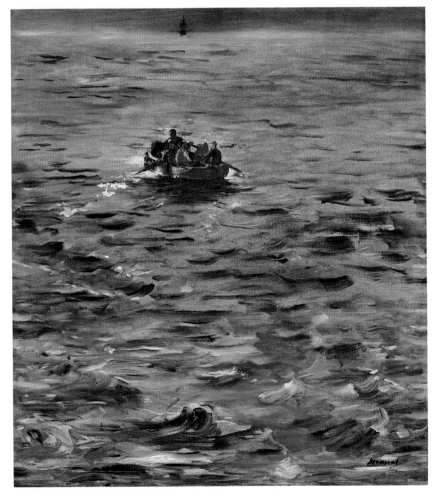

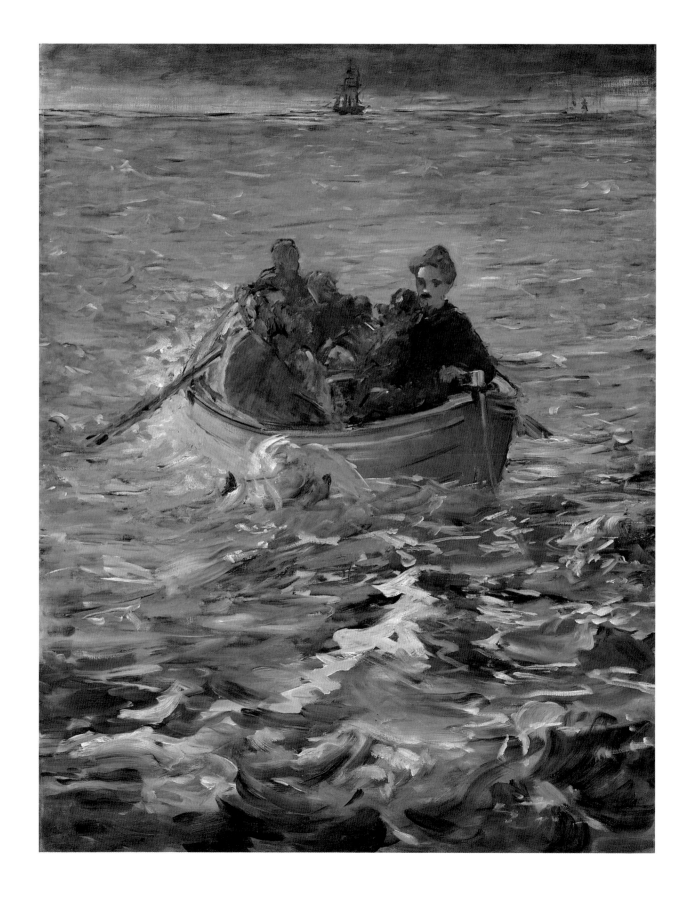

Notes

1. *Sancho*, Brussels, 13 January 1867; Pierre Véron in *Le Charivari*, 1 January 1867.
2. E. Zola, 'Une nouvelle manière en peinture: Edouard Manet', *Revue du XIXe siècle*, 1 January 1867. English trans. in Gronberg 1988, pp. 62–96.
3. Paris/New York 1983, Appendix I, no. 4; Wilson-Bareau 1991, p. 41. For a discussion of the regulations governing the Exposition's art section, see Mainardi 1987, pp. 128–31.
4. E. Zola in *L'Evénement*, 27 and 30 April, 7 May 1866; see Hamilton 1986, pp. 83–7.
5. From the autumn of 1866, Manet, his wife Suzanne and her son Léon lived with Mme Manet at 49 rue de St-Pétersbourg, near the Pont de l'Europe. A statement drawn up by Mme Manet at the end of that year showed that her son had been living at the rate of some 20,000 francs a year since the death of his father. See Moreau-Nélaton 1926, I, p. 105; Wilson-Bareau 1991, p. 12. On Manet's parents, see notes 98 and 99.
6. H. Daumier, *Projet de statue de la Paix*, in *Le Charivari*, 5 January 1867 (Delteil 3547); *O mon fils!* . . . , in *Le Charivari*, 16 January 1867 (Delteil 3549); see A. Stoll (ed.), *Die Rückkehr der Barbaren. Europäer und 'Wilde' in der Karikatur Honoré Daumiers*, Hamburg 1985, especially pp. 425–47.
7. See Ordrupgaard 1989, no. 17; Wilson-Bareau 1991, p. 15. Léon Leenhoff, then fifteen years old, was Suzanne Manet's son, born when Manet was still an art student. Manet was almost certainly not his father, now thought to have been Manet *père*. Léon was always presented as Suzanne's younger brother.
8. The French and foreign press, including the London *Times* of 2 July, carried the Emperor's speech, commented on by X. de Villarceaux, 'Les Prix de 1867', *L'Artiste*, September 1867, pp. 429–31.
9. See Providence 1981, pp. 10–21, 116–22, for some of the principal newspaper accounts, quoted or excerpted from the original French texts. These expand on Sandblad 1954, and Davies 1956 and 1970.
10. Proust 1897, p. 21; 1913, p. 133; 1988, p. 30.
11. The picture was exhibited at the rue de Richelieu premises of Alfred Cadart, the initiator of a revival of original printmaking.
12. Manet's first biography, Bazire 1884, p. 57, implies that the painting was banned from the 1867 exhibition, but was written without direct knowledge of the artist in the 1860s and is often inaccurate.
13. The cable, from Valentia on the south-west coast of Ireland to Hearts Content in Newfoundland, was in regular use from 1 August 1866. For the text of Maximilian's cable, see Corti 1968, p. 943.
14. For Beaucé's Mexican mission, see F. Robichon in the French military journal *Tradition*, no. 23, December 1988, p. 8; the documents cited are in the Archives Nationales, Paris (F21.117). Adler 1986, p. 166, notes the importance of Beaucé in relation to Manet, Mexico and Maximilian; he is also mentioned by Austin in Providence 1981, p. 109, note 52.
15. Salon of 1864, no. 108 *bis*, *Soldaderas de la bande du partisan Chavez* (location unknown); 1865, no. 122 *bis*, *Potrait du maréchal Bazaine en tenue de campagne*, possibly the equestrian portrait discussed in note 21.
16. A. de Neuville, *Combat de San Lorenzo (expédition du Mexique)*, Salon of 1867, no. 1134 (location unknown). For Jules Brunet, see note 60.
17. A variety of albums, beginning with *L'Autographe au Salon* (1863–5), normally reproduced artists' drawings related to their Salon exhibits. In 1867 the *Album autographique* was subtitled *L'Art à Paris en 1867*, and its twenty undated issues also covered the Exposition and the individual exhibitions of Manet (see note 28) and Courbet.
18. One of two military genre scenes painted for the Empress Charlotte was shown at the Salon of 1866, no. 98, *Campement du 3e Zouaves à San-Jacinto, près de la lagune de Chapala, versant du Pacifique* (Trieste, Castello di Miramare). Over twenty 'Mexican' works by Beaucé are recorded (not all currently located).
19. General Loysel, who served in Mexico from 1862 and was in close contact with Maximilian and Beaucé, wrote to Manet on 12 April 1876; copy in the Bibliothèque Nationale, Paris (Estampes: Cahier Leenhoff, I, pp. 5–6). At the Beaucé sale, Hôtel Drouot, 11–12 May 1876, Manet's small panel of *Cows in Pasture* (Rouart and Wildenstein I, 191) was acquired by G. de Bellio, according to the *procès verbal* (Archives de Paris).
20. Photographs of Beaucé's works by Richebourg include Salon paintings and state commissions (see fig. 100), paintings for the court in Mexico, sketches and drawings (Salon-de-Provence, Musée de l'Empéri).
21. A small equestrian portrait (Salon-de-Provence, Musée de l'Empéri), possibly Salon of 1865 (see note 15), was based on a photograph by Aubert (Paris, Gimon collection). For Mexican photographers see note 53.
22. Many of Manet's drawings have been lost, letters and notebooks have disappeared, and his photograph albums (Paris, Bibliothèque Nationale, and New York, Pierpont Morgan Library) are evidently not as Manet left them.
23. On the relationship between the Manet and Fournier families, see Proust 1913, pp. 2–3.
24. Proust 1897, pp. 128–30; 1913, pp. 22–7; 1988, pp. 13–17. On Couture, see *L'Enrôlement des Volontaires de 1792: Thomas Couture*, exhibition catalogue, Musée Départemental de l'Oise, Beauvais 1989. On Manet's military connections, see also Boime 1973, p. 176.
25. Lejosne was a commandant in the Paris military command from 1859 to 1870. The family was strongly republican and Manet frequented their salon in these years.
26. The project to publish a set of artistic lithographs, initiated by Cadart (see note 11), came to nothing. On the political implications of the print, see Druick and Zegers 1983; Paris/New York 1983, no. 44.
27. *Sancho*, Brussels, 14 June 1863.
28. For the smaller fragment of *Bullfighters* (New York, Frick Collection), see Rouart and Wildenstein I, 73; Wilson-Bareau 1991, pl. 71. *The Dead Man* was featured in a crude, reversed reproduction in the seventh issue of the *Album autographique*, in August 1867 (see note 17). A text announces Manet's direct appeal to the public in his pavilion on the avenue de l'Alma and lists the works in his catalogue.
29. The combined X-rays were first published by Reff, see Washington DC 1982, no. 77.
30. Thoré-Bürger and Baudelaire in *L'Indépendance belge*,

15 and 26 June 1864; see Bürger 1870, II, p. 98, Tabarant 1947, p. 85, Hamilton 1986, pp. 60–4, and C. Baudelaire, *Correspondance*, ed. C. Pichois, Paris 1973, II, pp. 386–7. Thoré-Bürger drew attention to the existence of a photograph by Goupil, published in 1863, see Washington DC 1982, no. 78, and Paris/New York 1983, no. 73. On Manet's access to the Pourtalès picture, see Wilson-Bareau 1988, p. 21.

31. For the possible political significance of Goya's bull-fighting etchings and lithographs, see N. Glendinning in *Journal of the Warburg and Courtauld Institutes*, XXIV, 1961, pp. 120–7, and J. Wilson-Bareau, *Goya's Prints*, London 1981, pp. 71–5. Napoleon III and Empress Eugénie attended bullfights at Bayonne-Saint-Esprit from 1856–62. In Mexico bullfighting was encouraged by the Conservatives (and by Maximilian) and suppressed again when Juárez and the Liberals returned to power in 1867.

32. Louis Martinet showed fourteen of Manet's works in March 1863. They included *Music in the Tuileries Gardens* (London, National Gallery) and several of his Spanish subjects. The show was adversely reviewed by Paul de Saint-Victor in *La Presse*, 27 April 1863. French text quoted in Moreau-Nélaton 1926, I, pp. 45–6; see also Hamilton 1986, p. 39.

33. Proust 1897, p. 169; 1913, p. 36; 1988, p. 27. Proust incorrectly implied that Manet visited Spain around 1860, see the documents in Wilson-Bareau 1988.

34. See P. Comte, *Ville de Pau, Musée des Beaux-Arts, catalogue raisonné des peintures*, Pau 1978, n.p. On the state commission, see also *Le Musée du Luxembourg en 1874*, exhibition catalogue, Grand Palais, Paris 1974, no. 64.

35. See A. Martínez-Novillo, *Le peintre et la tauromachie*, Paris 1988, pp. 109–19.

36. See C. Pichois (ed.), *Lettres à Charles Baudelaire*, Neuchâtel 1973, p. 236; Wilson-Bareau 1988, p. 48; Wilson-Bareau 1991, p. 36.

37. Wilson-Bareau 1988, p. 50; Wilson-Bareau 1991, pp. 36–7, pl. 86.

38. The first edition of Goya's *Tauromaquia* was published in Madrid in 1815, the second *c*.1855. Motifs from a number of the prints are seen in *Mlle V... en costume d'espada*, 1862 (New York, Metropolitan Museum of Art); see M. Ruggiero in Providence 1981, p. 27; Paris/New York 1983, nos. 33–5.

39. See Wilson-Bareau 1988, pp. 23–4.

40. C. Yriarte, *Goya*, Paris 1867, facing p. 86 (erroneously titled *Le deux mai*). Yriarte, whose name appears in Manet's address book, was the author of the first substantial monograph on Goya in France.

41. Goya entitled the prints now known as *The Disasters of War*, 'Fatal consequences of the bloody war in Spain with Bonaparte'; see Wilson-Bareau 1981 (cited in note 31), pp. 43–9.

42. On the meeting of Duret and Manet, see Paris/New York 1983, no. 108, Wilson-Bareau 1988, and Wilson-Bareau 1991, p. 35 and pl. 24.

43. Duret 1902, p. 71; 1906, pp. 114–15.

44. For the *Figaro* text (excerpted and without the caveat), see Providence 1981, p. 116–17. Lithographs of naïvely dramatic execution scenes are in the Musée Royal de l'Armée, Brussels. A set of six or eight unsigned lithographs (by Vinzenz Katzler?), published by H. Gerhart in Vienna and also reproduced as carte photo-

graphs, was probably partly based on the spurious account; some of the cartes bear Maximilian's alleged exclamation, which appears nowhere else: 'Tell López that I forgive him his treachery; tell the land of Mexico that I forgive her this crime' (Vienna, Albertina and Nationalbibliotek, Trieste, Castello di Miramare). See Providence 1981, pp. 180, 184 and 186; Anders and Eggert 1982, p. 111.

45. 'Les exécutions au Mexique', *Le Figaro*, 7 July 1867, p. 2; see Davies 1956, p. 171.

46. As many as twenty different images are known, principally by Aubert and Peraire. The portraits are often combined with those of Generals Mejía and Miramón.

47. The official report, written and signed on the Cerro de las Campanas at 07.05 on 19 June, simply states that 'the aforementioned prisoners were simultaneously executed, at the time and place indicated' (Mexico DF, Biblioteca Nacional).

48. The Cerro de las Campanas has often been incorrectly named, both in contemporaneous accounts and maps and in the recent literature.

49. Text excerpted in Providence 1981, p. 119.

50. The painting was analysed in the Conservation Department of the Boston Museum of Fine Arts in 1991, and part of the X-ray was remade (following the technically inadequate reproduction in Wilson-Bareau 1986, fig. 58). The X-ray will be published together with further scientific evidence about the picture.

51. See P. Willing, *L'Expédition du Mexique et la Gurre franco-allemande*, (*Les collections historiques du Musée de l'Armée*, vol. 3), Paris-Arcueil 1984, pp. 35 and 49.

52. Paris, Archives nationales, Dépôt Légal *Province* (F18*.XI.16): Vosges (Epinal) 23 August 1867, no. 106 (*Bibliographie de la France*, 5 October 1867, 'Imagerie', no. 1524); Moselle (Metz) 17 September 1867, no. 64 (*Bibliographie de la France*, 27 June 1868, 'Imagerie', no. 1080).

53. Wolff became the paper's principal art critic in 1868 and regularly attacked the work of Manet and, later, the Impressionists.

54. For an account of Aubert's career, see Ceysens 1987, and G. Gimon in *Prestige de la Photographie*, no. 3, December 1977, p. 80 ff; also Ratz 1991, pp. 20–5. Inferior copies of Aubert's cartes were circulated by Agustín Peraire (see fig. 23).

55. Scharf 1974, p. 49, refers to a condemnation of Disderi, without giving a source. For a report in *The Times*, see Davies 1956, p. 171. Liébert's condemnation on 26 October was reported in *La Gazette des Tribunaux*, 27 October 1867, p. 1035, and *Le Temps*, 28 October 1867.

56. An inscription on a carte photograph identifies the squad as 'sargentes de Galeano' and the officer as 'Teniente de la Guardia Supremos Poderes, Rodrigo Castillo' (Mexico DF, INAH, inv. 16276/174).

57. The squad and individual soldiers have been variously identified (see note 55). Salm-Salm 1868, I, p. 305, noted that the Supremos Poderes guards led the procession to the Cerro, the Cazadores de Galeano surrounded the carriages and the Nuevo León battalion carried out the execution; see also *Documentos gráficos* 1986, p. 218. Tüdös, reported in *Le Mémorial diplomatique* of 10 October 1867, identified the squad captain as Simón Montemayor; Davies 1970, p. 97, note 5,

gives the names of five soldiers (citing a 1911 Mexican source). In 1952, Manuel de la Rosa, who was aged twenty-six at the time, claimed to have fired the shot that killed Maximilian, see *Picture Post*, 28 June 1952 (see also Ratz 1991, p. 345).

58. *Le Mémorial diplomatique*, 31 July and 24 August 1867, quoted in Providence 1981, pp. 119–20; see also Salm-Salm 1868, p. 305; Blasio 1944, p. 179; and note 67.

59. See Duret 1902, p. 71; 1906, p. 115; and Tabarant 1947, p. 141.

60. *The Mexican Expedition. Butrón, robber baron, executed in the walled citadel in Mexico City*. Wood engraving after Jules Brunet in *Le Monde illustré*, 3 October 1863. See L. Johnson in *Burlington Magazine*, CXIX, 1977, pp. 560–4; also Sandblad 1948, p. 125; Boime 1973, p. 183 ff.; Providence 1981, pp. 187, 192–3.

61. Recorded by Zola in *L'Evénement illustré*, 10 May 1868, quoted in Wilson-Bareau 1991, p. 45.

62. The French *fusils d'infanterie* are also model 1842 weapons, with back action lock plates, correctly defined and clearly identifiable in Manet's painting. It is possible that some of the Mexican soldiers in Aubert's photograph have French muskets, model 1822/40 *transformé*.

63. The squad captain's regrets were recorded in both *L'Indépendance belge* and *Le Mémorial diplomatique* on 31 July, and repeated in the latter on 24 August. See notes 55 and 56.

64. The cartes reproduced bear the Dépôt légal stamp (Seine 1867, nos. 2230–1) and were announced in the *Bibliographie de la France* on 5 October.

65. On the Manet family's soirées, see note 98. No portraits or views connected with Mexico are included in Manet's photograph albums (see note 22).

66. M. de Montifaud, 'Salon de 1868: II', *L'Artiste*, May 1868, p. 253, cited in Darragon 1989, p. 150.

67. Salm-Salm 1868, I, p. 303, notes the discrepancies in the various published accounts. The statement of the Liberal officers concurs with accounts by Maximilian's Hungarian servant Tüdös, reported in *Le Mémorial diplomatique*, 10 October 1867, and told in Blasio 1944, pp. 179–80; see Providence 1981, pp. 121–2, also Ratz 1991, pp. 339–40, for a compilation of eyewitness accounts.

68. J. N. von Fürstenwärther, ms. diary, vol. II, between pp. 204–5; published as *Kaiser Maximilian von Mexiko*, Vienna 1910, drawing reproduced p. 155. A distant view of the Cerro by Aubert (see Ratz 1991, p. 135) was distributed as a carte de visite (cat. 22:8) and incorporated into a souvenir image (fig. 46).

69. As reported on 10 October 1867 in *Le Mémorial diplomatique*, in Spanish and French; quoted in Corti 1968, p. 822. See Ratz 1991, pp. 341 (ill.) and 411 n.16.

70. Several naïve oil paintings of the execution were evidently based on this carte, including one in the Philadelphia Museum of Art (inv. 50.124.827); see also F. Cachin, *Manet*, Paris 1990, p. 76, fig. 3. For another image of the execution taking place against a wall, see Boime 1973, pp. 183–7, and Providence 1981, p. 187.

71. A carte of this rare photograph is in the same album as fig. 23 (Mexico City, INAH, inv. 238224/9); see Providence 1981, p. 182. Another print is reproduced in *Documentos gráficos* 1986, p. 208.

72. See A.-B. Fonsmark in *Meddelelser fra Ny Carlsberg Glyptotek*, Copenhagen 1984, English summary pp. 83–4.

73. The second squaring up is indicated by measuring points around the edges of the picture, probably intended, according to Fonsmark, as a guide for threads, which would not disfigure the surface of the work, which Manet gave to Méry Laurent.

74. A handclasp is a central gesture in the Epinal print (fig. 47), where Maximilian is seen embracing his confessor.

75. According to Tüdös's eyewitness account, see note 67.

76. He may be compared with the victim in *The Suicide* (Zurich, Foundation E. G. Bührle Collection), usually dated 1881 but more probably painted around this time; see Rouart and Wildenstein I, 258; *The Passionate Eye. Impressionist and Other Master Paintings from the Collection of Emil G. Bührle, Zurich*, exhibition catalogue, Zurich and Munich 1990, no. 27.

77. From Tüdös's eyewitness account, see note 67.

78. In *La Chronique des arts et de la curiosité* (a supplement to the *Gazette des Beaux-Arts*), 7 February 1869,

79. For all the relevant documents cited here, see Paris/New York 1983, Appendix II, pp. 531–4; also a further reference in X. Feyrnet, 'La Chronique', *Le Temps*, 22 and 23 February 1869, referring to Lemercier's request to efface the drawing on the stone.

80. A copy of the lost original list is in Léon Leenhoff's notebook (cited in note 87); see Moreau-Nélaton 1926, I, p. 134, Rouart and Wildenstein I, p. 17.

81. Suzanne Manet to Mme Jules Michelet, 10 June [1873] (Paris, Bibliothèque Historique de la Ville de Paris). The letter is dated by the reference to Manet's *Reader* (Saint Louis Art Museum), shown in Vienna that year; see Rouart and Wildenstein I, 35.

82. O'Shaughnessy to Manet, 20 May 1876 (Paris, Bibliothèque d'Art et d'Archéologie); see J. Wilson-Bareau and B. Mitchell in *Print Quarterly*, VI, 1989, p. 266.

83. The rejected pictures were *Le linge (The Laundry)* (Philadelphia, Merion, the Barnes Foundation) and *The Artist* (São Paulo, Museum of Art). See Wilson-Bareau 1991, pp. 177–9 and pl. 169.

84. Unsigned article, 'La journée à Paris, M. Manet chez lui', *L'Evénement*, 20 April 1876, cited in Darragon 1989, pp. 264–6.

85. Proust 1897, p. 314; 1913, p. 122; 1988, p. 63.

86. A collection of press cuttings sent to Manet, mainly from Boston newspapers, is in the Tabarant archive at the Pierpont Morgan Library, New York.

87. See the letters from Gaston de Beauplan to Manet (Paris, Musée du Louvre, Cabinet des Dessins, 'Manet. Lettres et documents', pp. 20–3), copies by Léon Leenhoff (Paris, Bibliothèque Nationale, Estampes: Cahier Leenhoff, II, pp. 57–72), see Gronberg 1988, pp. 167–8; letters from Emilie Ambre to Manet (Louvre album, pp. 24–5). For Manet's portrait of the singer (Philadelphia Museum of Art), see Wilson-Bareau 1991, p. 256 and pl. 226.

88. Proust 1897, p. 175; 1913, p. 57; 1988, p. 36.

89. See Wilson-Bareau 1991, pp. 55–6. It is not known which pictures Manet sent to Jules de Jouy.

90. A. Tabarant (ed.), 'Une Correspondance inédite d'Edouard Manet: Les Lettres du siège de Paris (1870–1871)', *Mercure de France*, 1935, pp. 262–89; English trans. by M. Curtiss (ed.) in *Apollo*, vol. 113, June 1981, pp. 378–89; see also P. Cailler (ed.), *Manet raconté par*

lui-même et par ses amis, Geneva 1953, I, pp. 53–74, and Wilson-Bareau 1991, pp. 55–65.

91. Letter from Manet to F. Bracquemond, see J.-P. Bouillon in *Gazette des Beaux-Arts*, April 1983, p. 151; quoted in Wilson-Bareau 1991, p. 160.

92. Proust 1897, p. 176; 1913, pp. 64–5; 1988, p. 37.

93. D. Rouart (ed.), *Correspondance de Berthe Morisot*, Paris 1950, p. 58; K. Adler and T. Garb (eds.), *The Correspondence of Berthe Morisot*, London 1986, pp. 73–4.

94. See note 93; 1950, p. 59; 1986, p. 74; Wilson-Bareau 1991, p. 161.

95. The date on the lithograph is not necessarily that of its execution. For a discussion of its imagery, see J. Baas in *Art Journal*, Spring 1985, pp. 36–42. On Manet's response to the Commune, see M. R. Brown in *Arts*, December 1983, p. 8 ff.

96. The text describing the execution is quoted in Darragon 1989, pp. 200–1.

97. Manet to Félix Bracquemond, see note 91, Bouillon p. 151; Wilson-Bareau 1991, p. 161.

98. See the ms. recollections of Léon Leenhoff in 'Portrait de la mère de l'artiste' (New York, Pierpont Morgan Library, Tabarant archive); edited text in *Le Journal des curieux*, 10 March 1907, pp. 5–7.

99. On Manet's father, see Paris/New York 1983, no. 3; N. Locke in *Burlington Magazine*, CXXXIII, 1991, pp. 249–52. Ollivier met Manet and his brother Eugène in Italy in 1853.

100. For Manet as a caricaturist on his voyage to Rio in 1848–9, see Wilson-Bareau 1991, pp. 23–5. His caricature of Ollivier (Harris 1, Guérin 67) was reproduced in *Diogène*, April 1860.

101. Proust 1897, p. 177; 1913, p. 65; 1988, p. 37.

102. See Paris/New York 1983, nos. 185 and 186. One of the portraits (Paris, Musée d'Orsay) was later reduced in size; on the evidence of the Lochard photograph the other (the work reproduced) remained unaltered.

103. See the discussion of this Salon in Darragon 1989, pp. 204–7.

104. The fight was an extraordinary attraction and a special excursion train brought 1,200 Parisians to Cherbourg for the occasion (*Le Monde illustré*, 2 July 1864). See Adler 1986, pp. 107–10, and M. Ruggiero in Providence 1981, pp. 25–6, on the political implications of France's involvement on the Confederate side in the American Civil War.

105. The Alabama Arbitration forced Britain to pay $15.5 million in gold in compensation for lost American merchant ships.

106. Proust 1897, p. 179; 1913, p. 73; 1988, p. 40; see Rouart and Wildenstein II, 350–2.

107. For Manet's print and its reproduction in *L'Europe*, 22 February 1874, see P. Van den Abbeel and J. Wilson-Bareau in *Burlington Magazine*, CXXXI, 1989, pp. 283–8.

108. See the discussion by M. R. Brown in *Art Journal*, Spring 1985, pp. 43–8, also Van den Abbeel and Wilson-Bareau 1989 (cited in note 107), pp. 285–6.

109. Paris, Musée d'Orsay, and Rouen, Musée des Beaux-Arts; see *A Day in the Country*, exhibition catalogue, Los Angeles/Chicago/Paris 1984–5, pp. 118–22, and R. Kendall (ed.), *Monet by himself*, London 1989, p. 77.

110. On the rue Mosnier paintings and the 1878 Fête de la Paix, see B. R. Collins in *Burlington Magazine*, CXVII, 1975, pp. 709–14; R. Kasl in *Art Journal*, Spring 1985, pp. 49–58; and the far-reaching analysis by J. M. Roos, 'Within the "Zone of Silence": Monet and Manet in 1878', *Art History*, September 1988, pp. 372–407.

111. Manet's illustrated letters, dated from Bellevue, 14 July, carry the messages 'Vive la République' and 'Vive l'amnistie', see Rouart and Wildenstein II, 577 and 596; Paris/New York 1983, no. 205.

112. 'La France contient, dit l'Almanach impérial, 36 millions de sujets sans compter les sujets de mécontentement', *La Lanterne*, 31 May 1868.

113. Marcellin Desboutin to Manet, undated letter (Paris, Musée du Louvre, Cabinet des Dessins, 'Manet. Lettres et documents', f.º 9–10), and a postcard dated 30 November 1880 (f.º 11); see Moreau-Nélaton 1926, II, p. 78.

114. For Manet's letter to Mallarmé (Vulaines-sur-Seine, Musée Stéphane Mallarmé), see Wilson-Bareau 1991, p. 259; Monet to Duret (Paris, Musée du Louvre, Cabinet des Dessins, Monet no. 96, ms. 57), see D. Wildenstein, *Claude Monet*, I, Geneva 1974, p. 441.

115. Manet's paintings are reminiscent of the engraved frontispiece to Rochefort's memoir *De Nouméa en Europe*, Paris 1876. See the extensive account of Manet's projects by E. Darragon in *La Revue de l'art*, no. 56, 1982, pp. 25–40.

116. Rouart and Wildenstein I, 367 and 368.

117. Duret 1902, p. 143; 1906, p. 225; Paris/New York 1983, no. 206.

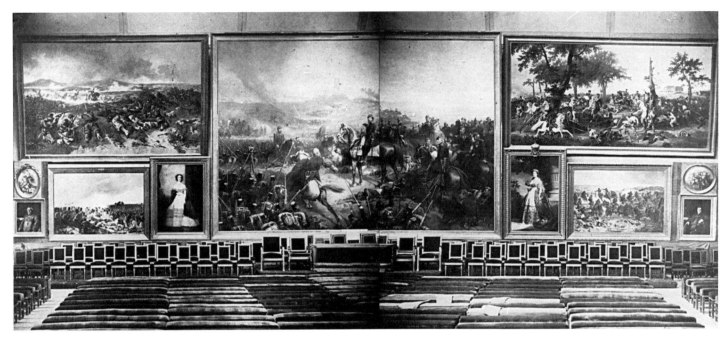

Fig. 96
The Salon d'Honneur at the
Salon of 1861, photograph
by Richebourg.
Paris, Bibliothèque
Nationale.

Yvon's *Battle of Solferino*
hangs in the centre of this
group of battle pictures.

Manet's Maximilian: History Painting, Censorship and Ambiguity

JOHN HOUSE

Napoleon III's regime banned Manet's *Execution of the Emperor Maximilian* from the Salon, the huge, jury-selected exhibition that was still, in the late 1860s, the only outlet for large-scale, ambitious paintings in Paris (see page 59). The subject was politically very contentious; but Manet's treatment of the theme was also problematic. To many late twentieth-century viewers, the directness and emotional understatement of the picture heighten its effect, but by nineteenth-century criteria it rejected the stock language of academic art – compositions with clear focuses, vivid gestures and facial expressions, and readily legible details – by which painters directed the interpretations of their viewers.

This essay seeks to explain why Manet's *Execution* was unacceptable to the French authorities, by placing it in the context of other paintings of subjects from contemporary history, and by examining the censorship of imagery that was critical of the imperial government and its policies and values. Celebratory paintings of French military might played a central part in propagating Napoleon's empire; Manet's painting starkly presented one of the regime's greatest political disasters, and treated it in a way that denied any ready apportionment of blame. Through its studied ambiguity it expressed the values of a particular segment of republican opposition in Paris.

History painting in decline

History painting was still generally seen as the painter's highest goal, but it was widely considered to be in a state of terminal decline. Traditionally, history painting was expected to treat significant events, usually from the past, that could serve as examples of heroism or morality, but by the 1860s there was no agreement about what subjects should be painted or how they should be treated. Many factors seemed to have brought about the decline of history painting. The modern world appeared to offer little scope for subjects of drama or morality, and the great events of the past were no longer felt to carry exemplary lessons for the present. At the same time, traditional history painting, with its dependence on a complex language of gesture and expression (see fig. 98), had become increasingly outmoded in the face of demands for an art more directly related to everyday experience.

Ingres, paradigm of the academic painter at the mid-century, propounded the 'high art' position in its most extreme form:

Most modern painters call themselves history painters: we must destroy this claim. The history painter is he who represents heroic deeds, and such deeds are only to be found in the history of the Greeks and Romans; it is only by representing them that the artist can demonstrate his skill in painting the nude and draperies. All other periods yield only genre paintings, because the costume conceals the body.[1]

Few commentators restricted the painter so narrowly to subjects from antiquity, but there was general agreement that true history painting should portray important actions and events, and should bring out their moral significance.

The critic Olivier Merson explicitly spelt out the social functions of history painting in 1861: 'So long as art is inspired by the lofty speculations of the soul and appeals to noble instincts, it will win the respect of the masses and they will pay homage to it as they would to a divine manifestation'; but if artists obey 'vulgar impressions', they will become slaves of the caprices of popular taste.[2]

As Ingres's tenets showed, the treatment of the theme was inseparable from the choice of subject. The wider significance of a scene could only be brought out if the painter conceived it with a breadth and generalisation that transcended its particular details; by this the work could be said to approach the 'ideal' and to attain 'style'.

However, these values were threatened from two sides, both from within and from without the academic camp. Even supporters of traditional history painting had come to feel that the heroic subject was no longer essential; as the poet and critic Théophile Gautier put it in 1855:

The expression 'history painting', as everyone knows, does not always mean a painting representing a historical subject; it can also be applied to pictures which are raised above genre painting by 'style', by the grandeur of their figures or the breadth of their execution.[3]

This view that a painting could become 'high art' by its treatment alone encouraged academically trained painters such as Alexandre Cabanel and Paul Baudry to concentrate on the sensual mythological scenes, the Venuses and nymphs, with which they won such success in the years around 1860. Even Ingres had painted such subjects throughout his career, for instance the female nude as *La Source* (Paris, Musée d'Orsay), much discussed when it was first shown in Paris in 1861.

The other threat to history painting came from techniques associated with the depiction of everyday genre scenes. Painters of subjects from the past came increasingly to focus on seemingly trivial themes, rather than on the significant actions that had been the lifeblood of traditional history painting. This shift reflected the widening public for art: the vast audiences attracted to the Salons mostly preferred paintings that depicted piquant incidents – sentimental or amusing – rather than heroic deeds. But it also corresponded to a significant change in the writing of history, towards the study of everyday life in the past. This appeared most notably in the writings of historians such as Augustin Thierry and Alexis Monteil from the 1820s onwards.[4] Pictures of historical incidents became widely popular with the 'troubadour' subjects of the 1810s, of which Ingres himself was a leading practitioner. By the 1850s, historical costume pieces of comparatively trivial subjects far outnumbered elevated history paintings.

This concern for everyday details was fed by the discoveries of archaeology, which had immeasurably extended the knowledge of past epochs. Historically correct details came to be seen as proof of a picture's authenticity. Such an emphasis on attributes, often incidental to the main theme of the narrative, worked against the 'high art' demand for generalisation and breadth of treatment. Gérôme's historical scenes of the 1860s, such as *The Death of Caesar* (fig. 97), were much criticised for overemphasising unimportant details; these criticisms were all the more pointed because Gérôme's earlier work (like *The Cock Fight*, Salon of 1847, Paris, Musée d'Orsay) had led many critics to see him as a potential saviour of the academic tradition.

A further shift away from 'high art' history painting was instigated by one of the largest series of state commissions of the century, the history paintings made for Versailles from 1833 onwards, after King Louis-Philippe had converted the whole palace into a museum dedicated *à toutes les gloires de la France*. In these paintings, which were an expression of Louis-Philippe's own ambition to create a popular form of monarchy, a heroic vision of history was decisively replaced by a more anecdotal, accessible version, pioneered by artists such as Horace Vernet (the National Gallery's four panoramic battle scenes by Vernet were painted for Louis-Philippe before he became king). It was also in these years that the term *genre historique* first became widely used to describe the new type of painting of historical subjects.[5]

A central issue in the debates about history painting was the question of narrative. Traditional history painting, such as David's major pictures of the 1780s and 1790s, had sought to present a distilled moment in time, and to epitomise the values and issues for which a subject stood by the gestures and expressions of the figures alone. By contrast, historical genre painting told its stories through devices that academic theorists regarded as extraneous to painting, notably through the addition of texts to spell out the story and through signs and details within the painting that evoked past or future events – for example pictures of other related scenes on a background wall, or letters newly written or received.

Contemporary history: a suitable theme for art?

The Versailles commissions highlighted another crucial problem facing history painting – the possibility of treating contemporary subjects. In part the problems here were practical, concerned with the question of costume. Few commentators shared Ingres's view that heroism was incompatible with any dress except classical drapery, but many found the idea of modern-dress history painting incongruous. Baudelaire played on this in the famous conclusion to his 1845 Salon review, by invoking the potential 'heroism' of even the most

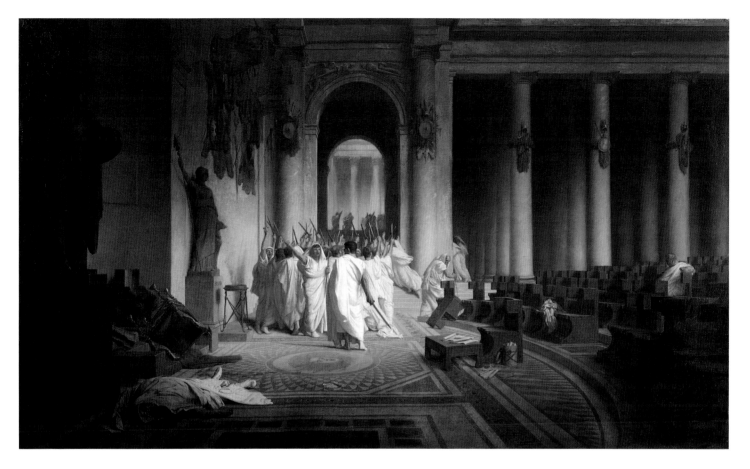

Fig. 97 (cat. 23)
Jean-Léon Gérôme,
The Death of Caesar,
Exposition 1867. Oil on
canvas, 85.5 x 145.5 cm.
Baltimore, Walters Art
Gallery.

Gérôme exhibited a larger
version of this subject (now
lost), showing only
Caesar's body and its im-
mediate surroundings, at
the 1859 Salon.

anonymous city dweller:

The painter, the true painter for whom we are looking, will be he who can snatch its epic quality from the life of today and can make us understand ... how great and poetic we are in our cravats and our patent-leather boots.[6]

But a more serious issue was also raised by Baudelaire's comments: where could the 'epic' be found in contemporary life? For the critic Ernest Chesneau, a supporter of Napoleon III's regime, this presented no problem:

There are so many dramas and great events that invite, and indeed imperiously demand the brush of the pain-ter.... The great events of modern life, civil, religious and military, must be represented and interpreted, and must be bequeathed by the means of art to the memory of our descendants. ...[7]

By contrast, the republican Jules Castagnary, writ-ing in 1857, argued that modern life had lost its epic quality:

Art [in the past] ... has placed itself in the service of heroism. It has depicted battles, great captains and

unfortunate kings; it has recounted the misfortunes of dynasties, the harshness of inexorable destiny. But, as society is increasingly organised by balancing its own forces, the keen nationalism of past races is fading away, the great feuds are calmed, the epic side of humanity diminishes. Today the greatness and decadence of peoples can no longer be explained in terms of politics, but rather by the deductions of social science. As time goes on, history is being transformed into political economy.[8]

Maximilian's fate in Mexico proved Castagnary's verdict mistaken. Indeed Castagnary himself declared in 1869 that recent events did offer suit-able subjects for *la grande peinture*, though without mentioning the Mexican episode. It was the elec-tions of May 1869 that inspired this change of view: 'The particular character and appearance of popular life ... are bound to stimulate the artist's imagination. Exalted feelings, strong passions, a diversity of costumes, natural groupings of figures, varied episodes – everything is there.'[9] The public scenes of contemporary life regained their potential as 'history' for Castagnary through the restoration of democracy that the elections seemed to represent. But although he advocated politically radical themes, he retained a very traditional set of requirements for history painting itself.

Castagnary's comments in 1857 about the loss of heroic potential in modern life introduce a leitmotiv in contemporary discussions about the state of society: that somewhere the elevated values of the past have been compromised or lost. Some commentators attributed this directly to the loss of political freedom,[10] while others extended Castagnary's analysis, focusing on the 'mercantile spirit' and rampant self-interest of the age,[11] and on its preoccupation with superficialities – literal details and accessories – at the expense of deeper truths.[12] These diagnoses were part of a wider pattern of anxiety that society was in a state of decline; the sequence of revolutions in France since 1789 seemed to many writers to be a symptom of an underlying malaise, of a national degeneration. These fears were to be greatly aggravated by France's catastrophic defeat in the Franco–Prussian War in 1870–1, and by the events of the Paris Commune (see pages 70–3).[13]

These wider social concerns are inseparable from the issues preoccupying the art world. The literalism of historical genre painting was seen as a symptom of society's superficiality, and the decline of 'high art' as the result of the invasion of commerce into the world of culture, which led artists to abandon their higher calling in favour of financial success.

However, the distinction between culture and capitalism was much clouded by the patterns of state and imperial patronage in the 1860s. The state commissioned and purchased many works of art every year, for museums and public buildings the length and breadth of France; and the Emperor also bought works for his own residences. Both favoured mythological and historical genre, peasant subjects and landscapes over traditional history paintings.[14] From the point of view of the Académie des Beaux-Arts, upholder of traditional 'high art' values, the state was thus betraying its duty; but official policy under Napoleon III supported aesthetic diversity, and encouraged the development of traditionally less significant, but more popular, types of painting.

These issues came into sharp focus in 1863. At the Salon, the medal of honour was awarded to Cabanel's *Birth of Venus* (Paris, Musée d'Orsay), a sensual neo-rococo nude, and the canvas was bought by the Emperor. At the same Salon, Bouguereau, like Cabanel a former Academy prizewinner, exhibited an ambitious 'high art' subject, *Orestes pursued by the Furies* (fig. 98), showing the tormented young hero pursued by vengeful Furies carrying the body of his mother whom he has murdered to avenge his father. Bouguereau wrote to the Director of Fine Arts asking that the state should buy his picture:

. . . it is only with the government and nowhere else that I can place this picture, which is a real attempt at sustaining *la grande peinture*. . . . The purchase of this picture would allow me to continue along a path that is more and more neglected, and which needs to be encouraged by the government, since it cannot find support from private collectors.[15]

The Director ignored this appeal, and Bouguereau turned increasingly to lucrative genre painting.

Later in the same year, the government instituted major reforms to art education, substantially diminishing the power of the Academy, whose control over the Salon jury was also drastically curtailed. The state assumed overall control of the Ecole des Beaux-Arts, creating new departments there – notably one for painting, which had previously only been taught in private studios – and also appointed the professors. In addition, the Ecole prizewinners, previously committed to spending their five-year fellowship in Rome, were now permitted to travel for half the time. The aim of the reforms, as spelt out by comte de Nieuwerkerke, Superintendent of Fine Arts, was to encourage originality and critical thinking in place of rigid dogma.[16]

Thus by the 1860s, the ideal of 'high art' history painting was increasingly a notional one, less a leading presence in contemporary art than a yardstick by which traditionalist critics might gauge the mediocrity of the paintings they saw around them. But history painting remained a central focus of debate. During the 1860s a number of young artists made ambitious attempts to reinvigorate the tradition, specifically by seeking to harness it to contemporary subjects.

The site of these attempts was the Paris Salon, the only forum where artists could regularly exhibit ambitious paintings and the primary focus of attention of the art critics. State commissions were generally shown here, and the state also made purchases directly from the exhibitions. Pictures

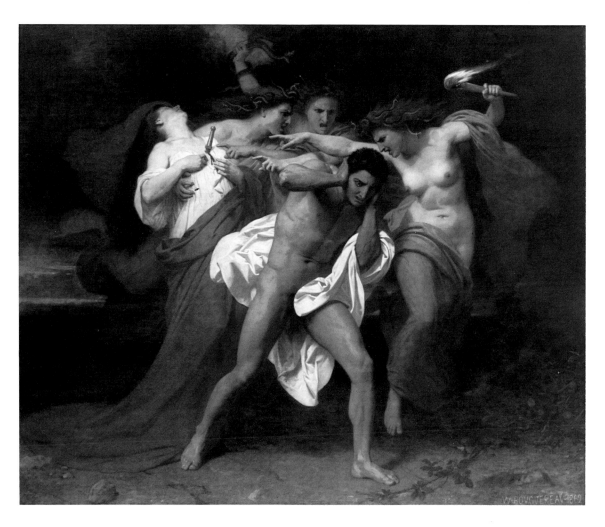

Fig. 98
William Bouguereau,
Orestes pursued by the
Furies, Salon of 1863.
Oil on canvas,
227.4 x 278.3 cm.
Norfolk, Virginia,
The Chrysler Museum.

The picture was exhibited
in 1863 with the title
The Remorse of Orestes.

shown at the Salon generated most public discussion about modern art, and it was these debates that defined public opinion of new works and encouraged potential buyers. Manet's *Execution of the Emperor Maximilian* was designed for the Salon, and it is in this context, and specifically in relation to contemporary modern-life history paintings, that his subject and the way in which he treated it must be viewed.

Military painting: the image of imperial power

The most visible modern subjects at the Salon were battle scenes, which were generally accorded pride of place in the big central hall of the exhibition (see fig. 96). Napoleon III continued to commission huge paintings of France's latest military engagements for Versailles, including subjects from the Crimean War, from the 1859 campaign against Austria in Italy, and some of Jean-Adolphe Beaucé's canvases of the Mexican campaign (figs. 12 and 29). Military subjects were not highly regarded by artistic theorists, but scenes of French victories gained great public attention and played on national military pride, which Napoleon III was determined to foster. They were often accompanied in the Salon catalogues by extensive texts describing the events depicted. These paintings are a central part of the context of Manet's *Execution*, since they defined the terms in which images of death and heroism, of leaders and ordinary soldiers, were expected to be treated.[17]

The painting of contemporary battle pictures presented an immediate problem: the changing patterns of modern warfare meant that significant action was now achieved by masses of men, not by the heroic action of individuals. Yet to depict these

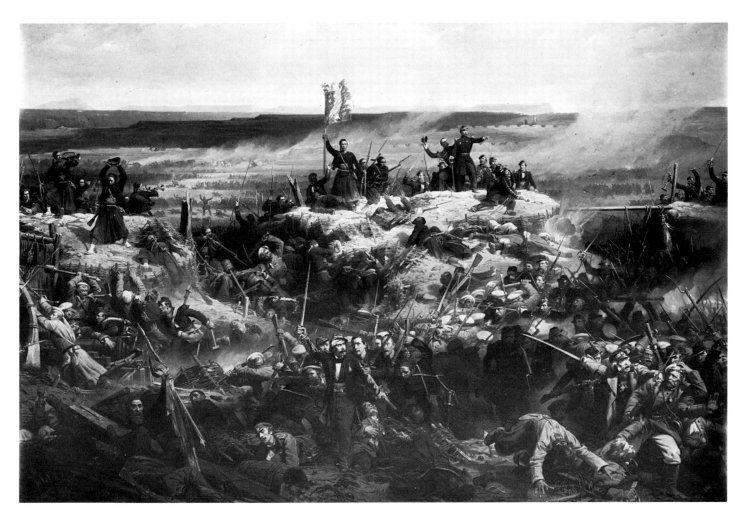

Fig. 99
Adolphe Yvon,
*Capture of the Malakoff
Tower, 8 September 1855
(Crimea)*, Salon of 1857,
Exposition 1867. Oil on
canvas, 600 x 900 cm.
Musée National du
Château de Versailles.

masses, even on a huge canvas, would involve hordes of tiny, indistinguishable figures, thus obliterating the significant human gestures and expressions that were central to the history-painting tradition. The usual compromise was to build up the vast composition out of sequences of episodes, as for instance in Adolphe Yvon's *Capture of the Malakoff Tower, 8 September 1855 (Crimea)* (fig. 99), shown at the Salon of 1857. Here, Gautier noted, 'in arranging his composition, he needed to include some warlike illustrations, some heroic deeds, some acts of superhuman valour that might have been forgotten by their authors, but were immortalised by art.'[18]

Olivier Merson's eulogy of Beaucé's *Battle of Solferino* (fig. 100), exhibited in 1861, describes how a composition such as this was expected to function:

What is remarkable in this picture is the *mise en scène*: it

expresses the character of reality so well that the events must have happened just as the painter depicts them. At a glance we see that this is not just a military review or a minor conflict . . . we instinctively grasp the importance of the struggle, and at once we realise the probable swings of fortune in this immense drama. Then, within this broad scene certain episodes stand out which occur at the right time and place, not to distract the attention, but to reinforce it. . . .[19]

Another account of the picture cited Beaucé's personal bravery at Solferino as warranty of the picture's authenticity, though criticising his focus on a single episode.[20]

Merson's final comment stresses the impact that such canvases were designed to have on their viewers. In 1863, Gautier *fils* ironically evoked the public's enthusiasm for these scenes of bravery, heightened by the realisation that the protagonists were their own family and friends:

The spectator, peacefully seated on his sofa, gets some-

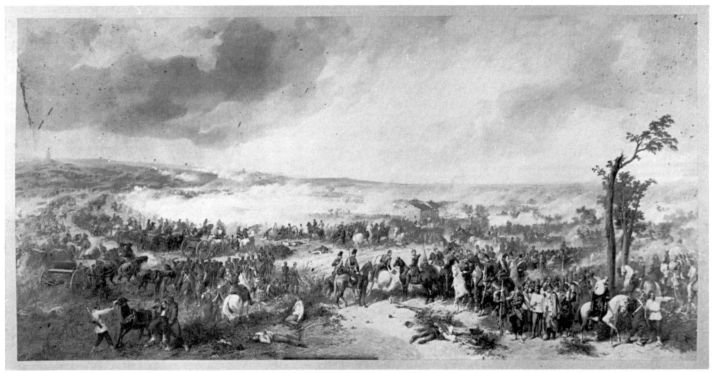

Fig. 100
Jean-Adolphe Beaucé,
Battle of Solferino,
Salon of 1861, Exposition
1867. Dimensions and
present whereabouts un-
known. Photograph by
Richebourg, *c.* 1870.
Mounted albumen print,
16.5 x 34.5 cm.
Salon-de-Provence, Musée
de l'Empéri.

thing of a shock: his warlike instincts are aroused without danger by the struggle on the canvas in front of him. He proudly says: We captured this, we burned that, we killed that many men and captured that many cannons.

In Yvon's *Battle of Magenta* (Versailles), Gautier praised the 'striking truthfulness' of 'the expression of the heads and the violence of the gestures', though he found the overall arrangement somewhat theatrical.[21]

However, such pictures became less popular during the 1860s, and when a number of the recent Versailles commissions were exhibited again at the Exposition Universelle of 1867 they aroused less enthusiasm. It was while they were on view that news arrived of Maximilian's execution, and Manet began work on his *Execution*. Yvon's huge pictures, including the 1857 *Capture of the Malakoff Tower* (fig. 99), now looked merely theatrical to Théodore Pelloquet:

In vain does he try to paint the terror . . . of the com-batants . . . [and] to make us witness the horror of a bloody battle. With the gesticulations of his figures, with their staring eyes surmounted by brows in the shape of circumflex accents, he leaves us cold and unmoved. Most often they seem to be playing a part, and their melodram-atic expressions recall those of the comedians in the axe and sabre fights at the small theatres.[22]

A further problem facing the battle painter was

the changing role of leaders and generals, who no longer led their troops from the front, but oversaw operations from a safe distance:

Today . . . it is the masses that brings back the vic-tories; . . . the general follows his soldiers instead of lead-ing them; so it is difficult to sum up a battle by a single great figure, as one could by Condé at Rocroi, by Kléber at Heliopolis, by Desaix at Marengo and by Napoleon at Waterloo.[23]

Yvon's enormous *Battle of Solferino*, exhibited in 1861, focused on the Emperor giving orders to his subordinates, rather than on the combat itself (see fig. 96), and Ernest Meissonier, in *HM The Emperor at Solferino* (fig. 101), a state commission, shown in 1864 and again in 1867, placed him well away from the combat, with only three corpses near the margins and a burst of smoke from a cannon on the right to suggest that battle has been engaged. Yvon's and Meissonier's canvases do, though, maintain one traditional device of 'high art' history painting: both place the Emperor as the unequivo-cal focus of the composition, silhouetted against the sky at the very centre of the picture.

Meissonier's *Solferino* is also exceptional among battle scenes in that it is very small; it is only 76 cm across – the size of a very modest genre painting. However, its treatment, combined with the fame of the artist, ensured that the picture was not seen to

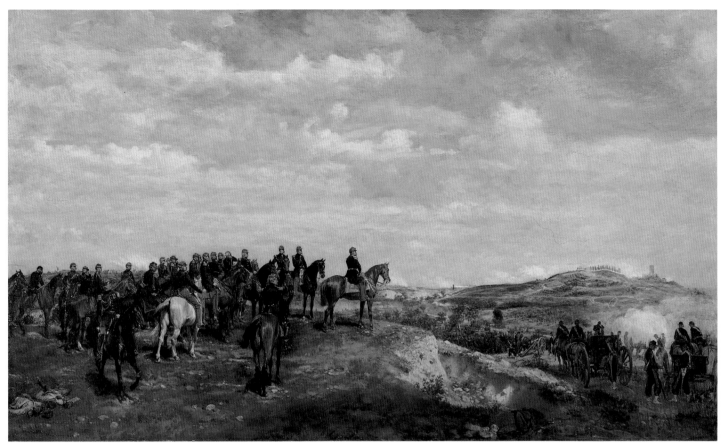

Fig. 101
Ernest Meissonier,
*HM The Emperor at
Solferino*, Salon of 1864,
Exposition 1867. Oil on
canvas, 43.5 x 76 cm.
Paris, Musée d'Orsay.

diminish the Emperor's status. The appropriate size of pictures was a vexed issue in the 1860s; painters such as Gérôme, like Meissonier, increasingly treated historical subjects on a modest scale (see fig. 97), while others, as we shall see, sought to elevate more trivial themes by treating them on the scale traditionally reserved for significant historical action.

An alternative type of military painting came into fashion in the 1860s, which evoked the private feelings of individual soldiers. Paul-Alexandre Protais first popularised this genre with *Morning, Before the Attack* (fig. 102) and *Evening, After the Combat* (Chantilly, Musée Condé), exhibited in 1863 and again in 1867. Most commentators found Protais's canvases true to the 'spirit' of the soldier or to the 'man' within the uniform; Claude Vignon contrasted the public's boredom at Yvon's huge dramas with their passion for Protais's images of 'the calm, dignified and resolute attitude' of ordinary soldiers.[24]

Images like Protais's came to represent the popular notion of the typical French footsoldier.

Some such conception lay behind Chesneau's attack on Jean-François Millet's *A Peasant resting on his Hoe* (fig. 103), exhibited in the Salon of 1863; Chesneau saw in this exhausted, seemingly brutalised fieldworker 'the typical country cretin', and indignantly protested against Millet's claim that this figure belonged to 'the hardworking country population, the strong popular stock from which our brave, intelligent soldiers are recruited.'[25] It was this 'strong stock' that Protais represented.

However, praise for Protais was not unanimous in 1863. For the critic and historian Paul Mantz, his soldiers were sentimental and artificial: 'They look like a company of poets . . . meditating about fallen leaves. The French army is not as elegiac as this, and M. Protais's picture [fig. 102], otherwise so well-conceived, is too intent on softening mothers' hearts.'[26] The problem for the journalist Maxime du Camp lay in the overemphasis of their individuality: 'The soldier is a collective being; he obeys and does not deliberate. . . . An isolated soldier is a man, that is to say a being with personal

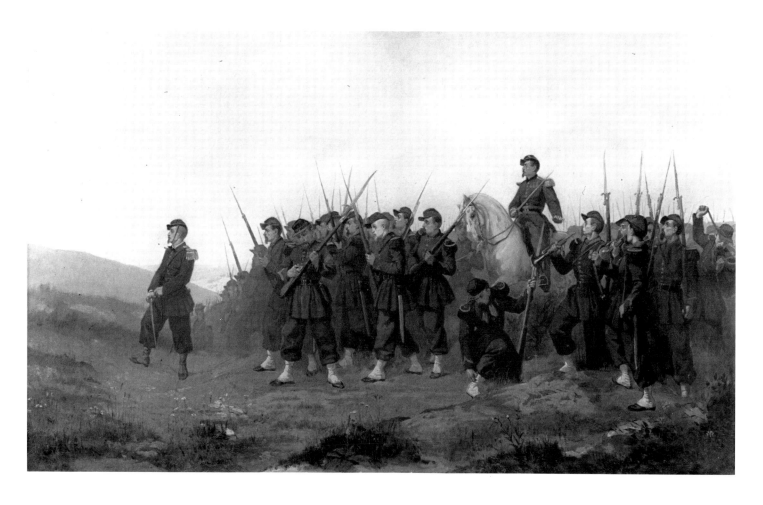

Fig. 102
Paul-Alexandre Protais,
Morning, Before the Attack,
Salon of 1863, Exposition
1867. Oil on canvas,
49 x 80 cm.
Chantilly, Musée Condé.

Fig. 103
Jean François Millet,
Man with a Hoe, Salon of
1863. Oil on canvas,
80 x 99 cm.
Malibu, California, Collec-
tion of the J. Paul Getty
Museum.

The picture was exhibited
with the title *A Peasant
resting on his Hoe*.

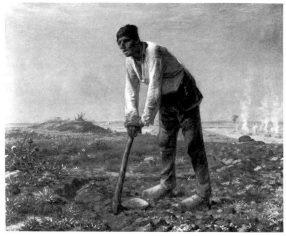

initiative; a company . . . will always be a group of
soldiers, that is to say beings whose initiative comes
from elsewhere.'[27] These comments are particularly
relevant to Manet's treatment of *The Execution of*

Maximilian, with its firing squad in strictly serried
ranks, their faces invisible, quite without recourse
to the rhetoric of bodily gesture and facial expression that gave Protais's figures their appeal.[28]

A revitalised history painting?

Two pictures exhibited by young artists at the 1866
Salon provoked discussion by seeking to raise contemporary scenes to the status of history painting:
Carolus-Duran's *The Assassinated Man; Souvenir of
the Roman Campagna* (fig. 104) and Tony Robert-
Fleury's *Warsaw, 8 April 1861* (fig. 105). Both are
scenes of violent death, and thus have added
relevance to Manet's *Execution* project.

Carolus-Duran's picture laid claim to 'high art'
status by its size and by the overt echoes of the *pietà*
in its composition. It was praised for its evocation
of a wide range of emotional responses to a tragedy
– vengefulness, horror, grief, pity, curiosity.
Gautier justified the 'excessive demonstrations of

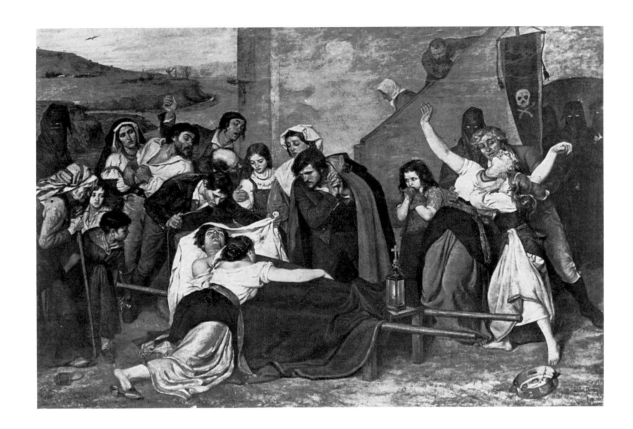

Fig. 104
Carolus-Duran,
*The Assassinated Man;
Souvenir of the Roman
Campagna*, Salon of
1866. Oil on canvas,
280 x 420 cm.
Lille, Musée des
Beaux-Arts.

Fig. 105
Tony Robert-Fleury,
Warsaw, 8 April 1861,
Salon of 1866,
Exposition 1867.
Oil on canvas, dimensions
and present whereabouts
unknown. Photograph
published by Goupil in the
1870s.
Paris, Musée d'Orsay.

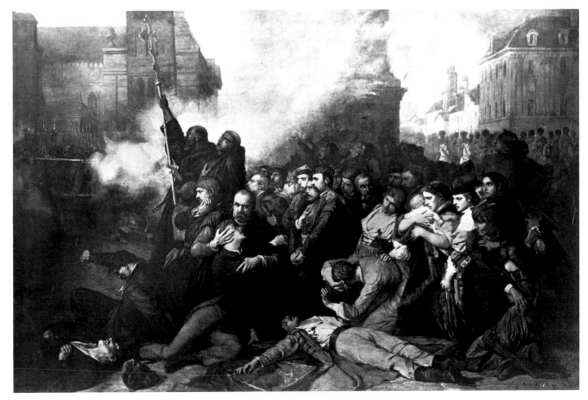

despair and rage', which might seem theatrical to the French, who expressed their grief with restraint, but were 'admissible among the Italians, who are great gesticulators'. He had reservations about the ugliness of the types, but for du Pays these represented the acceptable face of 'Realism'. For the critic and art historian Charles Clément, the canvas was inappropriately large for such a subject.[29]

The subject of Robert-Fleury's *Warsaw, 8 April 1861* immediately justified its vast scale: it represented Russian troops massacring Polish nationalist protestors, and was accompanied in the exhibition catalogue by a brief quotation from *Le Moniteur universel* describing the events. This episode had a resonance in the 1860s comparable to that of the Tiananmen Square massacre over the past few years.[30] The theme allowed the artist to show a diversity of local types and costumes, and to evoke a whole range of emotional responses among the Poles. The painting was generally agreed to be a powerful vindication of history painting of contemporary subjects, though Chesneau felt that its treatment of history allied it more to the 'prose' of historians such as Augustin Thierry than to a more 'poetic' vision.[31] Beyond this, critics felt free to expand on its political implications: its image of an atrocity committed by the Russians aroused indignation and hatred against the perpetrators, and ensured that the massacre was not forgotten.[32]

Both pictures, and the critical responses to them, show how gesture and expression were used to generate emotional and moral responses in their viewers.[33] Carolus-Duran's picture carried no obvious wider moral, since there is no indication of the circumstances of the assassination, beyond the suggestion that it is the result of an Italian peasant feud. But the acceptability of Robert-Fleury's picture, and the outspoken responses to it, show how readily a painting could tackle an active and polemical political issue, provided two conditions were met: first, that its message should be clearly legible, and second, that its position should be clearly in line with government policy. Anti-Russian sentiment could be readily expressed after Russia's defeat by the Anglo–French alliance in the Crimean War, and Russia's subsequent loss of power as an international political force in Europe. In his review of the picture, Charles Clément commented: 'I have heard it said that a Russian couldn't safely cross the central hall of the Salon.'[34] We do not know what the Tsar thought of the canvas on his state visit to the Exposition Universelle in 1867, where it was again exhibited. The continuing potency of the Polish issue was vividly demonstrated by the attempted assassination of the Tsar during his visit to Paris by a Polish exile.

Manet's 'indifference'

Examination of paintings such as these highlights the ways in which Manet's final picture (fig. 76:III) flouted current conventions, though its subject was pre-eminently the stuff of history painting. It avoided the use of the rhetoric of facial expression and dramatic gesture to engender emotion. Maximilian's expression is startlingly impassive, and only Mejía, seemingly first to be struck, jolts involuntarily backward. His contorted wrist and Maximilian's gesture as he grasps Miramón's left hand provide sharp, but by contemporary standards markedly understated, suggestions of the drama.

Much of the recent historical research on the picture has focused on the sources Manet used to document his composition,[35] but both the grouping and the details of the final picture suggest a studied neglect of much of the documentary information that would have been available to him (see page 59)[36] – most notably the fact that Maximilian had stood on the right of the three victims.[37] The background of the picture is also very generalised, with its plain stone wall and hints of Hispanic costume among the clutch of onlookers. Indeed Manet made the scene even less specific in the final version than it had been in the lithograph (fig. 77) or the first state of the Copenhagen sketch (fig. 75).

Moreover the technique of the painting worked against conventional methods of conveying meaning. It was expected that the most significant elements in a picture should be emphasised by their lighting and by being treated in more detail. Manet's whole scene is brightly and evenly lit, and the handling is largely undifferentiated in focus; the key point of the picture, Maximilian's face, is treated particularly indistinctly.

In one sense Manet's rejection of detailed attributes and narrative signs in favour of a spare, iconic image is a return to traditional notions of history painting, suggesting comparisons with images such as David's *The Oath of the Horatii* (Salon of 1785; Paris, Musée du Louvre). Yet the lack of clear focal points, and the refusal to use heightened gesture and expression to bring out the drama or pathos of the scene, mark a comprehensive rejection of the rhetorical language of 'high art' history painting.

In 1868, the year in which Manet first planned to submit *The Execution of Maximilian* to the Salon,[38] two critics focused on what they saw as the wider implications of his way of painting. In discussing his exhibits that year, *Portrait of Emile Zola* (fig. 106) and *A Young Woman* (*Woman with a Parrot*, New York, Metropolitan Museum of Art), their comments developed criticisms of his work that had become commonplace at previous exhibitions. The veteran republican critic and art historian Théophile Thoré deplored Manet's failure 'to give their relative value to the essential parts of human beings', and attributed this to 'a sort of pantheism which places no higher value on a head than a slipper . . ., which paints everything almost uniformly.' Paul Mantz wrote:

. . . he is little interested in nature, and life's spectacles do not move him. This indifference will be his undoing. M. Manet seems to us to have less enthusiasm than dilettantism. If he had even a little passion, he would arouse someone's enthusiasm, for there are still twenty or so people in France who have a taste for innovations and boldness.[39]

How can we reconcile Manet's choice of so politically and emotionally charged a theme as Maximilian's execution with this refusal to use the techniques which, in the eyes of his contemporaries, gave significance to such a subject? For critics earlier this century, Manet's treatment of his subjects showed that he was motivated by formal concerns alone; but more recent commentators have insisted on the relevance of his choice of so loaded a subject.[40] To assess the significance of the way in which he treated the theme, we must look at the wider contexts of Manet's image – the responses to the execution in France, the operation of censorship in the later Second Empire, and the uses of 'pantheism', 'indifference' and 'dilettantism' as strategies of social and political opposition.

Maximilian's execution: tragedy and censorship

Maximilian's execution could not readily be fitted into the notions of the modern that were current in the 1860s. The Warsaw massacre or the deaths of ordinary soldiers in battle could be understood in terms of the shift of 'history' to the experiences of everyman, but the apparent martyrdom of an emperor seemed like a flashback to another epoch, and to belong to a quite different system of representation. When the news broke, Eugène Forcade, political commentator of the *Revue des deux-mondes*, asked:

Why has this explosion of Shakespearian tragedy become entangled with the ideas, habits and customs of our own century, which are basically rationalist and positive? Who would have believed that in our age invisible witches could still sweep an honest Macbeth into the abyss in the guise of chivalric enticement, by telling him: you will be king?[41]

In *L'Indépendance belge* Jules Claretie wrote:

What a terrible denouement to the most incredible of adventures! Tragedy is certainly not dead, and the theatre of the future is there, bloody and traced out in full, a sombre and dramatic subject. Shakespeare would not have dreamed up a more shocking fifth act.[42]

For a writer in *L'Illustration*, it was a 'drama and a tragic history. Here, for the unhappy princess, was madness with its accompanying sorrows and terrors; there, for the prince, betrayal and death! Antique fate presents no more lamentable destiny!'[43]

Invocations of fate or destiny obscured the central problem of the apportionment of blame. Only in papers published outside French censorship could blame immediately be laid at Napoleon III's door. *L'Indépendance belge*, published in Brussels but with many French contributors and subscribers, led the condemnation, first in the form of reports of press comment in Vienna, and then in direct criticism.[44] In France itself, direct criticism was confined to two key speeches delivered in the Corps Législatif by Adolphe Thiers and Jules Favre, and to authorised press comment on these speeches. Both speeches focused on other aspects of the Mexican expedition, but both made it clear that they considered the ultimate responsibility to lie with France, and implicitly with the Emperor himself and his form of personal government.[45] In the months that followed this attribution of blame became ever more overt, even in France.[46] At the same time, beyond the obvious sympathy felt for Maximilian's personal tragedy, it was immediately argued by Napoleon's opponents that Juárez was doing no more in ordering Maximilian's execution than condemning him to the fate that he himself

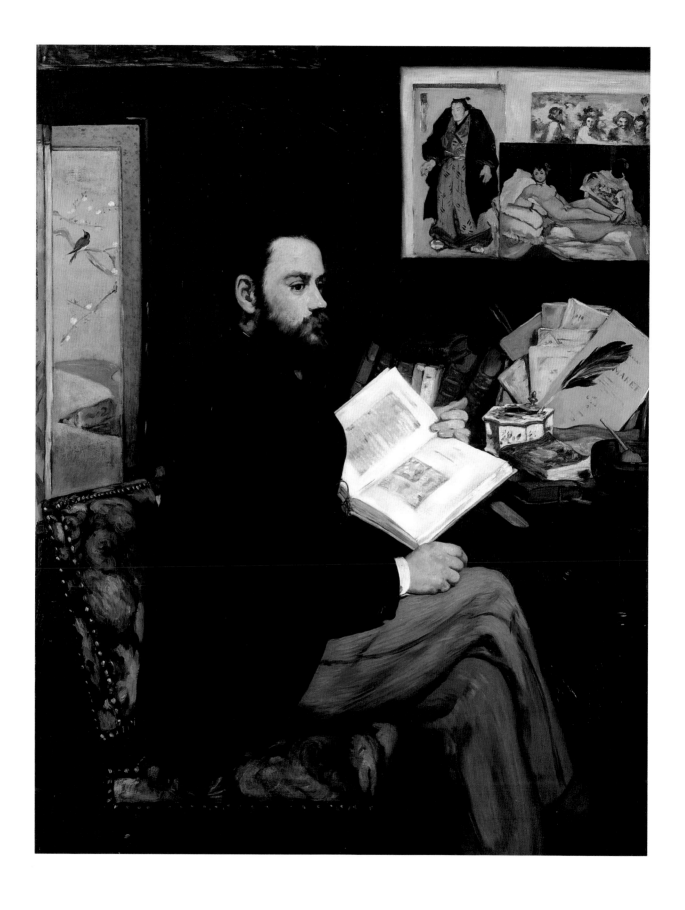

had imposed on the Juaristas by his savage decree of 3 October 1865 (see page 27).[47]

The execution of Maximilian took place in a strange period of limbo in French politics. Through the 1860s, tentative steps had been taken to liberalise the regime. On 19 January 1867, opening the new parliamentary session, the Emperor had promised major reforms of the laws concerning the press and public meetings, but the legislative bodies were unable to agree upon details, and the reforms were finally implemented only in the summer of 1868: the new press law was accepted by the Senate on 11 May and became law on 10 July. Though this law removed some restrictions imposed by Napoleon's press laws of 1852, in practice it did not lead to a wholesale liberalisation, and many of the newly launched radical journals were rapidly suppressed.[48]

At the same time, official authorisation was still needed before the performance of any play or the publication of any book, periodical or print. It was under these laws that the lithograph of Manet's *Execution of Maximilian* was banned. Exhibition paintings were not covered by the same regulations, but it seems that the jury of the Salon generally fulfilled a similar censorship function, though in a more informal way. However, the government censors might intervene directly here too, as is shown by the advance notification to Manet that the painting of the *Execution* would be rejected by the jury in 1869.[49]

We do not know why Manet did not submit his composition to the jury in 1868, as he initially planned (see page 58). Perhaps he was dissatisfied with it at this stage; but he would have had good reasons for wanting to show it then, when memories of the episode were still fresh. It is possible that he withheld it in 1868 in the hope that the new press laws, finally ratified shortly after that year's Salon opened, would herald a more general liberalisation in the display of politically sensitive imagery. The suppression of both print and painting in 1869 proved any such hopes ill-founded.

A report by the government theatre censors in 1862 shows how broad their terms of reference were. Distinct types of material were banned: those that threatened 'the interests of public morality; the interests of social order and the politics of the government; the interests of religion; and propriety and taste in references to individuals or things'.[50] When applied strictly, the regulations revealed an official sensitivity that verged on paranoia.[51] The authorities were particularly wary of the power of the visual image – in the form of a print, a painting or a stage representation. In the context of Maximilian's execution, this emerged most immediately in the suppression in September 1867 of the photographs of the firing squad and Maximilian's bullet-riddled clothes (figs. 51 and 53), while verbal descriptions were widely printed (see page 52). Manet, too, recognised the power attributed to images when he noted that his *Execution* lithograph (fig. 77) had been suppressed even before he had added any title to it – 'that speaks well for the work'.[52]

A few examples will show the types of imagery that were found threatening or problematic. In August 1864, shortly after Maximilian's arrival in Mexico, a play by Amédée Rolland and Gustave Aymard, *The Freebooters of Sonora*, was presented for the censor's approval; it was a melodrama, recounting the expedition of a French adventurer in Mexico. Although it was recognised to be based on the exploits of comte de Raousset-Boulbon, who had been executed in Mexico in 1854, the authorities, fearing that parallels would be drawn with current events, insisted that references to France should be omitted and that the final scene of the count's execution should be toned down. The theme of Raousset-Boulbon's adventures may have been all the more sensitive because there were suspicions that he had been supported by the French government.[53] Immediately after Maximilian's execution, a commentator in *Le Figaro* compared his fate with that of Raousset-Boulbon.[54]

Associations with Maximilian very probably lay behind the controversy that arose around a painting exhibited at the 1868 Salon – Gérôme's *7 December 1815, Nine o'Clock in the Morning (The Death of Marshal Ney)* (fig. 107). Depicting the immediate aftermath of the execution of Napoleon I's leading associate Marshal Ney, it showed the firing squad leaving the scene, and the body face down in the mud. Ney was executed in the 'white terror' that followed Napoleon's final defeat and exile and the restoration of the Bourbon monarchy. Gérôme himself later blamed the controversy on Ney's son, who had wanted the painting to be excluded from the Salon.[55] But the novelist and critic Edmond About gave a different account of why Gérôme's picture, and two images of Ney's death by other artists, were threatened with rejection:

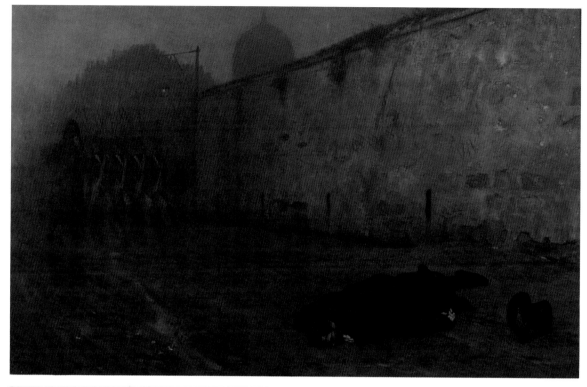

Fig. 107 (cat. 24)
Jean-Léon Gérôme,
The Death of Marshal Ney,
Salon of 1868. Oil on
canvas, 64 x 103 cm.
Sheffield, City Art
Galleries.

The picture was exhibited
with the title *7 December
1815, Nine o'Clock in the
Morning.*

Fig. 108
François Rude,
Marshal Ney, 1852-3.
Bronze, 267 cm high.
Paris, Place de
l'Observatoire.

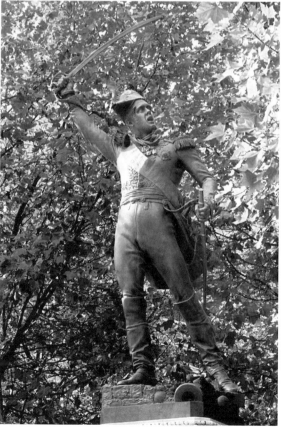

The administration thought that such a memory should not be evoked, and politely pointed out to the artists that the highest level of propriety dictated that this juridical assassination should not be put on display.[56]

The image of Ney had already played an important part in Napoleon III's imperial propaganda. A proposal for a Ney memorial, at the place of his execution, was first mooted in March 1848, and the idea was revived early in 1850 when Napoleon was Prince–President. François Rude was commissioned to work on a relief of Ney at the moment before his execution; this was to be seen as an atonement for his death, rather than as a celebration of his career. The project was radically altered early in 1852, soon after Napoleon's *coup d'état*, to a triumphant image of Ney as a great soldier. Rude's final bronze (fig. 108), inaugurated with great pomp and amid high security on the anniversary of Ney's death in 1853, vividly testified to Napoleon III's wish to co-opt for his own regime the imagery of Napoleon I's military might.[57]

About's description of Ney's execution as a 'juridical assassination' evokes comparison with Maximilian's fate at the hands of Juárez; moreover, immediately after Maximilian's death political commentators drew parallels between the two executions.[58] Whether or not the three artists who

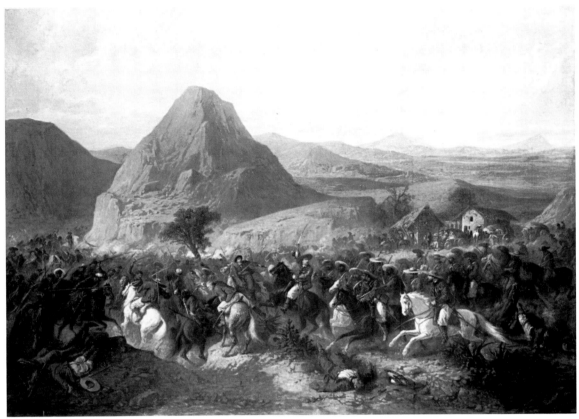

Fig. 109
Jean-Adolphe Beaucé,
Battle of Yerbabuena, 8 June 1865, between the Red Squadron of the French Counter-Guerrillas and the 1st Regiment of Mexican Lancers, Salon of 1868.
Oil on canvas,
130 x 188 cm.
Paris, Musée de l'Armée.

Michel Ney d'Elchingen, grandson of Marshal Ney (see figs. 107 and 108), leads his troops against Juarist forces.

painted subjects of Ney's death for the 1868 Salon were responding to this association, the anxiety that they caused shows how sensitive the administration was to historical imagery that was open to anti-Bonapartist interpretation. In Gérôme's picture, the crossed-out graffito '*Vive l'Empereur*' on the wall may have heightened the seeming topicality of the image. It remains an open question whether Gérôme intended any covert reference to Maximilian.[59]

Gérôme's treatment of the subject was also controversial. Many critics attacked it for its illegibility and for degrading the image of the heroic Ney. Castagnary eloquently spelt out how such a scene should be treated:

... anyone who has witnessed an execution at Vincennes ... would depict it in its gripping reality. He would show me the condemned man ... pale but intrepid; the voice of the commanding officer, the rifles taking aim, the report ringing out, the unhappy man crumpled and rolling in the mud and the blood. And if, instead of a poor unknown footsoldier ..., it was a great military leader who was being shot, a marshal of France, a leader of armies, then, in order to depict the heroic condemned

man, [and] his bewildered executioners with trembling hands and tearful eyes ..., in order to show me ... the anguish of this heartrending scene, he would find accents and words that would ring through my soul and raise my emotions to the level of his.[60]

Castagnary's account, like his evocation of the image of the 1869 elections quoted above (see page 89), vividly shows that even a committed republican critic might hold very traditional views about the appropriate rhetorical devices for the representation of historically significant subjects. As Manet himself later said of the radical politician Léon Gambetta, 'it's strange how reactionary republicans can be when it comes to art'.[61] Manet, like Gérôme, systematically avoided the rhetoric of heroic death that Castagnary evoked.

Ironically, another member of Ney's family appeared in the 1868 Salon in an appropriately heroic military context: his grandson Michel was shown in one of Beaucé's Mexican battle scenes, leading the French counter-guerrillas to victory at Yerbabuena on 8 June 1865 (fig. 109). The exhibition of paintings of French military successes in

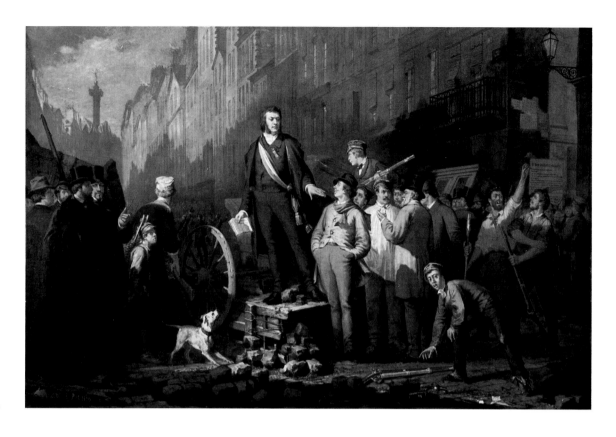

Fig. 110
Ernest-Louis Pichio,
*The Death of Alphonse
Baudin*, Salon of 1870.
Oil on canvas,
128 x197 cm.
Paris, Musée Carnavalet.

Fig. 111
William Bouguereau,
*Le Jour des morts (All Souls'
Day)*, Salon of 1859,
Exposition 1867. Oil on
canvas, 147 x 120 cm.
Bordeaux, Musée des
Beaux-Arts.

Le Jour des morts falls on
2 November.

Fig. 112
Aimé Millet and
Léon Dupré,
*Monument to Alphonse
Baudin*, 1872. Bronze and
stone, 163 x 210 x 70 cm.
Paris, Montmartre
Cemetery.

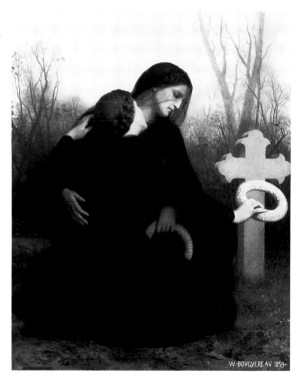

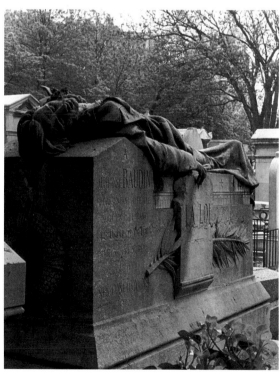

Mexico, such as this and fig. 29 (commissioned by the state for Versailles), even after the Mexican enterprise had ended in political and personal disaster, shows how important the image of France's victorious armies remained, and how far it could be presented as if it were quite independent of the political circumstances of the combat depicted. Indeed, even a heroic defeat in Mexico such as Camarón could still be shown, as in Beaucé's painting exhibited in 1869 (fig. 11). Manet's *Execution*, with its military firing squad, decisively and unacceptably reintroduced political overtones.

A further episode in 1868 revealed the imperial regime's sensitivity to historical imagery – this time to memories of its own history. In summer 1868, Eugène Ténot published a detailed narrative of Louis Napoleon's seizure of power. Although the implications of this book were very damaging to Napoleon's regime, it could not be suppressed because of the precision of its documentation and because of the author's insistence on his own 'impartiality'.[62] The book recounted a little-remembered episode of the *coup d'état*, the death on 3 December 1851 of Alphonse Baudin, 'representative of the people', who was shot on one of the first barricades erected in opposition to the coup. Ténot's account triggered a republican demonstration around Baudin's simple grave in the Montmartre cemetery on 2 November 1868, the *Jour des morts*. This in turn led three republican journals to launch a subscription for a more appropriate monument to the republican hero. The authorities prosecuted both those who had spoken at the initial demonstration and the editors of the papers that had launched the subscription, despite its seeming legality. The ensuing trial provided the forum for a series of savage attacks against the imperial regime by the defending lawyers, among them Léon Gambetta. Although the defendants were convicted, the trial marked a crucial stage in the growth of political opposition.[63]

Two images frame the Baudin episode. Bouguereau's *Le Jour des morts (All Souls' Day)* (fig. 111), first shown in 1859 and again at the 1867 Exposition Universelle, shows the acceptable form of observance of the *Jour des morts* – as a time for private family grief. On 2 November 1867, two days after the closure of the Exposition and a year before the Baudin demonstration, the *Jour des morts* was the occasion of a previous republican protest in the Montmartre cemetery, later seen as the starting

point of direct action against the Empire.[64] Only in 1870, when the gradual process of reform had led, with the so-called 'Liberal Empire' and the ministry of Emile Ollivier, to a marked increase in freedom of expression, could these issues be confronted directly in painting. In the 1870 Salon Ernest-Louis Pichio exhibited *The Death of Alphonse Baudin* (fig. 110); Baudin stands on the barricade, the moment before the bullets struck, holding a copy of the 1789 Declaration of the Rights of Man, while in the shadows on the wall on the right hangs the *coup d'état* proclamation of 2 December 1851. The Bastille column, seen at back left, and the obvious references to Delacroix's *Liberty guiding the People* (Salon of 1831; Paris, Musée du Louvre), would have heightened the polemical character of Pichio's image. Yet as far as we know there was no attempt to suppress the picture. A monument to Baudin was erected, by public subscription, in the first years of the Third Republic; the bronze by Aimé Millet shows Baudin's corpse clutching a stone tablet inscribed 'La Loi' (fig. 112).[65]

Another painting, accepted and much praised at the 1869 Salon from which Manet's *Execution* was excluded, hints at the sensitive borderline between artistic and political radicalism: Henri Regnault's *Juan Prim, 8 October 1868* (fig. 113). Regnault, one of the first Ecole de Rome prizewinners after the reforms of 1863, was widely seen as the potential saviour of French painting, and his death in 1871 in the Franco–Prussian War was greeted as a national tragedy. He travelled extensively during his fellowship, and studied works outside the Ecole's canon, notably paintings by Velázquez (a taste he shared with Manet). While he was in Spain a revolution overthrew the Spanish Queen Isabella, and he was commissioned to paint one of the leaders of the revolution, Juan Prim.[66] Prim had been commander-in-chief of the allied expeditionary forces at the beginning of the Mexican campaign in 1861–2, before the Spanish and British withdrew (see page 21). France initially offered conditional support to the new regime in Spain, though distancing itself from its revolutionary overtones.

Regnault's *Juan Prim, 8 October 1868* (the date marked Prim's triumphant entry into Madrid), a large equestrian portrait, attracted great attention at the 1869 Salon, both for its subject and its treatment. The vigorous, sketchy brushwork aroused much debate, being seen by the supporters of the

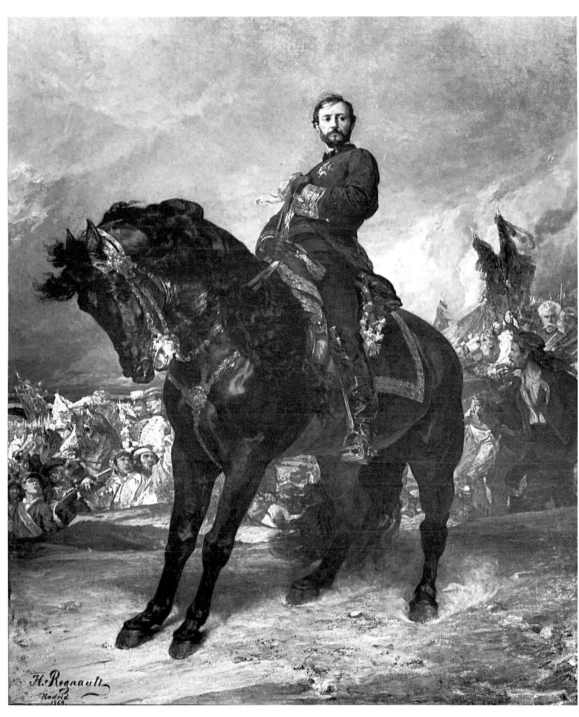

Fig. 113
Henri Regnault,
Juan Prim, 8 October 1868,
Salon of 1869. Oil on
canvas, 315 x 258 cm.
Paris, Musée d'Orsay.

old Ecole regime as final evidence of the loss of true discipline, and by supporters of the 1863 reforms as proof that the liberalisation of art education was ushering in a new, reinvigorated 'high art'. Both the subject and its presentation were widely seen as a valid form of modern history painting. But the sensitivity of the issues involved was revealed in the critics' determination to keep artistic and political questions categorically separate. For Georges Lafenestre and Marius Chaumelin, it was in its technique – its colour, drawing and paint handling – that the picture was 'revolutionary'; Gautier saw Prim as 'truly a hero', but insisted he was 'speaking purely from a picturesque point of view'.[67]

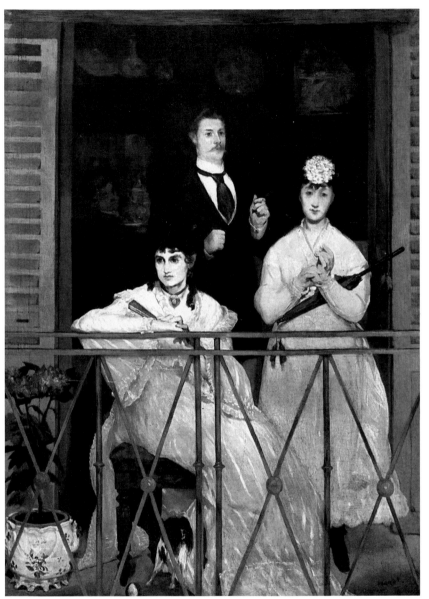

Fig. 114
Edouard Manet,
The Balcony, Salon of 1869.
Oil on canvas,
170 x 124.5 cm.
Paris, Musée d'Orsay.

Manet's 'Maximilian': detachment as opposition

We can now suggest why the authorities decided to forestall Manet's *Execution of Maximilian* even before he submitted it to the Salon jury. Most obviously, it presented an episode that reflected badly on Napoleon's foreign policy. But this is not an adequate reason in itself, for, at the Salon of 1868, Jules-Marc Chamerlat was allowed to exhibit two scenes relating to the execution, *The Emperor Maximilian at the Convent of Las Capuchinas* and *The Evening of the Execution of the Emperor Maximilian (Querétaro, 19 June 1867)*. Since these paintings are untraced and no press comment on them has been found, we can only surmise what made them acceptable; but it seems likely, from the titles, that they portrayed Maximilian's innocence and piety and the pathos of his fate, as did Jean-Paul Laurens's *The Last Moments of Maximilian*, shown at the 1882 Salon (fig. 115).

As we have seen, Manet avoided most of the traditional means of evoking meaning and morality – through gesture, expression, and so on. The picture cannot be read either as an iconic image of tragedy or betrayal, in terms of Davidian history painting, or as a poignant narrative, in terms of historical genre. By contemporary standards the treatment of the subject was very problematic, in its seeming detachment from the drama and its refusal to present a clear moral. This was accentuated by the way it was painted – by its summary brushwork and seeming lack of finish.

Certainly its ambiguities could be seen as artistic failure, and many of Manet's exhibited pictures were attacked in these terms, most notably *The Luncheon* (Munich, Neue Pinakothek) and *The Balcony* (fig. 114), shown together in 1869. Moreover, when preparing a brief press statement about the suppression of his *Execution* lithograph in 1869 Manet himself described it as '*une oeuvre absolument artistique*', seemingly inviting it to be viewed in exclusively 'artistic' terms.[68] But why should it have suffered political censorship if its failings were artistic? Since the canvas was not exhibited in France, we cannot appeal to the verdicts of his contemporaries. However, some possible answers emerge from responses to other paintings by Manet, and from contemporary social debate.

These answers lie in the question of legibility

itself, and the debates about it in the late Second Empire. The conventions of 'high art' painting presented a world whose terms of reference were unambiguous, through carefully orchestrated compositions revolving around key figures, and through the parade of emotional feeling within an orderly framework of values and hierarchies. Yet much social debate in the 1860s focused on the ways in which the modern world could not be clearly read or understood – most immediately in the context of woman's place in the modern city, and the difficulties of distinguishing between respectable women and 'prostitutes'. These debates turned on just the same issues as were involved in the conventions of 'high art' – on gesture, expression and clothing – but their conclusions were different. In place of the comforting world of art, where everyone knew their place and the viewer knew everyone's place, modern social life presented a constant threat to legibility and hence potentially to social order.

Critics' disquiet at Manet's images of modern urban life raised such questions of definition and classification: the viewer could not tell what the women in *The Balcony* were doing, gazing out onto the insecure public space of the street.[69] But how does such social uncertainty relate to Manet's claim that his pictures were 'absolutely artistic'; did this 'artistic' sphere locate them apart from questions of politics, or did this very notion of the 'artistic' represent a political position?

This 'artistic' sphere belonged to a particular sector of Parisian culture, which cultivated a distance and detachment from dominant social and political values, and yet set itself up as anatomist of contemporary society; their opponents characterised this detachment as 'indifference'. Among the theorists of this position were the writers of Manet's immediate circle, notably Baudelaire, who propounded it in his celebrated essay 'The Painter of Modern Life'. In part their stance developed from a rejection of the stereotypes and hierarchies that underpinned current social norms, but it was also crucially bound up with the question of censorship: an assumed and ironic distance was a cogent, but less tangible, mode of opposition than overt confrontation.[70] The appeal to the 'artistic' was a repudiation of bourgeois values and a statement of the transcendence of 'artistic' vision, but it was also a strategic position that attempted to divert the all-pervasive attentions of the censor. Zola's 1867

essay on Manet, which was so insistent on his lack of concern for his subject matter, must be seen as part of this strategy, and perhaps more specifically as a bid to help Manet gain access to the 1867 Exposition Universelle.[71]

Viewed in this context, *The Execution of Maximilian* presents a comparable set of uncertainties. Though its subject is utterly clear, its message and moral are difficult to interpret. Beyond the (by contemporary standards) inexpressive physiognomies and gestures, it offers a number of signs or details that invite interpretation but ultimately thwart it. The placing of Maximilian's sombrero in the final version (fig. 76:III) evokes the idea of a halo and of martyrdom, and the grouping of the victims (seemingly inappropriately) even echoes Christ between the thieves, all within the context of an ostensibly descriptive depiction. Contemporary discussion of Maximilian's fate had highlighted the French government's false propaganda about his initial reception in Mexico as 'a messiah awaited by the population', and contrasted this with his real situation. The sombrero in Manet's painting plays on these uncertainties.[72] The other issue is the uniform of the soldiers. As Zola emphasised in his 1869 article about the suppression of Manet's image, the uniforms of the executioners were indeed very similar to standard French uniforms.[73] However, this very similarity allowed a ready slippage between two ways of reading the image: the literal one, which could identify them as authentic uniforms of the regular Mexican Republican army, and the metaphorical one, which could readily see the executioners as French and thus read the image as placing the ultimate responsibility on the French.

It was this disconcerting combination of ambiguous signs with lack of expressive rhetoric that made Manet's image particularly problematic. Its uncertainties were inseparable from the historical situation itself. Maximilian was universally seen as a victim, but to a considerable degree he was the victim of his own decisions – not only of the heroic, if quixotic, decision to stay on in Mexico to meet his fate, but also of his savage decree of 3 October 1865 against his opponents (see page 27). The soldiers who executed him were only obeying orders, just as any well-trained French soldier would; and even Juárez, by condemning him to death, was doing no more than Maximilian had with the 1865 decree. The only clear blame lay back in Paris – where Manet meant the image to be seen

– with Napoleon III, whose ambitions precipitated the whole episode, and whose censors suppressed Manet's image.

It was by its ambivalence, by the studied lack of dramatic rhetoric or moral signposting, that Manet's purely 'artistic' *Execution of Maximilian* could function politically. Its detachment and its open-endedness, a distinctively Parisian language of opposition to Napoleon's empire, set up this image of Maximilian's fate, by a rough wall at Querétaro, as an icon of the perils of imperial and dynastic ambitions.

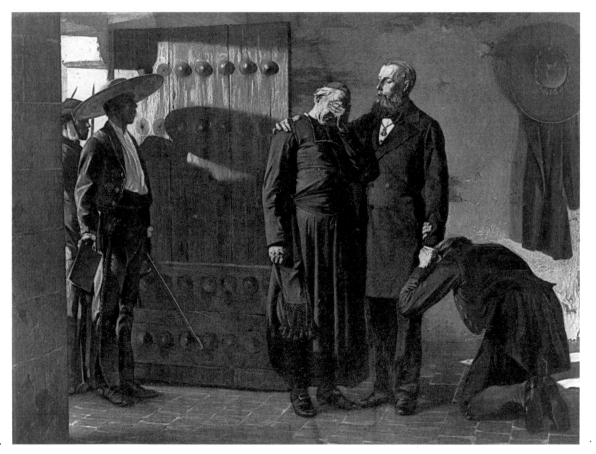

Fig. 115
Jean-Paul Laurens,
The Last Moments of Max-
imilian, Emperor of Mexico,
Salon of 1882. Oil on
canvas, 222 x 300 cm.
Moscow, Tretiakov Gallery.

Notes

I am indebted to Elizabeth C. Childs and Suzanne Glover Lindsay for their searching comments on the first draft of this essay.

1. Ingres, quoted by T. Silvestre, *Les Artistes français*, Paris 1926, II, p. 21 (essay first published in 1856); quoted in part by Austin, in Providence 1981, p. 52.
2. O. Merson, *La Peinture en France: Exposition de 1861*, Paris 1861, p. 146.
3. T. Gautier, *Les Beaux-Arts en Europe, 1855*, I, Paris 1855, p. 10.
4. Thierry described the development of his ideas about history during the 1820s in 'Histoire de mes idées et de mes travaux historiques', in *Dix ans d'études historiques*, Brussels 1835. The first volume of Monteil's *Histoire des français des divers états aux cinq derniers siècles* was published in 1828.
5. See especially M. Marrinan, *Painting Politics for Louis-Philippe: Art and Ideology in Orléanist France, 1830–1848*, New Haven and London 1988; on *genre historique*, cf. pp. 19–25, 210–13 and *passim*; on Versailles, especially pp. 57ff., 114ff., 123ff., 150ff., 164ff.; and also T. W. Gaehtgens, *Versailles: de la résidence royale au musée historique*, Paris 1984.
6. C. Baudelaire, *Salon de 1845*, Paris 1845, quoted from C. Baudelaiare, *Art in Paris 1845–1862*, trs. Jonathan Mayne, London 1965, p. 32.
7. E. Chesneau, 'Le Réalisme et l'esprit français dans l'art', in *L'Art et les artistes modernes en France et en Angleterre*, Paris 1864, p. 40.
8. J. Castagnary, 'Philosophie du Salon de 1857', in *Salons (1857–1870)*, Paris 1892, I, p. 9.
9. Castagnary, 'Salon de 1869', in Castagnary 1892 (cited in note 8), I, pp. 353–4.
10. M. du Camp, *Le Salon de 1859*, Paris 1859, pp. 13–16.
11. e.g. E. About, 'Le Salon de 1868', *Revue des deux-mondes*, 1 June 1868, p. 719; G. Lafenestre, 'Le Salon de 1868', in *L'Art vivant: La Peinture et la sculpture aux Salons de 1868 à 1877*, Paris 1881, I, p. 9; A. Duparc, *Le Salon de 1869*, Paris 1869, p. 5.
12. e.g. M. du Camp, 'Salon de 1865', in *Les Beaux-Arts à l'exposition universelle et aux Salons de 1863, 1864, 1865, 1866 et 1867*, Paris 1867, pp. 138–40; C. Clément, 'Exposition de 1866, V', *Journal des débats*, 26 May 1866; Chesneau 1864 (cited in note 7), p. 257, where he repeats his optimism for the potential of contemporary subjects.
13. For a valuable recent study of these issues, see D. Pick, *Faces of Degeneration: A European Disorder, c.1848–c.1918*, Cambridge 1989.
14. For a remarkable anthology of state purchases from these years, see G. Lacambre, *Le Musée du Luxembourg en 1874*, exhibition catalogue, Grand Palais, Paris 1974, with a brief discussion of the complexities of state purchases, pp. 8–9; for purchases for provincial museums, see D. J. Sherman, *Worthy Monuments: Art Museums and the Politics of Culture in Nineteenth-Century France*. Cambridge, Mass., 1989, Chapter 1.
15. Letter from Adolphe-William Bouguereau to the comte de Nieuwerkerke, 25 May 1863, quoted in L. d'Argencourt, 'Bouguereau et le marché de l'art en France', in *William Bouguereau*, exhibition catalogue, Petit Palais, Paris 1984, pp. 99–100.
16. Nieuwerkerke's report and the Decree itself are published in *Gazette des Beaux-Arts*, December 1863, pp. 563–72.
17. For another discussion of Manet's picture in relation to military painting, see Boime 1973, pp. 176–82.
18. T. Gautier, 'Salon de 1857, XIX', *L'Artiste*, 7 November 1857, p. 145; for another useful statement of the problems of battle painting see M. du Camp, *Le Salon de 1861*, Paris 1861, pp. 12–15.
19. Merson 1861 (cited in note 2), p. 85.
20. Du Camp 1861 (cited in note 18), p. 14. Beaucé's *Solférino* (present location unknown), his most famous work, was exhibited again in the Exposition Universelle of 1867.
21. T. Gautier fils, 'Salon de 1863 (1er article)', *Le Monde illustré*, 23 May 1863, p. 330.
22. T. Pelloquet, 'Exposition Universelle de 1867: Beaux-Arts: France – Peinture (3e article)', *Le Monde illustré*, 27 July 1867, p. 59. Boime 1973, pp. 181–2, suggests that the similar comments by Manet's friend Théodore Duret in his review of the Exposition may have influenced Manet's treatment of the *Execution*; however, as Pelloquet's comments show, such criticisms were not confined to Manet's immediate circle.
23. Du Camp 1861 (cited in note 18), p. 13.
24. C. Vignon, 'Le Salon de 1863', *Le Correspondant*, June 1863, pp. 373–5; cf. also T. Gautier, 'Salon de 1863, I', *Le Moniteur universel*, 23 May 1863.
25. Chesneau 1864 (cited in note 7), pp. 283–4.
26. P. Mantz, 'Le Salon de 1863 (1er article)', *Gazette des Beaux-Arts*, June 1863, p. 491.
27. Du Camp, 'Salon de 1863', in du Camp 1867 (cited in note 12), pp. 22–3.
28. Several writers, notably Boime 1973, pp. 188–9, have suggested that a figure in the centre of Protais's *Morning, Before the Attack* was a source for the figure of the sergeant on the right of Manet's painting. However, it seems unlikely, given the contrast between Protais's appealing, pensive physiognomies and Manet's own spare execution and suppression of facial expression.
29. T. Gautier, 'Salon de 1866, IV', *Le Moniteur universel*, 4 July 1866; A.-J. du Pays, 'Salon de 1866, II', *L'Illustration*, 19 May 1866, p. 310; C. Clément, 'Exposition de 1866, V', *Journal des débats*, 26 May 1866; on the varied emotions, see du Pays, ibid., and E. Chesneau, *Les nations rivales dans l'art*, Paris 1868, p. 332.
30. The events in Poland were extensively discussed by C. de Mazade in a series of articles in the *Revue des deux-mondes*, republished with a new foreward as *La Pologne contemporaine: Récits et portraits de la révolution polonaise*, Paris 1863; for a vivid description of the massacre of 8 April 1861, see pp. 112–15.
31. Chesneau 1868 (cited in note 29), p. 218.
32. For political readings, see Gautier 1866, du Pays 1866 and Clément 1866 (cited in note 29), and P. Challemel-Lacour, 'Le Salon de 1866', *La Revue moderne*, 1 June 1866, p. 541.
33. For reviews emphasising the 'ethnographic truth' of Robert-Fleury's picture, see Clément 1866 (cited in note 29) and du Camp, 'Salon de 1866', in du Camp 1867 (cited in note 12), p. 199.
34. Clément 1866 (cited in note 29).

35. Sources of information are also discussed in particular in Sandblad 1954, pp. 109ff., and Providence 1981, pp. 10ff., 116ff., which quotes the principal reports.

36. This is noted by N. Austin in Providence 1981, p. 51.

37. See the account in *Le Mémorial diplomatique*, 10 October 1867, pp. 1122–3, quoted in Providence 1981, pp. 121–2.

38. M. de Montifaud, 'Salon de 1868, II', *L'Artiste*, May 1868, p. 253, announced that Manet was planning to exhibit *The Death of Maximilian*, cited by Darragon 1989, p. 150.

39. T. Thoré, 'Salon de 1868', *l'Indépendance belge*, 29 June 1868, in Bürger 1870, II, pp. 531–2; P. Mantz, 'Salon de 1868, V', *L'Illustration*, 7 June 1868, p. 361, both quoted in Hamilton 1986, pp. 121, 124.

40. The formalist (or modernist) readings of the picture are summarised by Sandblad 1954, pp. 117–19, whose pioneering account of the picture first opened out the questions of the significance of the subject for Manet and the sources he used for it. For a recent critique of modernist readings of the picture, see Larsen 1990, pp. 32–48.

41. E. Forcade, 'Chronique de la quinzaine', *Revue des deux-mondes*, 15 July 1867, p. 517, cited by Darragon 1989, p. 143.

42. J. Claretie, 'Courrier de Paris', *L'Indépendance belge*, 6 July 1867, p. 1.

43. R. du Merzer, 'Exécution de l'Empereur Maximilien', *L'Illustration*, 13 July 1867, p. 18.

44. 'Nouvelles de France', *L'Indépendance belge*, 4 July 1867, p. 2; 'Nouvelles de France', *L'Indépendance belge*, 6 July 1867, p. 2; the paper had many French subscribers and was circulated in Paris, though several issues containing early reports of Maximilian's execution were banned.

45. *Discours parlementaires de M. Thiers*, XI, Paris 1881, pp. 164–248, on responsibility, see especially pp. 219, 222; J. Favre, *Discours parlementaires*, III, Paris 1881, pp. 230–48, on responsibility, see especially p. 248. Both speeches were immediately published in *Le Moniteur universel*, 10 July 1867, pp. 910–13.

46. The first detailed history of the expedition to appear in France was comte E. de Kératry, *L'Empereur Maximilien, son élévation et sa chute*. Published initially as articles in the *Revue contemporaraine* between 15 July and 15 October 1867, it was first published in book form outside France; it appeared in book form in France late in 1867, with a new preface by Prévost-Paradol, dated November 1867, in which ultimate blame was clearly attributed to Napoleon III's 'personal government'.

47. This argument was first used in *L'Indépendance belge* on 4 July 1867, and reiterated several times in the following days.

48. See especially R. Bellet, *Presse et journalisme sous le Second Empire*, Paris 1967. In my discussion of censorship I am indebted to Elizabeth C. Childs, who generously allowed me to read her unpublished dissertation, *Honoré Daumier and the Exotic Vision: Studies in French Culture and Caricature*, Columbia University, New York 1989, which contains an important section on 'Sense and Censorship in the Publication of Caricature' (pp. 65ff.). On censorship in this period, see also A. Rifkin, 'Cultural movement and the Paris Commune', *Art History*, June 1979, pp. 202–7.

49. Likewise in 1863 Courbet was prevented from exhibiting his picture of drunken priests, *The Return from the Meeting*, even at the Salon des Refusés, created that year for the display of works rejected by the Salon jury.

50. *La Censure sous Napoléon III: Rapports inédits et in extenso (1852 à 1866)*, Paris 1892, p. 185.

51. For a justification of the most repressive surveillance, see 'Rapport à l'Empereur sur le régime de la presse', 1856, in *Documents pour servir à l'histoire du Second Empire: Circulaires, rapports, notes et instructions confidentielles, 1851–1870*, Paris 1872, pp. 187–93; for an attack on this repression and arguments that the government should concentrate on positive propaganda, see 'La presse et les écrivains sous l'empire: Note remise au Ministre de l'Intérieur par la Direction de la Presse', 1867, in ibid., pp. 197–221.

52. Manet, letter to Zola, January 1869, in Paris/New York 1983, p. 531, Wilson-Bareau 1991, p. 50; on the power of the image without any text, see also Bann 1987, p. 53 (I am grateful to Stephen Bann for bringing his discussion of Manet's picture to my attention).

53. *La Censure* 1892 (cited in note 50), pp. 249–50. For an account of Raousset-Boulbon's remarkable career, with suspicions of French government involvement in his Mexican exploits, see P. Larousse, *Grand dictionnaire universel du XIXe siècle*, XIII, Paris 1875, pp. 689–90.

54. 'Mexique: le dernier jour d'un condamné', *Le Figaro*, 9 July 1867, p. 2.

55. Jean-Léon Gérôme, quoted in C. Moreau-Vauthier, *Gérôme*, Paris 1906, p. 254. Gérôme also claimed that the picture had been criticised by Bonapartists and Legitimists alike, each side seeing it as supporting the other.

56. About 1868 (cited in note 11), p. 729.

57. For a richly documented account of the Ney monument, see L. de Fourcaud, *François Rude, sculpteur: ses oeuvres et son temps*, Paris 1904, pp. 368–89.

58. e.g. *L'Indépendance belge*, 6 July 1867, p. 2; 8 July 1867, p. 1; Boime 1973, p. 189, notes another such reference.

59. Whether or not Gérôme intended such a reference, it is implausible that his picture – an overt updating of his *Death of Caesar* (fig. 104) – was somehow a response to Manet's *Execution* project, as suggested by G. M. Ackerman, 'Gérôme and Manet', *Gazette des Beaux-Arts*, September 1967, pp. 169–70.

60. Castagnary, 'Salon de 1868', in Castagnary 1892 (cited in note 8), I, p. 262; for other criticisms of Gérôme's picture, see e.g. Lafenestre 1868, in Lafenestre 1881 (cited in note 11), I, p. 27; R. de Navery, *Le Salon de 1868*, Paris 1868, p. 21; M. Chaumelin, 'Salon de 1868, II', *La Presse*, 3 June 1868.

61. Proust 1897, p. 177; 1913, p. 66; 1988, p. 38.

62. E. Ténot, *Paris en décembre 1851: Etude historique sur le coup d'état*, Paris 1868, Foreword, pp. v–ix; for a contemporary discussion of the implications of Ténot's book, see C. de Mazade, 'Chronique de la quinzaine', *Revue des deux-mondes*, 15 September 1868, pp. 502–4.

63. For accounts of the Baudin affair, see T. Delord, *Histoire du Second Empire*, V, Paris 1874, pp. 345–74; E. Ollivier, *L'Empire libéral*, XI, pp. 78–104; Rifkin 1979 (cited in note 48), pp. 206–7; for contemporary comment, see de Mazade 1868 (cited in note 62), 15 November 1868, pp. 491–4 and 1 December 1868, pp. 751–3.

64. See Delord 1874 (cited in note 63), pp. 257–61.
65. On the Baudin monument, see *Sculpture française au XIXe siècle*, exhibition catalogue, Grand Palais, Paris 1986, pp. 238–9.
66. On Regnault's interest in Velázquez, and on the commission for the Prim portrait, see A. Duparc (ed.), *Correspondance de Henri Regnault*, Paris 1873, pp. 192–247.
67. Lafenestre, 'Le Salon de 1869', in Lafenestre 1881 (cited in note 11), I, p. 97; M. Chaumelin, 'Salon de 1869: Peinture IV', *La Presse*, 22 June 1869; T. Gautier, 'Le Salon de 1869', in *Tableaux à la plume*, Paris 1880, p. 292. For negative criticism, see A. Baignères, 'Peinture et sculpture à l'exposition de 1869', *Revue contemporaine*, 15 May 1869, pp. 260–1; for positive statements, seeing it as marking the renewal of the Ecole de Rome, see M. Chaumelin, 'Le Salon de 1869, III', *L'Indépendance belge*, 1 June 1869, and, more equivocally, C. Blanc, 'Salon de 1869, III', *Le Temps*, 26 May 1869.
68. Paris/New York 1983, p. 532; another report (p. 531) said that Manet had treated his subject 'from an exclusively artistic point of view'.
69. A vivid example of the application of these criteria is Castagnary's review of Manet's 1869 exhibits ('Salon de 1869', in Castagnary 1892 (cited in note 8), I, pp. 364–5, quoted in part by N. Austin in Providence 1981, p. 51): 'M. Manet ... arranges his people at random without any reason or meaning for the composition. The result is uncertainty and often obscurity of thought.... In the *Balcony* ... one woman has seated herself apparently just to enjoy the view of the street; the other is putting on her gloves as if she were just about to go out. This contradictory attitude bewilders me.... A feeling for functions, for fitness is indispensable. Neither the painter nor the writer can neglect them. Like characters in a comedy, so in a painting each figure must be in its place, play its part, and so contribute to the expression of the general idea. Nothing arbitrary and nothing superfluous, such is the law of every artistic composition.' For further discussion of the illegibility and moral uncertainties of these pictures, see J. House 1986, and J. House, 'Social Critic or Enfant Terrible: the Avant-garde Artist in Paris in the 1860s', in *Actes du XXVIIe congrès international d'histoire de l'art*, Strasbourg 1991/2.
70. For a valuable discussion of genre painting in the context of censorship, see L. W. Kinney, 'Genre: A Social Contract?', *Art Journal*, Winter 1987, pp. 267 ff.
71. Zola's article was first published in *Revue du XIXe siècle* on 1 January 1867; initial selection for the Exposition Universelle was made in December 1866 and January 1867, see Mainardi 1987, p. 131.
72. As recalled by Jules Favre in his speech on 9 July 1867, Favre 1881 (cited in note 45), p. 242; for discussion of the Christ associations in the picture, see Sandblad 1954, pp. 147–8, and Bann 1987, p. 52, for discussion of the hat, see pp. 63–4.
73. Zola, in *La Tribune*, 4 February 1869 (reprinted and translated in Paris/New York 1983, pp. 531–2) where he emphasises the accuracy of the uniforms, but notes that the image could readily be seen as 'France shooting Maximilian'.

The Maximilian Paintings:
Provenance and Exhibition History

JOHN LEIGHTON AND JULIET WILSON-BAREAU

The Execution of Maximilian (fig. 70:I)

Rouart and Wildenstein I, 124
Boston, Museum of Fine Arts (No. 30.444)

The painting is not listed in either the manuscript register of works in Manet's studio, made in 1883 after his death by Mme Manet's son, Léon Leenhoff (see page 82, note 7), or the testamentary inventory compiled in the same year. According to Tabarant (1931, p. 176, and 1947, p. 141) the canvas remained rolled up until it was discovered in an attic in Mme Manet's home at Asnières in 1899. She gave it to Léon who stored it in his office in Paris, first at 10 bis rue Amélie, then at 94 rue St Dominique, where '. . . it obstructed the corridor alongside the small employees' dining room, until the day Léon Koëlla [Leenhoff] decided to hang it on the wall where it could be admired, although it had suffered considerably, having been rolled the wrong way, with the painted surface inside for many years' (Tabarant 1947, p. 141). A note in Léon Leenhoff's hand describes it as *Maximilien-esquisse* and indicates that it was sold to Vollard for 500 francs, to be paid by the end of July 1900 (New York, Pierpont Morgan Library, Tabarant archive, dossier Koëlla-Leenhoff). Tabarant records that Vollard paid 800 francs (1947, p. 141). In 1909 Vollard sold the picture to Frank Gair Macomber of Boston, who presented it to the Museum of Fine Arts, Boston, in 1930. The painting was cleaned and restored in 1980 and has been re-examined for this exhibition.

EXHIBITIONS

Salon d'automne, Paris 1905, no. 17; *Manet*, Orangerie des Tuileries, Paris 1932, no. 27; *Manet*, Paris/New York 1983, no. 104.

The Execution of Maximilian (fig. 73:II)

Rouart and Wildenstein I, 126
London, National Gallery (No. 3294)

The painting was in Manet's studio at his death and is recorded in the 1883 testamentary inventory of the studio contents under *études peintes* as *L'éxecution de Maximilien (esquisse)*. It is listed as no. 300 in Léon Leenhoff's manuscript register of Manet's works, made that same year: *Esquisse du Maximilen, 287½ x 197, non encadré, non [deleted] photographié*, with an additional note that it was photographed on 20 December (fig. 71). This photo-

graph by Lochard was mistakenly numbered 309 – the register number for the Mannheim painting (see below).

From Lochard's photograph it is clear that the picture had already suffered considerable neglect. The left-hand section with the figures of Maximilian and Mejía was already missing or was damaged and masked out on the photographic print. In the original Lochard album (Paris, Bibliothèque Nationale Estampes, DC 300h, p. 73) the photograph has a caption in Léon's hand: 'First project for the Execution of Maximilian. Damourette [see page 58] posed for one of the Generals. Painted in the rue Guyot studio in 1867.'

There are differing accounts of the fate of the picture. According to Vollard (*Souvenirs d'un marchand de tableaux*, Paris 1936, p. 70) the left-hand section was cut away by Léon who told the dealer:

...the firing squad looked better without the group of generals and what was left of the head of Maximilian. . . . If I'd thought that a few scraps of canvas, half-eaten by the saltpetre in the wall, could be of any value, I wouldn't have used them to light the fire.

Vollard states that what remained of the picture was rolled up and stored in Mme Manet's house at Asnières, until Léon decided to cut off the figure of the sergeant at the right, observing that he 'gained from being presented without his legs, which were hanging in tatters', and to sell it as 'a genre subject' to the dealer Portier in the late 1880s or early 1890s.

Vollard himself later acquired the central section with the firing squad from Léon and sold it to Degas, who had already purchased the sergeant from Portier.

Degas gives a slightly different account in one of his notebooks (private collection, photograph in National Gallery dossier):

This picture, which for years had remained rolled up at Mme Manet's home at Genevilliers, was cut up and sent for sale, most probably by her brother Leenhoff [see page 82, note 7]. At first the canvas, already cropped on the left, was deposited for a long time with [the dealers] Mme Martin and Camentron. Then it was cut up. The sergeant loading his rifle, behind the firing soldiers, was hawked about and eventually sold for 500 francs to Portier who let me have it.

An entry in Julie Manet's diary indicates that Degas had acquired two sections of the picture by November 1894 and records his intention 'to try to put the painting back as it was' (*Growing Up with the Impressionists: The Diary of Julie Manet*, London 1987, p. 54). Degas had the surviving fragments mounted onto a single piece of canvas of approximately the original dimensions of the painting.

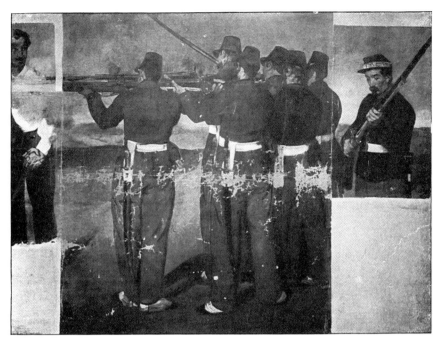

Fig. 116
Edouard Manet,
*The Execution of
Maximilian* (II).
Reproduction in the sale
catalogue of the Edgar
Degas Collection, 1918,
showing the painting as
pieced together onto a
single canvas for Degas
around 1895.

This is how they appear in an unmasked photograph in J. Meier-Graefe, *Edouard Manet* (London 1912, p. 191) and in the catalogue of the sale of the Degas collection (Paris, Galerie Georges Petit, 26-7 March 1918, lot 74). These reproductions (fig. 116) reveal the extent of the damage to the central section showing the firing squad. The mounted fragments were acquired by the National Gallery at the Degas sale (see C.J. Holmes, *Self & Partners*, London 1936, p. 338) and shortly afterwards they were again separated and placed onto three stretchers.

The two fragments depicting Miramón were cleaned and restored in 1979; the remaining fragments were cleaned in preparation for the present exhibition when the pieces were once again mounted onto a single support (fig. 73:II).

EXHIBITIONS

No. 3294B (*The Sergeant loading his Rifle*) was in the exhibition, *Nineteenth-Century French Paintings*, National Gallery, London 1942, no. 2; nos. 3294A (*The Firing Squad*) and B were exhibited in *Manet and his Circle* at the Tate Gallery (Arts Council Exhibition), London 1954, nos. 6, 7; nos. 3294A and B shown in *Edouard Manet*, Philadelphia/Chicago 1967, nos. 85A

and B; all the fragments were brought together for the exhibition *The Artist's Eye*, selected by Howard Hodgkin, at the National Gallery, London 1979, no. 8; and were shown in *Manet at Work*, National Gallery, London 1983, cat. 14.

The Execution of Maximilian (fig. 76:III)

Rouart and Wildenstein I, 127
Mannheim, Städtische Kunsthalle (No. M281)

This final version of the composition is first recorded in an inventory made by Manet in 1872 with a valuation of 25,000 francs. Godet photographed the painting for the artist, probably in the same year (Paris, Bibliothèque Nationale Estampes, DC 300f, III, micr. P176122). In the 1883 testamentary inventory of Manet's studio it is listed as no. 18 (valued at 1,000 francs) and is recorded as no. 309 in Léon Leenhoff's manuscript register as *Exécution de Maximilien. Signé et daté 19 juin 1867. Cadre ancien, non photographié* (i.e. by Lochard). Although originally included in the studio sale at the Hôtel Drouot (4-5 February 1884, no. 16), it was withdrawn by Manet's widow who eventually sold it in 1898 to Durand-Ruel for 5,000 francs. He exhibited it that same year at the International Exhibition in London, where it was favourably reviewed in the *Art Journal, Nation* and *Manchester Courier* (Kate Flint (ed.) *Impressionists in England. The Critical Reception*, London 1984, pp. 153, 155 and 261). It was acquired (at an unknown date) by Baron Denys Cochin for 12,000 francs and then by the Bernheim-Jeune family. In January 1910 the painting was sold through Paul Cassirer in Berlin to the Kunsthalle, Mannheim. The picture was cleaned and restored at the Doerner Institute in Munich in 1985.

EXHIBITIONS

Clarendon Hotel, New York 1879; Studio Building gallery, Boston 1880 (see page 69); *Exhibition of International Art*, Prince's Club, Knightsbridge, London 1898, no. 16, repr. (lent by Durand-Ruel); *Salon d'Automne*, Paris 1905, no. 18 (lent by M. Denys Cochin); *Ausstellung der Berliner Secession*, Berlin 1910; *Art moderne*, Manzi-Joyant, Paris 1913, no. 60; *Impressionnistes et Romantiques Français dans les Musées Allemands*, Orangerie des Tuileries, Paris 1951, no. 49; *Französische Malerei von Delacroix bis Picasso*, Stadthalle Wolfsburg 1961, no. 87; *Französische Malerei des 19 Jahrhunderts von David bis Cézanne*, Haus der Kunst, Munich 1964-5, no. 162.

Chronology 1821–84

Numbers in brackets refer to figures.

1821
Mexico gains independence from Spain after General Agustín de Iturbide proclaims the Plan of Iguala; Iturbide becomes president of Regency Council, then Emperor (July 1822–March 1823).

1823
Iturbide forced to abdicate and go into exile after a rebellion of leading generals, including Antonio López de Santa Anna. Monroe Doctrine proclaimed by US President James Monroe, to counter European designs in the Americas.

1824
October Federal constitutional system established in Mexico.

1830
July 27–9 July Revolution in France; Charles X replaced by Louis-Philippe d'Orléans (1830–48).
August 18 Birth of Franz Joseph of Habsburg, future Emperor of Austria.

1832
January 23 *Birth of Edouard Manet in Paris.*
July 6 Birth of Ferdinand Maximilian, a younger brother of Franz Joseph and future Emperor of Mexico, in Vienna.
After the death of the duc de Reichstadt, son of Napoleon I and Marie-Louise of Austria, the Emperor's nephew, Louis Napoleon Bonaparte (born 1808, future Emperor Napoleon III) assumes leadership of the Bonapartist cause.

1836
October 31 Louis Napoleon Bonaparte's attempted seizure of power fails; he goes into exile.
Abolition of federalism in Mexico.

1840
Louis Napoleon is imprisoned at the fortress of Ham, on the Somme, after another failed *coup d'état* (escapes to England in 1846).
June 7 Birth of Princess Charlotte of Belgium, daughter of Leopold I (future Empress of Mexico).

1841–4
Santa Anna in power in Mexico.

1846–7
War between the United States and Mexico, following US annexation of Texas, leads to loss of New Mexico and California by Mexico (Treaty of Guadalupe Hidalgo 1848). Restoration of federalism in Mexico (1846–53).

1848
'Year of Revolutions'
February 22–4 Fall of Louis-Philippe in France.

February 25 Second Republic proclaimed in France; return of Louis Napoleon from exile in England.
April 23 Election of a French Constituent Assembly that includes Louis Napoleon.
June 22–6 Riots in Paris. *Manet and Antonin Proust witness the street fighting.* Conservative reaction; Party of Order established.
December 2 Accession of Franz Joseph I, Emperor of Austria.
December 9 *Manet embarks as a naval cadet for Rio de Janeiro.*
December 10 Louis Napoleon, supported by the Party of Order, elected President of the French Republic for four years.

1849
March 23 Battle of Novara, in Lombardy, following Austrian intervention to curb Italian Nationalism.
May 26 Dissolution of the Constituent Assembly in Paris, followed by repressive, anti-Republican measures.
June 13 *Manet back in France; fails entrance examination to the Ecole naval at Brest.*
July France intervenes against Republican forces in Rome.

1850
Maximilian joins the Austrian Navy.
September *Manet enters Couture's studio.*

1851
December 2 *Coup d'état* in Paris, organised by Louis Napoleon and the duc de Morny.
December 4 Street fighting on the Paris boulevards; death of Alphonse Baudin on the barricades (110). *Manet sees the victims' corpses in the cemetery at Montmartre.* Freedom of the press abolished.
December 21 Plebiscite confirms Louis Napoleon as Prince–President of France.

1852
January 14 Promulgation of a new French Constitution giving virtually all powers to Louis Napoleon; repressive press laws enacted.
November 21 Plebiscite elects Louis Napoleon as Emperor of the French (2).
December 2 Proclamation of Second Empire in France.

1853
Santa Anna resumes power in Mexico (1853–5); Benito Juárez (born 1806) (7) and other Liberal leaders go into exile in New Orleans.
January 29 Marriage of Napoleon III and Eugénie (Eugenia María de Montijo, condesa de Teba, born 1826).

1854
March Uprising (Revolution of Ayutla) led by Juan Alvarez and Ignacio Comonfort against Santa Anna in Mexico.

Crimean War (1854–6): France and Great Britain allied against Russia; siege of Sebastopol.

1855

August Fall of Santa Anna in Mexico; he goes into exile. Liberals in power; beginning of the Mexican Reform movement.

September 8 Taking of the Malakoff Tower by French troops under General Mac-Mahon (99), leads to the fall of Sebastopol in the Crimea.

November Restriction of ecclesiastical prvilege, decreed by Juárez as Minister of Justice, provokes clerical opposition in Mexico.

December Comonfort becomes acting President of the Mexican Republic.

1856

February Constituent Congress meets in Mexico City.

February *Manet leaves Couture's studio after six years.*

March 16 Birth of the Prince Imperial in Paris (3).

June Lerdo Law forces sale of ecclesiastical properties in Mexico.

1857

February 5 Promulgation of the federal Constitution of the Republic of Mexico.

February 28 Franz Joseph of Austria appoints Maximilian Governor of Lombardy-Venetia.

July 27 Marriage of Maximilian and Princess Charlotte of Belgium.

November 18 Congress appoints Comonfort as President of Mexico. Juárez, elected President of the Supreme Court, becomes his constitutional successor.

December Comonfort closes Congress to curb Liberal radicalism.

1858

Civil War of the Reform in Mexico (1858–60) between Republicans and Conservative rebels led by Generals Miguel Miramón and Tomás Mejía (56, 57).

January General Félix Zuloaga seizes power in Mexico, forces Comonfort into exile and establishes a Conservative regime in Mexico City; Juárez claims the presidency and establishes a Liberal, Republican administration in Veracruz.

1859

January 14 Failed assassination of Napoleon III by an Italian, Felice Orsini, followed by French action in favour of a united Italy.

January 31 Miramón elected President of the Mexican Republic by a junta in Mexico City.

April 6 Juárez's Republican government in Veracruz recognised by the United States.

June 4 Victory of French forces under Generals Canrobert and Mac-Mahon over Austrian troops at Magenta (Lombardy).

June 24 French and Sardinian forces defeat the Austrian army at Solferino (100–101): Austrian loss of Lombardy–Venetia.

October President Miramón's bankrupt government in Mexico City agrees to the emission of bonds to the financier Jecker, owner of a bank in Mexico.

1860

April 14 *Publication of Manet's caricature of Emile Ollivier in the satirical journal 'Diogène'.*

December 22 Defeat of Miramón by Juárez's constitutionalist forces in Mexico.

December 24 Maximilian and Charlotte take up residence in the castle of Miramare, near Trieste.

1861

January 11 Juárez makes a triumphal entry into Mexico City.

April 11 Beginning of the American Civil War.

May *Manet occupies a large studio on the rue Guyot (until 1870).*

June 11 Juárez declared Constitutional President of the Republic of Mexico.

July 17 The Mexican Congress votes a two-year moratorium on repayment of all public debts; Great Britain, France and Spain break off diplomatic relations.

September 1 The Mexican monarchist José Manuel Hidalgo proposes a French intervention and the establishment of a Second Empire in Mexico to Napoleon III and Eugénie at Biarritz.

October 4 Maximilian at Miramare is informed of Napoleon III's plans for Mexico.

October 31 France, Great Britain and Spain sign the Tripartite Convention in London in order to force Mexico to pay her debts.

November 12–29 Eleven French ships sail from Toulon for Mexico.

December 17 Disembarkation of the first allied troops at Veracruz.

1862

January 6–8 British and French troops disembark at Veracruz; arrival of the Spanish General Juan Prim (113) to head the expeditionary force, supplemented by further French troops in March under General Charles-Ferdinand Lorencez.

January 25 Juárez decrees the death penalty for all who aid and abet the foreign intervention (the law that would be applied to the Emperor Maximilian in 1867).

February 19 The Convention of La Soledad, signed by Prim on behalf of the allies, opens negotiations to resolve the dispute.

April 9 Negotiations fail; the Tripartite Convention is annulled and Spanish and British troops leave Mexico; General Lorencez begins the French advance on Mexico City.

May 5 French forces are routed at Puebla.

August 15 Napoleon III's official birthday is celebrated in Paris. *Manet's lithograph 'The Balloon' (93) executed August-September.*

September 21 General Elie-Frédéric Forey disembarks with 3,400 French troops at Veracruz, followed in October by 20,000 men under three generals including General Achille-François Bazaine, a veteran of French campaigns in Algeria, the Crimea and Italy. French Foreign Legion forces arrive.

September 23 Bismarck appointed Prime Minister of Prussia by King Wilhelm I.

1863

March 1 *Manet's first major exhibition at Martinet's gallery in Paris.*

March 16 French siege of Puebla begins.

March 29 Storming of San Xavier (9, 29); resistance of Puebla.

March 30 Sixty-five French Foreign Legionnaires attacked by 2,000 Republican troops at Camarón (11), between Veracruz and Puebla.

May *Manet exhibits at the Paris Salon des Refusés.*

May 17 Surrender of Puebla to the French.

May 31 Juárez and his government leave Mexico City for San Luis Potosí.

June 7 General Bazaine enters Mexico City with the French vanguard.

June 10 General Forey receives the keys of Mexico City (12); he names a junta to elect a provisional government and establishes courts martial.

July 10 An Assembly of Notables in Mexico City votes for a constitutional, hereditary monarchy; a commission embarks for Miramare in August.

October 1 Bazaine takes over the supreme command from Forey.

October 3 The Mexican commission led by José María Gutiérrez de Estrada offers the imperial crown to Maximilian at Miramare (13).

October 28 *Marriage of Manet and Suzanne Leenhoff in Holland.*

1864

March 5 Maximilian and Charlotte meet Napoleon III in Paris.

April 4 The United States House of Representatives votes unanimously against recognition of a monarchy in Mexico.

April 10 Maximilian accepts the crown of Mexico, having renounced his rights to the Austrian succession; signs the Convention of Miramare accepting French protection.

April 14 Departure of Emperor Maximilian and Empress Charlotte (Carlota) from Miramare for Mexico (14), via Rome. Interview with Pope Pius IX.

May *Manet's 'Incident in a Bullfight' (31, 32) and 'Dead Christ and the Angels' shown in the Paris Salon.*

May 29 Maximilian and Charlotte arrive at Veracruz.

June 12 Entry of Maximilian and Charlotte into Mexico City.

June 19 Battle between an American Union and a Confederate ship off the coast of France. *Incident depicted by Manet in 'The Battle of the Kearsarge and the Alabama', exhibited in Paris (90).*

July 25 Maximilian appoints a moderate, liberal ministry to the disgust of the clericals.

October Juárez establishes his Republican government at Chihuahua in northern Mexico.

December Arrival of 2,000 Belgian and 6,000 Austrian volunteers in Mexico.

1865

February-March Maximilian ratifies Liberal ecclesiastical policy.

April 9 American Civil War ends.

April 11 Belgian troops routed by Juárez's forces at Tacámbaro (Michoacán) in Mexico.

April 14 Assassination of President Lincoln.

May *Manet's 'Olympia' and 'Jesus mocked by the Soldiers' shown in the Paris Salon.*

July 16 President Andrew Johnson reaffirms America's recognition of Juárez's government.

September *Manet visits Spain; studies works by Velázquez and Goya in Madrid.*

October 3 Maximilian decrees the death penalty for all unauthorised armed persons and their supporters in Mexico (a decree held against him at his court martial).

1866

April 14 Marshal Bazaine ordered by Napoleon III to prepare for French withdrawal from Mexico.

Manet's 'Fifer' and 'Tragic Actor' rejected by the Salon jury; Zola's defence of Manet appears in 'L'Evénement'.

May 17 Maximilian requests Bazaine to organise a Mexican national army.

July 3 Austrian forces routed by the Prussian army at Sadowa, in Bohemia. Bazaine withdraws French and Imperial troops from the north of Mexico.

July 27 Telegraph cable laid between Ireland and Newfoundland.

August 9–18 Charlotte arrives in Paris from Mexico to seek aid for Maximilian and has three unsuccessful interviews with Napoleon III.

September 27–30 Charlotte in Rome to see the Pope; succumbs to madness, and is taken to Miramare in October.

October 21 General François de Castelnau arrives in Mexico City to press for Maximilians's abdication and organise the French withdrawal.

November-December Maximilian decides not to abdicate and appoints the Conservative Generals Miramón, Márquez and Mejía as commanders of a Mexican army.

1867

January-March French expeditionary forces progressively withdrawn; Bazaine joins final embarkation at Veracruz on 13 March.

February 19 Maximilian goes to Querétaro, north of Mexico City, with Generals Miramón and Mejía, to make a last stand against the advancing Liberal army.

March 11 Juárez and his government move south to San Luis Potosí.

March 14 Beginning of the siege of Querétaro (25,000 Republican troops under General Mariano Escobedo against 9,000 defenders).

April 1 Inauguration of the Paris Exposition Universelle.

May 1 Inauguration of the Paris Salon.

May 15 Maximilian, betrayed by Colonel Miguel López, surrenders to General Escobedo; imprisoned with Miramón and Mejía, first in La Cruz and later in the Convent of Las Capuchinas.

May 22 (or 24) *Opening of Manet's one-man exhibition near the Exposition Universelle.*

June 6 Assassination attempt on the Tsar of Russia by a Polish extremist in Paris.

June 12–15 Maximilian and his generals tried by court

martial in Querétaro; death sentence on the three prisoners confirmed by Juárez.

June 19 Execution of Maximilian, with Miramón and Mejía, on the Cerro de las Campanas. Juárez's government refuses to hand over the body to the Austrian government.

June 21 Entry of the Republican army into Mexico City.

June 29 News of Maximilian's execution is cabled to Vienna.

July 1 Napoleon III is advised by cable. Prize-giving ceremony for the Exposition Universelle.

July 4 Official cable from the Austrian Minister in Washington to Vienna confirms news of the execution.

July 5 The President of the French Legislature announces the news in Paris.

July 8 Spurious 'eyewitness' account of the execution appears in *Le Figaro*.

July–October Detailed despatches from Mexico and USA reported in the French and Belgian press.

October *Manet's exhibition and the Exposition Universelle close.*

December 20 Juárez declared President of the Republic of Mexico, after re-election.

1868

January 20 Maximilian's body entombed in the Habsburg crypt in Vienna.

May *Manet's 'Portrait of Emile Zola' and 'A Young Woman' shown in the Paris Salon; 'The Execution of Maximilian' announced in the press but was not shown.*

May 9 Liberalisation of French press laws.

July 1 Henri Rochefort launches the radical journal *La Lanterne*.

July 15–30 *Manet's 'Dead Man' (31) exhibited at Le Havre.*

September 19 Prim's uprising in Spain; Isabella II leaves the throne.

November 2 Republican demonstration at the tomb of Baudin (112); León Gambetta indicts the imperial regime in France.

1869

January–February *Manet advised that his painting of 'The Execution of Maximilian' (76: III) cannot be shown or his lithograph (77) published; Zola castigates French authorities in 'La Tribune'.*

May *Manet's 'The Balcony' (114) and 'The Luncheon' shown in the Paris Salon.*

May–June Election victories for the Republicans; Gambetta elected deputy for Belleville on a liberal, democratic programme.

July 12 The Conservative Prime Minister Eugène Rouher resigns.

1870

January 2 Emile Ollivier invited by Napoleon III to form a new 'Liberal' government.

January 12 Rochefort leads a funeral procession of 100,000 Republicans in protest at the shooting of the journalist Victor Noir by a Bonaparte prince.

March *Manet and Jules de La Rochenoire involved in attempts to liberalise the Salon jury.*

May *Manet's 'The Music Lesson' and 'Portrait of Eva Gonzalès' shown in the Paris Salon.*

May 8 Plebiscite in favour of the Empire.

July 3 Announcement of the candidacy of a Hohenzollern to the throne of Spain.

July 8 Meeting of the French Minister and Wilhelm of Prussia at Ems, near Cologne followed by the incident of the Ems telegram.

July 19 France declares war against Prussia.

August Prussian armies move into Alsace and Lorraine; Marshal Bazaine is blockaded at Metz.

August 9 Fall of Ollivier's government in France.

September 1 Napoleon III surrenders with Marshal Mac-Mahon at Sedan.

September 4 Insurrection in Paris: a provisional government proclaims the end of the Second Empire and inaugurates the Third Republic; sets up defence committees.

September 7 Gambetta, Minister of the Interior, leaves Paris by balloon.

September 8 *Manet sends his family to safety in the Pyrenees.*

September 15 Paris, governed by a central committee, votes to continue the war against Prussia.

September 16 *Manet closes his studio on the rue Guyot.*

September 19 Paris is surrounded by Prussian troops.

October 27 Bazaine surrenders at Metz.

October 31 Radicals fail to overthrow the provisional government in Paris.

November 7 *Manet and Degas enlist in the National Guard; Manet joins the general staff in December.*

1871

January 18 Wilhelm I proclaimed Emperor of Germany at Versailles.

January 24–8 Paris capitulates; armistice signed with Prussia.

February A National Assembly with a conservative, monarchist majority is elected; Adolphe Thiers forms a government of National Unity, which sits in Bordeaux. *Manet rejoins his family in south-west France, and visits the Assembly in Bordeaux.*

March 1 Thiers's government votes the end of the Empire; humiliating peace terms with Germany provoke a violent reaction in Paris.

March 10 The National Assembly moves to Versailles.

March 18 Thiers fails to disarm Paris.

March 28 The Council of the Commune proclaimed, supported by the International Workers Organisation.

April 2 The Versailles army begins a siege of Paris.

April 17 *Manet elected in absentia to the Artists' Federation in Paris.*

April 19 Proclamation of the Commune.

May 21–8 The *semaine sanglante* (bloody week): Versailles troops enter Paris to suppress the Commune; around 30,000 are killed, 40,000 arrested.

May–June *Manet returns to Paris (by 5 June).*

June 7 Courbet arrested as a prominent Communard.

July Thiers begins payment of the Prussian war indemnity and frees five out of twenty-one departments from German occupation.

October 12 Juárez reconfirmed for a second presidential

term in Mexico, but challenged by Porfirio Díaz (later dictator of Mexico, 1877–1911).

November 28 Execution of the Communard Louis Rossel, with Bourgeois and Ferré, at the Camp de Satory, near Versailles. *Manet present at the execution.*

1872

January *Manet sells twenty-four paintings to Durand-Ruel.*
May *Manet's 'The Battle of the Kearsarge and the Alabama' shown in the Paris Salon.*
July 1 *Manet moves to a studio at 4 rue St-Pétersbourg, near the Pont de l'Europe.*
July 18 Death of Juárez in Mexico City.

1873

January 9 Death of Napoleon III in England.
May *Manet's 'Le Bon Bock' and 'Repose' in the Paris Salon.*
May 24 Thiers, forced to resign as President of the French Republic, replaced by Marshal Mac-Mahon.
September France freed from German occupation.
October Failed restoration attempt by the monarchists and appointment of Mac-Mahon as President of the Republic for seven years; regime of *Ordre moral* initiated by the duc de Broglie.
October–December Trial by court martial of Bazaine at Versailles (death sentence commuted to imprisonment). *Manet attends the trial (89).*

1874

February 20 *Publication of Manet's lithographs 'Civil War' (83) and 'Boy with Dog'.*
March 19–20 Escape of Rochefort and his Communard companions from the prison colony at Nouméa in New Caledonia (94, 95).
April 12 *Mallarmé publishes a defence of Manet, following the Salon jury's rejection of two works.*
May *Manet's 'The Railroad' and a watercolour 'Polichinelle' shown in the Paris Salon.*
June 16 *Publication of Manet's colour lithograph 'Polichinelle', after initial seizure by the police.*

1875

May *Manet's 'Argenteuil' shown in the Paris Salon.*
December French National Assembly dissolved.

1876

January Election of the French Senate with a small monarchist majority, and of the Chambre des Députés with a large Republican majority.
April *The Salon jury rejects Manet's paintings, 'l'Artiste' and 'Le Linge', and he opens his studio to the public.*

1877

May *Manet's 'Faure in the Role of Hamlet' shown in the Paris Salon; 'Nana', rejected, is exhibited in a shop window.*
May–June Mac-Mahon nominates the duc de Broglie as president of the Council of Ministers; dissolves the Chamber of Deputies after a vote of no confidence.
October 14 Elections confirm the Republican majority in France.

1878

Exposition Universelle of 1878 in Paris. *Manet does not submit works.*

June 30 Fête de la Paix.

1879

January 30 Mac-Mahon resigns; Jules Grévy elected President of the French Republic; Gambetta made President of the Chamber of Deputies.
June Death of the Prince Imperial ends Bonapartist hopes of restoration.
April 1 *Manet moves into his last studio on the rue d'Amsterdam.*
May *Manet's 'Boating' and 'In the Conservatory' shown in the Paris Salon.*
June French Government votes to return to Paris (from Versailles) and to celebrate the Fête Nationale on 14 July.
December *Manet's 'Execution of Maximilian' (76: III) exhibited in New York (79, 80) and in January 1880 in Boston.*

1880

April 8–30 *Manet's one-man exhibition at 'La Vie moderne'.*
May *Manet's 'Portrait of Antonin Proust' and 'Chez le père Lathuile' shown in the Paris Salon.*
May–November *Manet at Bellevue for treatment of his leg.*
July 13 Full amnesty for all deported and exiled Communards voted by the government.
July 14 Rochefort returns to Paris for the first Fête Nationale.
November *Manet plans to paint 'The Escape of Rochefort' (94, 95) for the Paris Salon.*

1881

May *'Pertuiset the Lion Hunter' and 'Portrait of M. Henri Rochefort' (88), shown in the Paris Salon, earn Manet a second-class medal.*
June–July New laws establish freedom of association and of the press.
June–September *Manet at Versailles for treatment and rest.*
November Gambetta becomes Prime Minister and nominates Antonin Proust as Minister of Arts.
December 30 *Manet is made a Chevalier of the Legion of Honour.*

1882

January Fall of Gambetta's government.
May *Manet's 'A Bar at the Folies-Bergère' and 'Jeanne' shown in the Paris Salon.*
June–September *Manet very ill at Rueil; returns to Paris and draws up his will (30 September).*

1883

March 1 *Manet paints his last picture (a flower piece).*
April 30 *Manet dies ten days after an operation on his leg, and is buried in the cemetery at Passy (3 May).*

1884

January *Memorial exhibition of Manet's work at the Ecole des Beaux-Arts.*
February 4–5 *Sale of the contents of Manet's studio at the Hôtel Drouot in Paris.*

Bibliography

A short bibliography of works consulted or cited in the text.

Historical monographs and articles

F. Anders and K. Eggert, *Maximilian von Mexiko. Erherzog und Kaiser*, St Pölten-Vienna 1982 (with a critical bibliography)

N. N. Barker, *The French Experience in Mexico, 1821–1861: A History of Constant Misunderstanding*, Chapel Hill 1979

J. Bazant, 'Mexico from Independence to 1867', *The Cambridge History of Latin America*, ed. L. Bethell, vol. iii, Cambridge 1988

J. L. Blasio, *Maximilian: Memoirs of his Private Secretary*, New Haven 1934

Count E. C. Corti, *Maximilian and Carlota of Mexico*, 2 vols., New York 1928 (with a critical bibliography)

Documentos gráficos para la Historia de México, vol. 2, *1854–1867. La Reforma y el Imperio*, Mexico 1986 (with a detailed chronology and extensive iconography)

A. Duchesne, *Au service de Maximilien et de Charlotte. L'expédition des volontaires belge au Mexique 1864–1867*, doctoral thesis, Musée Royal de l'Armée, Brussels, I, 1967, II, 1968 (with a remarkable critical bibliography)

R. Fabiani, *The Castle of Miramare. The Historical Museum*, Trieste 1989

A. J. Hanna and K. A. Hanna, *Napoleon III and Mexico*, Chapel Hill 1971

P. F. Martin, *Maximilian in Mexico*, London 1914

M. Quirarte, *Historiografía sobre el imperio de Maximiliano*, Mexico 1970

K. Ratz (ed.), *Maximilian in Querétaro: Bilddokumentation über den Untergang des Zweiten Mexikanischen Kaiserreiches*, Graz 1991

Comtesse H. de Reinach Foussemagne, *Charlotte de Belgique, Impératrice du Mexique*, Paris 1925 (with many documents)

R. Roeder, *Juárez and his Mexico*, 2 vols., New York 1947

Prince F. Salm-Salm, *My Diary in Mexico in 1867*, 2 vols., London 1868

M. J. Strang, 'Napoleon III: The Fatal Foreign Policy', see Providence 1981 (exhibition catalogue), pp. 83–99

P. Willing, *Les Collections historiques du Musée de l'Armée*, vol. 3, Paris-Arcueil 1984

Art historical monographs and articles

G. M. Ackerman, 'Gérôme and Manet', *Gazette des Beaux-Arts*, September 1967, pp. 163–76

K. Adler, *Manet*, Oxford 1986

N. A. Austin, 'Metaphor and Fact at Mid Century: Manet and Contemporary History Painting', see Providence 1981 (exhibition catalogue), pp. 50–9

S. Bann, 'The Odd Man Out: Historical Narrative and the Cinematic Image', *History and Theory*, vol. 26, 1987

E. Bazire, *Manet*, Paris 1884

C. Becker (ed.), 'Letters from Manet to Zola', see Paris/New York 1983 (exhibition catalogue), pp. 518–30

A. Boime, 'New Light on Manet's *Execution of Maximilian*', *Art Quarterly*, Autumn 1973, pp. 172–208

K. L. Brush, 'Manet's *Execution* and the Tradition of the *Histoire*', see Providence 1981 (exhibition catalogue), pp. 39–49

W. Bürger (T. Thoré), *Salons de W. Bürger 1861 à 1868*, Paris 1870

F. Cachin et al., *Manet*, see Paris/New York 1983 (exhibition catalogue)

A. Ceysens, 'François Aubert et photographie au Mexique', see Woluwe-Saint-Lambert 1987 (exhibition catalogue), pp. 113–22

E. Darragon, *Manet*, Paris 1989

M. Davies, 'Recent Manet Literature', *Burlington Magazine*, XCVIII, 1956, pp. 169–71

M. Davies, London, National Gallery, *French School: Early 19th Century, Impressionists, Post-Impressionists, etc.*, London 1970

D. Druick and P. Zegers, 'Manet's "Balloon": French Diversion, The Fête de l'Empereur 1862', *Print Collector's Newsletter*, XIV, May–June 1983, pp. 37–46

T. Duret, *Manet*, Paris 1902 and 1906

T. A. Gronberg, *Manet. A Retrospective*, New York 1988

G. H. Hamilton, *Manet and his Critics*, (New Haven 1954), New Haven and London 1986

J. House, 'Manet's *Naïveté*, see London 1986 (exhibition catalogue), pp. 1–19

P. M. Jones, 'Structure and Meaning in the *Execution* Series', see Providence 1981 (exhibition catalogue), pp. 10–21 and 116

N. Larsen, 'Modernism, Manet and the *Maximilian*: Executing Negation', in *Modernism and Hegemony: A Materialist Critique of Aesthetic Agencies*, Minneapolis 1990, pp. 32–48

P. Mainardi, *Art and Politics of the Second Empire*, New Haven and London 1987

E. Moreau-Nélaton, *Manet raconté par lui-même*, 2 vols., Paris 1926

A. Proust, *Edouard Manet: Souvenirs*, in *Revue blanche*, 1897, pp. 125–35, 168–80, 201–7, 306–15, 413–24 (reprint Geneva 1968); ed. A. Barthélemy, Paris 1913; Caen 1988 (the 1897 text)

T. Reff, *Manet and Modern Paris*, see Washington D C 1982 (exhibition catalogue)

E. A. Reid, 'Realism and Manet', see Providence 1981 (exhibition catalogue), pp. 69–82

M. Ruggiero, 'Manet and the Image of War and Revolution', see Providence 1981 (exhibition catalogue), pp. 22–38

N.G. Sandblad, *Manet: Three Studies in Artistic Conception*, Lund 1954

A. Scharf, *Art and Photography*, Harmondsworth (England) 1974

A. Tabarant, *Manet et ses oeuvres*, Paris 1947

M. Wilson, *Manet at Work*, see London 1983 (exhibition catalogue)

J. Wilson-Bareau (ed.), 'Documents Relating to the "Maximilian Affair"', see Paris/New York 1983 (exhibition catalogue), pp. 531–4

J. Wilson-Bareau, *The Hidden Face of Manet*, see London 1986 (exhibition catalogue)

J. Wilson-Bareau (ed.), *Edouard Manet: Voyage en Espagne*, Caen 1988

J. Wilson-Bareau (ed.), *Manet by himself*, London and New York 1991; *Manet par lui-même*, Paris 1991

M. Wivel, *Manet*, see Ordrupgaard 1989 (exhibition catalogue)

E. Zola, see 'Documents Relating to the "Maximilian Affair"' in Paris/New York 1983 (exhibition catalogue), pp. 531–4

Catalogues raisonnés

L. Delteil, *Le Peintre-graveur illustré*, vols. XX–XXIX, *Daumier*, Paris 1925–6

M. Guérin, *L'Oeuvre gravé de Manet*, Paris 1944

J.C. Harris, *Edouard Manet: Graphic Work*, New York 1970; revised San Francisco 1990

T. Harris, *Goya Engravings and Lithographs*, Oxford 1964, reprint San Francisco 1983

D. Rouart and D. Wildenstein, *Edouard Manet: Catalogue raisonné*, 2 vols., Lausanne 1975

Exhibition catalogues

London, Courtauld Institute Galleries, *The Hidden Face of Manet* (*Burlington Magazine*, CXXVIII), 1986

London, National Gallery, *Manet at Work*, 1983

Ordrupgaard, Samlingen, Copenhagen, *Manet*, 1989

Paris, Grand Palais, and New York, Metropolitan Museum of Art, *Manet*, 1983

Providence (Rhode Is.), Bell Gallery, List Art Center, Brown University, *Edouard Manet and the Execution of Maximilian*, 1981

Trieste, Castello di Miramare, *Massimiliano da Trieste al Messico*, 1986

Washington, DC, National Gallery of Art, *Manet and Modern Paris*, 1982

Woluwe-Saint-Lambert (Belgium), *Charlotte et Maximilien. Les Belges au Mexique 1864–1867*, 1987

List of Works in the Exhibition

1 (fig. 70) Edouard Manet,
The Execution of Maximilian (I), *c.* July–September
1867. Oil on canvas, 196 x 259.8 cm.
Boston, Museum of Fine Arts, Gift of Mr and Mrs
Frank Gair Macomber.

2 (fig. 73) Edouard Manet,
The Execution of Maximilian (II), *c.* September 1867–
March 1868, with a (probably non-autograph)
signature to the right of the sergeant: Manet. Oil on
canvas, four fragments mounted on a single support,
193 x 284 cm.
London, National Gallery.

3 (fig. 76) Edouard Manet,
The Execution of Maximilian (III), 1868–9, signed and
dated lower left: Manet 19 juin 1867 (the date of
Maximilian's execution). Oil on canvas, 252 x 302 cm.
Mannheim, Städtische Kunsthalle.

4 (fig. 2) Charles Edouard Boutibonne and John
Frederick Herring,
Napoleon III on Horseback, 1856. Oil on canvas,
109.9 x 89.5 cm.
Lent by Her Majesty The Queen.

5 (fig. 7) Artist unknown,
President Benito Juárez, *c.*1868. Oil on canvas,
50.5 x 41.5 cm.
Mexico City, INAH, Castillo de Chapultepec.

6 Constantino Escalante and Hesiquio Iriarte,
The Battle for Puebla, 1862. Coloured lithograph, 54 x
73 cm. Lettered: 'Battle gained over the French in the
neighbourhood of Puebla on 5 May 1862', with lists
of the various incidents in the battle.
Mexico City, INAH, Castillo de Chapultepec.

7 Constantino Escalante and Hesiquio Iriarte, *Mexican
Guerilla Scouts capturing a French Officer near Orizaba*,
1862–3. Coloured lithograph, 22.4 x 31 cm.
Mexico City, INAH, Castillo de Chapultepec.

8 (fig. 4) *The French Army in Mexico*, 1863. Coloured
and gilded lithograph, 40.5 x 27.9 cm, published by
Pinot & Sagaire, Epinal and Paris.
Paris, Musée National des Arts et Traditions Populaires.

9 (fig. 9) *War in Mexico, Siege and Capture of Puebla*,
1863. Coloured and gilded lithograph, 27.6 x 41 cm,
published by Pinot & Sagaire, Epinal and Paris.
Paris, Musée National des Arts et Traditions Populaires.

10 (fig. 12) Jean-Adolphe Beaucé,
*General Forey leading the French Expeditionary Force into
Mexico City*, 1867–8. Oil on canvas, on panel, 79 x 148 cm.
Property of the French Foreign Legion.

11 (fig. 5) Alfred Graefle (after Winterhalter),
Maximilian, Emperor of Mexico, 1867–8. Oil on canvas,
100 x 76.2 cm.
Lent by Her Majesty The Queen.

12 (fig. 6) Alfred Graefle (after Winterhalter),
Charlotte, Empress of Mexico, 1867–8. Oil on canvas,
99.4 x 74.3 cm.
Lent by Her Majesty The Queen

13 (fig. 13) Cesare dell'Acqua,
The Mexican Delegation at Miramare, photograph by
Ghémar Frères, Brussels, *c.*1865. Mounted albumen
print, 34 x 50 cm (with letters 43.6 x 58 cm).
Lettered: 'Portraits of the Archduke Maximilian and
the Members of the Mexican Delegation who offered
the Crown of the Empire to His Imperial and Royal
Highness on 3 October 1863 at Miramare', with the
names of the delegation.
Brussels, Musée Royal de l'Armée.

14 (see fig. 15) Jean-Adolphe Beaucé,
The Emperor Maximilian on Horseback, signed and dated
lower right: J. A. Beaucé/Mexico 1865. Photograph by
François Aubert, *c.* 1865, signed in the negative:
Aubert foto Mexico. Albumen print, 33 x 27.5 cm.
Brussels, Musée Royal de l'Armée.

15 (fig. 16) François Aubert,
The Castle at Chapultepec, *c.*1864. Albumen print,
26.2 x 36.8 cm.
Brussels, Musée Royal de l'Armée.

16 (fig. 17) François Aubert,
Maximilian and his Court playing Cricket, *c.*1865.
Albumen print, 28.2 x 37.3 cm.
Brussels, Musée Royal de l'Armée.

17 (fig. 18) François Aubert,
General Tomás Mejía, *c.*1864. Albumen print,
17.3 x 13 cm.
Brussels, Musée Royal de l'Armée.

18 (fig. 20) François Aubert,
Exterior View of the Convent of La Cruz, June 1867.
Albumen print, 16.5 x 22.8 cm.
Brussels, Musée Royal de l'Armée.

19 (fig. 22) François Aubert,
The Three Crosses on the Cerro de las Campanas,
June 1867. Albumen print, 16 x 22.4 cm.
Brussels, Musée Royal de l'Armée.

20 (fig. 69) François Aubert,
The Emperor's Shirt after the Execution, June 1867.
Albumen print, 22.5 x 16 cm.
Brussels, Musée Royal de l'Armée.

21 (fig. 24) François Aubert,
The Corpse of Maximilian in his Coffin, June 1867.
Albumen print, 22.3 x 16.5 cm.
Brussels, Musée Royal de l'Armée.

22 *Souvenirs of the Emperor Maximilian and his
Execution*. 13 carte de visite photographs.
Brussels, Musée Royal de l'Armée:

1. The Archduke Maximilian, photo. Bingham (as fig. 58)
2. The Archduchess Charlotte, photo. Ghémar, Brussels, 1857
3. Medallion portraits of Maximilian and Charlotte, Generals Mejía, Miramón and Méndez, photo. Aubert, 1867
4. Miramar – Querétaro, photo. Jägern (as fig. 44)
5. Memorial portrait of Maximilian, with his last words, photo. Aubert, 1867
6. Maximilian's prison cell in the Convent of Las Capuchinas (drawing by an unidentified artist), photo. Aubert, 1867
7. The execution squad, photo. Disderi (as fig. 51)
8. A view of the Cerro de las Campanas, where Maximilian surrendered and was executed, photo. Aubert, 1867 (see fig. 46)
9. General Escobedo, to whom Maximilian surrendered at Querétaro, photo. Aubert, 1867
10. Maximilian's waistcoat, photo. Disderi (as fig. 54)
11. The corpse of Maximilian in his coffin, photo. Aubert (see fig. 24)
12. The embalmed corpse of Maximilian, photo. Aubert (see fig. 24)
13. President Benito Juárez, photo. Aubert, c.1867–8 (see cat. 5)

23 (fig. 97) Jean-Léon Gérôme,
The Death of Caesar, signed and dated lower left: J.L. GEROME MDCCCLX[?]. Exposition 1867. Oil on canvas, 85.5 x 145.5 cm.
Maryland, Baltimore, Walters Art Gallery.

24 (fig. 107) Jean-Léon Gérôme,
The Death of Marshal Ney, signed and dated lower left: J. L. GEROME. 186[?]. Salon of 1868 (*7 December 1815, Nine o'Clock in the Morning*). Oil on canvas, 64 x 103 cm.
Sheffield, City Art Galleries.

25 (fig. 33) Artist unknown (Italian School, 17th century),
A Dead Soldier, also known as *Roland mort*. Oil on canvas, 104.8 x 167 cm.
London, National Gallery.

26 (fig. 31) Edouard Manet,
The Dead Man (The Dead Toreador), 1864–5, signed lower right: Manet. Oil on canvas, 76 x 153.3 cm.
Washington DC, National Gallery of Art, Widener Collection.

27 (fig. 35) Alfred Dehodencq,
Bullfight in Spain, Novillada at the Escorial, signed and dated lower left: Alfred Dehodencq, juillet 1850 Madrid. Salon of 1850–1. Oil on canvas, 149 x 208 cm.
Pau, Musée des Beaux-Arts.

28 (fig. 36) Edouard Manet,
Bullfight, 1865, signed lower right: Manet. Oil on canvas, 48 x 60.4 cm.
Art Institute of Chicago, Mr and Mrs Martin A. Ryerson Collection.

29 (fig. 82) Edouard Manet,
The Fifer, 1865–6, signed twice at lower right: Manet. Oil on canvas, 161 x 97 cm.
Paris, Musée d'Orsay.

30 (fig. 81) Eva Gonzalès,
The Bugler, Salon of 1870, signed lower right: Eva Gonzalès. Oil on canvas, 130 x 98 cm.
Villeneuve-sur-Lot, Musée Gaston-Rapin.

31 (fig. 37) Francisco Goya,
Pedro Romero killing the halted Bull, plate 30 of *La Tauromaquia*, first edition, Madrid 1816. Etching and aquatint, 24.5 x 35.5 cm.
London, British Museum.

32 Francisco Goya,
The Unfortunate Death of Pepe Illo in the Ring at Madrid, plate 33 of *La Tauromaquia*, first edition, Madrid 1816. Etching and aquatint, 24.5 x 35 cm.
London, British Museum.

33 (fig. 40) Francisco Goya,
Y no hai remedio (And it can't be helped), c.1810–11, plate 15 of *The Disasters of War*, first edition, Madrid 1863. Etching, 14.1 x 16.8 cm.
London, British Museum.

34 Francisco Goya,
No se puede mirar (One can't look), 1810–12, plate 26 of *The Disasters of War*, first edition, Madrid 1863. Etching, 14.4 x 21 cm.
London, British Museum.

35 (fig. 47) *Death of Maximilian, Emperor of Mexico, and of Generals Miramón and Mejía, on 19 June 1867. View of the Town of Querétaro*. Coloured and gilded lithograph, 28 x 41 cm, published by Pinot & Sagaire, Epinal and Paris, August/October 1867
Paris, Musée National des Arts et Traditions Populaires.

36 (fig. 48) *Execution of the Emperor Maximilian – Querétaro, 19 June 1867*. Reproduction of a lithograph, 26.9 x 38.9 cm, published by Gangel and Didion, Metz, September 1867, Paris, June 1868.
Courtesy of Bibliothèque Nationale, Paris.

37 (see figs. 51, 53, 54) *Souvenir of the Execution of Maximilian*, 1867. Modern reproduction of a photograph by Disderi after Aubert, 15 x 22.1 cm.
Courtesy of Bibliothèque Nationale, Paris.
The print combines four of Aubert's carte de visite views: the Convent of Las Capuchinas where Maximilian was imprisoned (see cat. 22:6) and subsequently embalmed (fig. 24, cat. 22:11, 12), the execution squad and the Emperor's coat and waistcoat.

38 (fig. 60) Edouard Manet,
Sergeant holding his Musket, 1868. Pen and sepia ink on tracing paper (laid on card), 26.6 x 9.8 cm.
Mannheim, Städtische Kunsthalle.

39 (fig. 77) Edouard Manet,
The Execution of Maximilian, 1868. Lithograph, 33.3 x 43.3 cm, proof before letters, 1868–9?
Amsterdam, Rijksprentenkabinet, Rijksmuseum.

40 (fig. 74) Edouard Manet,
The Execution of Maximilian (sketch), 1868–9, signed
and dated lower right: Manet 1867 (the date of
Maximilian's execution). Oil on canvas, 50 x 60 cm.
Courtesy of Copenhagen, Ny Carlsberg Glyptotek.

41 (figs. 85, 86) Edouard Manet,
*The Barricade, c.*1871. Graphite, watercolour and
gouache on two joined sheets of paper, 46.2 x 32.5
cm. Verso: *The Execution of Maximilian* (outline
tracing). Black chalk and stylus.
Budapest, Museum of Fine Arts.

42 (fig. 84) Edouard Manet,
*The Barricade, c.*1871–3. Lithograph, 46.5 x 33.4 cm,
edition of 1884.
Mannheim, Städtische Kunsthalle.

43 (fig. 83) Edouard Manet,
Civil War, 1871–4, signed and dated lower left: Manet
1871 (the date of the Paris Commune). Lithograph,
39.9 x 58 cm, edition of 1874.
London, British Museum.

44 (fig. 93) Edouard Manet,
The Balloon, signed and dated lower right: éd. Manet
1862. Lithograph, 40.3 x 51.5 cm, one of five known
proofs.
London, British Museum.

45 (fig. 90) Edouard Manet,
The Battle of the Kearsarge and the Alabama, 1864,
signed lower right: Manet. Salon of 1872. Oil on
canvas, 134 x 127 cm.
Philadelphia Museum of Art, John G. Johnson
Collection.

46 (fig. 89) Edouard Manet,
The Trial of Marshal Bazaine, 1873. Graphite on two
pages from a sketchbook, 18.5 x 23.8 cm.
Rotterdam, Boymans-van Beuningen Museum.

47 (fig. 87) Edouard Manet,
Georges Clemenceau at the Tribune, 1879–80. Oil on
canvas, 115.9 x 88.2 cm.
Fort Worth, Texas, Kimbell Art Museum.

48 (fig. 88) Edouard Manet,
Henri Rochefort, signed and dated lower right: Manet
1881. Salon of 1881. Oil on canvas, 81.5 x 66.5 cm.
Hamburg, Kunsthalle.

49 (fig. 95) Edouard Manet,
The Escape of Rochefort, 1880–1. Oil on canvas,
143 x 114 cm.
Zurich, Kunsthaus, Vereinigung Zürcher
Kunstfreunde.

50 (fig. 94) Edouard Manet,
The Escape of Rochefort, 1880–1, signed lower right:
Manet. Oil on canvas, 80 x 73 cm.
Paris, Musée d'Orsay.

Lenders to the Exhibition

Picture Credits

Index